TRENT AND ALL THAT

Rubens, *The Holy Family with Saint Anne*

TRENT

AND ALL THAT

✠

*Renaming Catholicism in
the Early Modern Era*

JOHN W. O'MALLEY

Harvard University Press
Cambridge, Massachusetts
London, England
2000

Frontispiece: Peter Paul Rubens, *The Holy Family with Saint Anne,* © Museo del Prado, no. 1639. All rights reserved.

Library of Congress Cataloging-in-Publication Data

O'Malley, John W.
Trent and all that : renaming Catholicism in the early modern era
/ John W. O'Malley.
p.   cm.
Includes bibliographical references and index.
ISBN 0-674-00087-0 (alk. paper)
1. Counter-Reformation.   I. Title.
BR430.045   2000
282′.09′031—dc21   99-41584

For Helen and Mary North

CONTENTS

✠

TRENT AND ALL THAT

"*Must* a name mean something?" Alice asked doubtfully.
"Of course it must," Humpty-Dumpty said with a short laugh:
"*My* name means the shape I am—and a good handsome shape
it is, too. With a name like yours, you might be any shape, almost."

Lewis Carroll,
Through the Looking-Glass

INTRODUCTION

✠

What's in a Name?

Protestantism in the early modern period is known in English as the "Reformation" and in other languages by an equivalent term.[1] It is a designation that sparks comparatively little comment. Catholicism for the same period is not so lucky, for it is sometimes called the "Counter Reformation," sometimes the "Catholic Reformation," sometimes the "Tridentine Reformation," sometimes something else still. No matter which term scholars choose from this menu, they often feel obliged to justify or explain it. Why so? Could it be that such justifications and explanations indicate an unresolved problem?

What's in a name? Sometimes very little. A rose still smells as sweet. Even designations for historical phenomena like "the Middle Ages" that were once loaded with prejudices lose them through repeated usage. They become the equivalent of dead metaphors, where the image loses its punch. Is it not further true that all such historical constructs are imperfect, not much more than pointers to what can never be fully grasped by them, impositions on a fluid reality that they can never adequately capture? What difference does it make, then, what we call the Catholic side of the early modern period? Should we not stop worrying about labels, mere terms of convenience, and get on with the real business of history?

I long felt satisfied with this nonchalant attitude and even promoted it. For the past thirty years I have been dealing with aspects of the Catholic side of early modern history, but for a long time most of my work was on the Italian Renaissance. More recently, however, my editing of Erasmus and especially my book on the Jesuits have drawn me into the more contentious later times. This development in my interests forced me to wrestle with new questions about a phenomenon that has always fascinated me—the ideals and the realities of reform and reformation, whether in the sixteenth century with Giles of Viterbo, Luther, and preachers at the papal court, or in the twentieth with the *aggiornamento* of the Second Vatican Council.

Among the questions I had to face with a new urgency was what to call the Catholic side of the early modern epoch. This question kept imposing itself upon me not as an academic issue but as the result of some practical decisions I had to make. What title was I to give to a "guide to research" that tried to do for Catholicism what Steven Ozment's *Reformation Europe* did for Protestantism?[2] What entries from the Catholic side should be included in the *Oxford Encyclopedia of the Reformation,* for which I was a consulting editor? How did the early Jesuits, about whom I was writing a book, fit the categories of "Counter Reformation" and "Catholic Reformation"?[3]

I gradually came to the conclusion that those two terms, the most widely used, were inadequate and sometimes misleading as designations for what the early Society of Jesus was about. Perhaps, as I had already begun to suspect, they were also misleading when taken as all-inclusive terms for the much larger reality of Catholicism itself.

True, they caught in an indispensable way crucially important aspects of the subject, but by a kind of synecdoche did they not take the part for the whole?

I came to see, moreover, that such terms, even when accompanied by disclaimers, were not simple labels, for they acted as implicit questions and implicit categories of interpretation. They thus subtly directed attention to some issues and away from others, highlighted certain phenomena and cast others into the shadows, admitted some evidence but filtered out the rest. I thought I had indications to show that historians see things one way when they wear the hermeneutical spectacles, for instance, of "Counter-Reformation Rome," and very differently when they wear those of "early modern Rome."

The traditional terms sometimes blind us to incongruities staring us in the face, as I believe happened, for instance, with the juxtaposition I noticed of a wall text and painting at the magnificent "Age of Rubens" exhibit a few years ago at the Museum of Fine Arts, Boston. The text, entitled "Painting and the Counter Reformation," described a newly vigorous Catholic Church that, unlike Protestant churches, brought art and artists into its service. It concluded, however, with the following qualification: "Bishops and Church leaders constantly monitored the 'decorum' of religious painting, guarding against inappropriate imagery and unconventional interpretations." In other words, they censored it. So far, so good, for some church leaders tried to do precisely that.

I found it ironic, however, that within two feet of the wall text hung Rubens's *Holy Family with Saint Anne,* painted probably in the late 1620s. Rubens was a devout Catholic employed on an international basis by Catholic prelates and princes. In the painting, which is reproduced as a frontispiece to this book, a frontally nude Jesus stands on his mother's lap with his left hand caressing her neck. The Virgin is one of Rubens's typically ample young women in contemporary dress. To steady himself, her infant son rests his right hand on her exposed right breast. How, I could not help asking, do this painting and this text fit together? Would this painting have been any different had there been no "Counter Reformation"? Yet it is surely a Catholic painting in that it would be accepted by Catholics as expressing their religious sentiments, but it would hardly be accepted as such by Protestants.

What's in a name? I gradually and reluctantly arrived at the conclusion that at least in this instance there was a great deal in a name. Names may be no more than pointers, but this name pointed in certain directions and not in others. This name told us what we were talking about. Conversely, if we did not know what name to use, we to some extent did not know what we were talking about. I came to agree, that is, with Alfred North Whitehead: ". . . definitions—though in form they remain the mere assignment of names—are at once seen to be the most important aspect of the subject. The act of assigning names is in fact the act of choosing the various complex ideas which are to be the special object of study. The whole subject depends on such a choice."[4]

If names are oblique definitions of the subject, they are sometimes even more than that. As R. W. Scribner observed about issues in the sixteenth century similar to ours: "This is no idle quibble about mere words, since words with such specialized meaning are often the shorthand expression for ideology and myth."[5] The truth of Scribner's observation has become ever more evident to me. The pages that follow provide irrefutable evidence that, although the terms for the Catholic side of the early modern epoch arose from historians' honest efforts to generalize about their subject, they also were radically conditioned by the secular and religious politics of the historians' milieux. They are not neutral.

Historians ply by and large a cautious trade, and, though required to make generalizations, they are wary of them. Yet the books they write and the courses they teach must have names. When historians in such instances are constrained to assign names, they must throw their habitual caution to the winds and engage in mega-history on the broadest conceivable scale. *This,* they say, is what these two hundred—or thousand—years were all about. By means of this naming process, the academic equivalent of the sound-bite, they make mega-definitions. Like the sound-bite, the mega-definition sticks in mind and memory long after everything else evanesces.

This book is about the problem of naming in early modern Catholicism. It proposes a solution to the problem by arguing that, first, we need to accept the multiplicity of names as a good thing, for each of them captures an important aspect of the reality. Second, for such acceptance to be fruitful, we must apply these names more reflectively than heretofore, careful to indicate precisely what we mean to convey by each of them. Third, we need to add "Early Modern Catholicism" to the list as a more comprehensive designation than the others, a designation that provides for aspects they let slip through their grasp.

In this book I hope to sway readers to my solution principally through a review of the history of the naming process. The review constitutes the substance of the book, so that I must perforce also review some of the historiographical trends and political situations that have been the matrix for the process. In this regard the book bears some faint family resemblance to Norman F. Cantor's *Inventing the Middle Ages*[6] or even more, though my chronological scope is much more limited, to Wallace K. Ferguson's *The Renaissance in*

Historical Thought[7] and to A. G. Dickens and Jóhn M. Tonkin's *The Reformation in Historical Thought.*[8]

The book differs from these studies, however, in at least two significant ways. First, it has a much more specific focus: naming. It deals with *names*—where they came from, who used them, what prejudices they entailed. Its focus on names allows me to omit or glide over many methodological debates that a full historiographical review would require. By reason of its very specificity the focus acts, nonetheless, as a sharp instrument to probe into the complexity of early modern Catholicism as historians—particularly in the past few decades—have begun to uncover it. It also allows me to write a considerably shorter book, which I hope will attract more readers than would something of more sweeping scope.

This book differs from the others in a second way. Cantor, Ferguson, and Dickens and Tonkin accept the traditional names that designate their phenomena and then discuss historians' interpretations of what the phenomena entail. I, on the contrary, propose a solution that includes adding a new name. I am engaged in problem-solving in a way they were not. But what, more precisely, is the problem I am hoping to solve? At its core is the careless way terms like "reform" and "reformation" are applied to Catholicism for this period. When historians use these words, they assume that they and their audience know what they are talking about; even when they bother to provide definitions, they rarely analyze them with any sophistication. Sometimes the terms seem to indicate nothing more than religious fervor. Thus Filippo Neri becomes a reformer. But was he? According to what criteria? If religious fervor that issues in some betterment of society makes one a reformer, does that not make St. Benedict a reformer? Yet we usually do not speak of him in that way. He did not live in an "age of reform and reformation," as did Neri, who becomes a reformer by osmosis.

A crucial task in solving the problem, then, is to determine what we might mean by our terms and how they then apply to Catholicism. A large part of the task is conceptual, and, I maintain, it is more incumbent upon the Catholic side than upon the Protestant. Despite the complexity and diversity of the Protestant side, a self-definition related to change, that is, reform, is at its core. In mainline churches this meant reforming doctrine by repudiating the supposed "works-righteousness" of the Catholic Church and embracing righteousness by faith; following from that change were others, often radical, in church order and religious practice.

Change, that is, "reform," is crucial to Catholicism in this period. When historians apply the term to Catholicism, however, they generally do so without telling us with any precision what the concept means in this new context, so that it sometimes seems to stand for something quite specific, like disciplining bishops and pastors of parishes to do their jobs, and sometimes for something as global as a "Great Awakening." In any case, they often use "reform" as if it operated in Catholicism in the same way it did in Protestantism. But is that not to be shown rather than assumed?

I believe that if this fundamental task receives adequate attention, the usefulness of traditional categories like "Counter Reformation" and "Catholic Reformation" will be reaffirmed, once they cease being used promiscuously. The usefulness of newer categories like "Confessional Catholicism" will also be vindicated, in large part because they have been constructed from the beginning with greater precision of definition. But other aspects of Catholicism escape these nets, for none of them is capacious enough.

Is there such a name? I propose "Early Modern Catholicism." Like any such name, it has liabilities, as will become clear. But I think its advantages outweigh the liabilities sufficiently to make it worth introducing into our historiographical vocabulary. For one thing, it does not reduce the reality to one of its aspects, which is the scourge that has beset the other terms, each employed as if it expressed the whole truth.[9]

I first argued for "Early Modern Catholicism" in 1991.[10] Since then I have heard objections and tried to take them into account, yet I remain convinced of its usefulness. I have been strengthened in my opinion by the discovery that other historians, seemingly independent of me, use "Early Modern Catholicism" or a close equivalent of it.[11] Florencia E. Mallon, writing about a quite different problem, proposed that in these postmodern times, historians "must admit that riding many horses" is the only way to negotiate our way.[12] My solution allows us to do just that, while at the same time keeping all the horses on the same early modern Catholic ranch.

In order to forestall misunderstandings, I need at the outset to give some indication of what I intend by the component parts of my term. By "early modern" I mean simply the period convention- ally designated as such, which historians interpret as beginning and ending at different times depending upon what places and what issues are being considered. It designates some time after the Great Schism/Hundred Years War and before the French Revolution. In Italy, even though the "modernity" of the Italian Renaissance is today a disputed question, it might be understood to begin in the early Quattrocento; in Germany, France, Spain, and England, con- siderably later, where "late medieval" is still clearly appropriate. The early modern period begins at one point if we are considering science, at another if we are considering "letters," at another if art, at still another if politics.

By "modern" I do not mean to assert anything one way or the other about Catholicism's manifesting more "modern" or more "medieval" traits. Rather, I am simply acknowledging that the Catholic Church was subject to all the forces at play in the period and, to some degree or other, agent for them. Early Modern Catholicism, in other words, was part of Early Modern History.

By "Catholicism" I mean to include all people, institutions, and cultural and religious manifestations that before 1517 were Christian and that after 1517 were not Protestant. This includes, of course, "the Catholic Church," that is, the institution comprising in the first instance popes, bishops, and pastors, as well as the apparatus these churchmen employed, such as synods and inquisitions. "Church" might be taken in an extended sense even to include secular rulers, insofar as they governed the church through, for instance, the nomination of bishops. It would include perhaps some aspects of the male religious orders but not so clearly the orders and congregations of women.

By "Catholicism" I also, like many others, mean to go beyond such realities, which have constituted the ecclesio-political perspective of traditional "church history," to a more inclusive perspective. Briefly, I mean to include in Catholicism both church and, as they say, religion, both doctrine and devotion, parish and confraternity, prince and pauper, laws and art, clergy and laity. I mean to go beyond Europe to include the newly discovered lands.

I believe my solution is a good one, but I do not, even so, consider it to be the main contribution of this book. The main contribution, I hope, is that the book will help us view "the Catholic side" with new eyes, so that we become more aware of a breadth, depth, and complexity that earlier historians frequently either missed or, more often, forced into an inappropriate or inadequate interpretative framework—by inadequate naming.

I must immediately add that one of the most important reasons historians missed the complexity of early modern Catholicism was not improper naming as such but larger historiographical traditions of which the naming was but a manifestation. The two broadest of these traditions are the obvious ones: first, the tradition of historical writing represented by Protestant and secular historians and, second, the tradition represented by historians writing out of a Catholic background.

For serious historians of the Protestant and secular tradition, Catholicism until quite recently lacked interest as a subject of research, except possibly as a foil against which to understand the changes the Reformation caused or brought in its wake.[13] For them, Catholicism was the backward and lackluster stepsister to the Reformation. These historians seemed to take seriously Catholics' claim that their church did not change. If nothing changed, there was nothing for historians to write about, for fascination with *la longue durée* was yet to come, especially to historians in German and English universities, who set the pace, particularly for the North American world.

The truth is that books and articles of the highest academic standards dealing with the Reformation have been rolling off the presses since the nineteenth century. This is true even of a Catholic country like Italy, where the internationally respected scholars came from the "lay" *(laico)* or anticlerical ranks and often were more interested in Italian heretics than in the overwhelmingly Catholic heritage of their country.

In this regard the fundamental fact that must be reckoned with is that modern historical methods, first effectively codified by

Leopold von Ranke, originated in Protestant circles and were often used in ways or led to conclusions that made them offensive to Catholic sensibilities and suspect to Catholic authorities. Even the better historians writing out of the Catholic tradition were therefore often engaged in a game of catch-up and refutation. Moreover, much Catholic scholarship for this period was done by local, amateur, and apologetic authors, who were ignorant of the canons of modern historical methods.

Catholic historians were also often writing under the influence of the same assumption of an unchanging church as were their Protestant and secular counterparts. Yet they felt constrained to show how effectively the old church responded to the Reformation. For historians of Protestantism things got radically better (or even radically worse) in the sixteenth century because they radically changed. This was high drama, exciting to write about. For Catholic historians things did not change, but they got better. This was a paradox frustrating to deal with.

My generalizations about these historians need thousands of qualifications, and I hope that what follows in this book will provide at least a few of them. On the one hand, sometimes the most distinguished historians in the Protestant-secular tradition have led the breakthroughs into a more sophisticated approach to Catholicism; on the other, this book stands, I hope, as a tribute to the great historians from the Catholic tradition who belie my words.

Nonetheless, until quite recently teachers of undergraduate history courses had for their students an almost limitless supply of fine articles and monographs dealing with every aspect of the Reformation but were hard pressed indeed to provide even a few titles of similar caliber for Catholicism. That situation has changed considerably. Certainly in North America books and articles have been appearing in good numbers. Catholicism in the early modern period has become a hot topic for doctoral students on a scale impossible to imagine even a decade ago. The dumpy stepsister, though perhaps not yet quite a Cinderella, has somehow acquired a certain allure.

This new interest in early modern Catholicism is another reason the topic of this book is timely. In the relationship between adequate naming and the quality and quantity of scholarship on the subject, we are dealing, obviously, with a hermeneutical circle. The scholarship challenges the adequacy of the categories of interpretation, and the categories influence the direction of the scholarship.

While such shifts in interest surely result from larger cultural factors, in this case the change has, when viewed more narrowly, been inspired in part by the massive scholarship of Hubert Jedin and his disciples on all aspects of the Council of Trent. It has also been influenced by shifts in historical method, in which practitioners from the *Annales* school of the École Pratique des Hautes Études would be the most easily named. In any case, scholarship began to reveal a reality more intriguing, sprawling, and complicated than was earlier suspected, and this produced further scholars to pursue the clues. Documentation in unsuspectedly vast amounts, most of it never before examined in any systematic way, has fueled the curiosity of scholars intrepid enough to mine it.

Hubert Jedin is of special importance for this book for several reasons, but principally because in 1946 he published *Katholische Reformation oder Gegenreformation?* (Catholic Reformation or Counter Reformation?), an essay about the proper naming of the Catholic side that I take as my central point of reference for this book.[14] Jedin, a professor of church history at the University of Bonn from 1949 until 1965, was the most respected and probably most prolific scholar of the twentieth century writing on sixteenth-century Catholicism. He was forty-six years old when he published the essay and already had some 150 items in print, many of them works of substantial scholarship. His two-volume study of Giro-lamo Seripando, prior general of the Augustinian order, cardinal, and leading figure at Trent, was only the largest and best known.[15] He was on his way toward completion of the first volume of the central project of his life, the standard history of the Council of Trent, which turned out to be one of the greatest and most lasting monuments of historical scholarship produced since World War II. He published the fourth and final volume in 1975, five years before his death in 1980.[16]

Jedin's essay of 1946 did not attract a great deal of attention at first, but because of its intrinsic merits and Jedin's increasingly recognized stature, it gradually became accepted as the classic statement on the subject. In the essay Jedin first reviewed the history of the two terms then most current for designating Catholicism in the sixteenth and seventeenth centuries—"Catholic Reform/Reformation" and "Counter Reformation." He then elaborated on how he understood them and their relationship to each other, concluding this section by affirming that a combination of the two, "Catholic-Reform-and-Counter-Reformation," was the proper designation. In part three he dealt with rival designations such as "Catholic Restoration" and "Baroque Catholicism." He ended with a resounding reaffirmation of the importance of the Council of Trent and with a proposal that the council indicated a new, transitional period in church history. He thus at least implicitly justified another name, "the Tridentine Era."

Jedin's essay serves as a line of demarcation for our subject. While the essay itself never became particularly well known outside Ger-

many and Italy, the viewpoint it espoused was transmitted internationally in other ways, especially through the multivolume history
of the church that Jedin edited and that became a teachers' vade
mecum in the several languages into which it was translated. Serious reflection on the subject almost perforce must take the essay as
its point of departure. There is no other work quite like it. Some
important reviews of the debate about what to call the Catholic side
have appeared in the meantime, especially the excellent article in
1964 by Pier Giorgio Camaiani, but no one has argued with more
effect than Jedin for a specific solution.[17]

The first chapter of this book roughly corresponds to the first
part of Jedin's essay in that I review the process of naming up to the
time Jedin wrote, at the end of World War II. In the next chapter I
take a closer look at Jedin himself and at his methods and assumptions. Jedin thought that he had solved the problem, but the debate
has continued for more than fifty years, sometimes with Jedin himself taken as problem rather than solution.[18] That is the topic of the
third chapter. The fourth explores historiographical traditions that
break with earlier models. Finally, in the conclusion I assess the
situation and argue for a solution.

This book originated at Campion Hall, Oxford University, in
the fall of 1993 in a series of lectures I delivered entitled "What
Ever Happened to the Counter Reformation? Fifty Years Trying to
Name It." In what follows I have retained much of the structure of
the lectures. In keeping with the original occasion, I have tried to
avoid overwhelming the reader with more detail than is essential
for grasping the argument. This means I have written a book that
by reason of its size and my limitations deals modestly with problems of surely immodest dimensions.

Hermeneutical and other philosophical issues of deepest gravity cry for attention with almost every statement I make. Ideological issues do the same. Of this I am acutely aware. If I seem to dance through such issues with blithe and uncomprehending spirit, I ask the reader to give me occasionally the benefit of the doubt. To probe the issues more deeply would mean writing a very different book.

ONE

✠

How It All Began

One of the most consistent themes of the Bible is the need for conversion, that is, the need for individuals to reform themselves, with the help of God's grace, by turning to a better way of life. This basic understanding of reform persisted throughout the patristic period, but it was not without institutional applications and ramifications, especially in the West.[1] Not until the Investiture Controversy of the eleventh century, however, did the idea clearly emerge that the church itself, as a corporation, might be subject to reform and, indeed, require it.[2]

This portentous idea entered history when the papal party, eventually led by Pope Gregory VII, tried to abolish long-standing procedures in the name of a return to the even more ancient provisions of canon law. Thus the idea that the church needed to be radically reformed had its genesis in the revival of the study of canon law in Germany and Italy, the first great renaissance of learning in the Middle Ages that would henceforth have a continuous history.

The idea would be peculiar to the Western Church and Empire, unknown in the East. The canons upon which the idea of reform was based, some of which were medieval forgeries, were presumed to be holier and more authentic than contemporary practices that contravened them. The popes and their allies, who waged against recalcitrants a vigorous war not only of propaganda but sometimes of spear and sword, became the first church reformers.[3]

The Gregorian Reform and its long aftermath ushered in several profound changes in Western culture that would establish the parameters of our subject into the sixteenth century and, for Catholics, almost up to the present. First, the Gregorians set in motion a process whereby canon law would achieve a normative centrality in Christian life that it had not had before. Second, reform *(reformatio)* would thus be inextricably identified with a reassertion (or a further elaboration) of ancient discipline, usually considered to be best formulated in the canons. Reform thus dealt with *mores,* which meant not so much "morals" or morality as public discipline, that is, behavior or, more specifically, practices in accord with norms of law. Within religious orders the later movement known as Observantism took as its basic premise the idea that reform of the order would be accomplished through more precise observance of the order's original statutes. Third, although the terms were sometimes used interchangeably, reform *(reformatio)* was very different from renewal or rebirth *(renovatio),* which meant something much broader than implementation of legal norms—for example, a rebirth of learning or of imperial glories.

The idea that the church had to be reformed along the lines of more ancient discipline took on new urgency in the fourteenth and fifteenth centuries. With the scandal of the Great Western Schism, in which two and then three men simultaneously claimed to be pope, the idea was turned against the very institution that had principally created it, the papacy. Reform now also began to extend beyond *mores* to include belief, resulting in the exclusion from the church of heretics like Wyclif and Hus. Thus emerged at the Council of Constance (1414–1418) the slogan that would be a battle cry for the next century: "reform in faith and practice, in head and members" *(ecclesia sit reformata in fide et in moribus, in capite et in membris).*[4]

Even with the settlement of the Schism, cries for reform of the church, especially reform of the "abuses" practiced by the papal curia, continued in swelling crescendo into the next century, when they finally branched into Protestant and, at least until the Council of Trent (1545–1563), Catholic forms.[5] Half of the decrees of Trent were about reform—*de reformatione.*

With the passage of time, the word "reform/reformation" in Latin and its vernacular equivalents came to be appropriated and claimed ever more effectively by Protestants. Calvinist communities almost from the beginning referred to themselves as "reformed churches" *(églises réformées),* and Lutherans by the last quarter of the sixteenth century were following a similar path. Early in the next century Johann Gerhard and Konrad Dieterich would play an important role in the development of the latter.[6]

Clearly reform had taken on a new meaning in the Protestant world, for it had been cut from any connection with the canons. At the same time, Catholic rulers in Germany were still claiming the term by calling the sometimes forcible restoration of Catholicism in areas gone Lutheran "the reformation of religion" *(die Reformation der religion).* Nonetheless, the Protestant purchase on Reformation was destined ultimately to triumph.

In 1692 Veit Ludwig von Seckendorff, in a polemical work replying to the equally polemical *Histoire de Luthéranisme* by the Jesuit Louis Maimbourg, in his very title helped establish "Reformation" in the vocabulary of church history as pertaining to Luther and his accomplishments—*Commentarius . . . de reformatione religionis ductu D. Martini Lutheri.*[7] He thus made the crucial identification of Protestantism with Reformation, which in its modern sense had already been slipping gradually and unobtrusively into Lutheran historiographical vocabulary.

Seckendorff made the identification, moreover, at just the moment when historians and theologians were abandoning older and more mythical schemes, especially the biblically inspired megadivision of history into the Four Monarchies—Persia, Babylon, Greece, and Rome. At the same time a German pedagogue named Christoph Keller, seizing on the idea that had been germinating at least since Petrarch in the fourteenth century of an epoch between antiquity and modernity, used Middle Age (*medium aevum*) for the intermediate period. He thus crystallized the division of the past into ancient, medieval, and modern, a construct that has been with us ever since.[8] Although it would take church historians, unlike political historians, more than a century definitively to embrace this tripartite division, for Keller and later Lutheran historians the Reformation fell, obviously, on the modernity side of the great divide.[9]

By the middle of the eighteenth century, Lutheran theologians and historians had gone a step further and accepted the Reformation as a distinct historical epoch, which required providing for it beginning and ending dates. A gently evolving consensus set the dates at 1517, Luther's posting of the Theses, and 1555, the Peace of Augsburg, when Catholics and Lutherans laid down their arms and accepted the fact of religious division—*cuius regio, eius religio.* True, not until the nineteenth century did Leopold von Ranke definitively consolidate this chronology for both secular and church history in his six-volume "German History in the Epoch of the Reformation" (*Deutsche Geschichte im Zeitalter der Reformation*) and

through his immense prestige send it on its way outside Germany
to win almost universal acceptance from historians. But the epoch
and its chronology were well enough established within Germany
by the last quarter of the eighteenth century to make it possible for
a dependent concept like "Counter Reformation" *(Gegenreformation)* to surface and begin to gain currency. This was the accom-
plishment of a Lutheran lawyer and legal historian from Göttingen,
Johann Stephan Pütter, who first used the term in 1776 in the
introduction to his edition of the Augsburg Confession.[10]

✝

By *Gegenreformation* Pütter meant the forced return of Lutherans to
the practice of Catholicism in areas that had once been Lutheran.
Three things must be noted about Pütter's understanding of
"Counter Reformation." First, whether he used the term in the
singular or plural form, he meant to designate a series of uncon-
nected actions, namely, the military, political, and diplomatic measures Catholic princes were able to marshal against German Lutherans in certain localities. Second, he gave the term a quite precise
and narrow definition, for the words meant exactly what they
say—Anti-Reformation. Third, this usage suggested a chronology
that ran from the Peace of Augsburg through the Thirty Years War,
1555–1648. The usage laid the groundwork that made it possible
for von Ranke to deliver it to the world at large at a much later
date. In 1843 he ended his *Deutsche Geschichte im Zeitalter der Reformation* with the solemn pronouncement: "After the era of the Reformation came the era of the Counter Reformations."[11]

Pütter surely captured the sentiments of many oppressed Lutherans in the years in question. The context in which his idea of
Counter Reformation was born and transmitted was, however,

laden with presuppositions about the Catholic Church coming from both the Enlightenment and the Lutheran theological tradition. In this regard the two ideologies tended to converge, for both saw Catholic resurgence after Augsburg as due exclusively to political causes, specifically to powerful princes, who for their own ends waged war against the Protestants and who under the name of reform promoted within the Catholic Church nothing more than a rigid enforcement of discipline that would help consolidate their authority.

For Lutherans, moreover, there could be no genuine reform but theirs; thus "Reformation" could never be meaningfully applied to the Catholic Church. Calvinists and others made similar claims, and the term gradually extended to the whole Protestant enterprise of the sixteenth century. Not until the Restoration following the Napoleonic Wars did Catholics find a term with which to challenge this usage—"Protestant Revolution."

After the shattering blows the Catholic establishment had suffered in the French Revolution, no nastier term could be imagined by most Catholics than "revolution," a wild and irrational force destructive of public order and intent especially on the obliteration of the Catholic Church. In the last quarter of the nineteenth century, Johannes Janssen published his immensely popular eight-volume "History of the German People since the Close of the Middle Ages" (*Geschichte des deutschen Volkes seit dem Ausgang des Mittelalters*), a social history before Social History, which provided a framework for Catholic interpretation of the Reformation that remained dominant for generations. Janssen put his considerable prestige behind "Revolution" as its correct name.[12]

But the term was a historiographical dud, never making it into the mainstream. "Reformation" was already too firmly in place.

Moreover, important Catholic historians like Cardinal Joseph Hergenröther abstained from using "Revolution," instead referring to
the whole phenomenon as "Schism" or "Religious Division" *(die
grosse abendländische Glaubensspaltung)*.[13] Nonetheless, the failure of
the alternative cannot be dissociated from the larger context of
discrimination against Catholic intellectuals and the seemingly ar-
rogant dismissal of their achievements in the Germany newly
unified in 1870 under Prussian dominance.[14]

At that very same time, with the *Kulturkampf* at its height, Johann
Joseph Döllinger, "indisputably the most learned ecclesiastical historian of his time," who also advocated "Revolution," was excom-
municated after refusing to accept papal infallibility as defined in
Vatican Council I. He took with him a number of other Catholic
historians.[15] Besides weakening the Catholic historical enterprise,
Döllinger's exodus raised questions about the freedom of the historians who remained Catholic to express the truth as they saw it and
hence gave further cause for disdain.

On an international scale, the failure of "Protestant Revolution"
was just another minor manifestation of the ever more marginal
role Catholics were playing in the world of learning as the nineteenth century wore on. The reasons for this situation were many,
but surely an important cause was the increasing intransigence of
Pope Pius IX during his seemingly endless pontificate (1846–1878)
and his distrust of "the modern world"—that is, everything that had
happened since the Reformation, which culminated with the sei-
zure of the Papal State in 1870 by the forces of the Risorgimento.

The pope's pronouncements gave aid and comfort to historians
already inclined to believe that the Catholic Church had not, could
not, would not essentially change from what it was in the Middle
Ages except to enforce more stringently what it otherwise refused

to change. This is what happened, they asserted, after 1555. Even before Pius IX, the English Whig historian Thomas Babington Macaulay concluded, like many others, that the "decay" of southern Europe in his day arose largely from this fact.[16]

Not all persons on the two sides of the cultural divide were so self-enclosed. Early in the century Johann Adam Möhler, the Catholic theologian and church historian at Tübingen and then Munich, for instance, wrote of Luther and Lutheranism with insight and a certain sympathy, and he insisted that the church needed reform in the sixteenth century.

On the Protestant side, Ranke's greatness is perhaps nowhere more evident than in his appreciation that spiritual forces for renewal were powerfully at work in sixteenth-century Catholicism. He described these forces in his first major work, "The Roman Popes" *(Die römischen Päpste)*. He insisted that they were operative before 1555 and were not simply a reaction to the Reformation.[17] He judged them against Lutheran criteria, true, and saw them as fundamentally frustrated by the end of the century, but he nonetheless broke with the prevalent interpretations of Catholic resurgence as the product of nothing but political and military forces.

Ranke gradually moved to almost exclusive use of "Counter Reformation" in the singular form, which suggested a kind of unity in the Catholic reality that he saw springing up after 1555 from three major sources—the Council of Trent, the Jesuits, and the papacy. Such a coalition might even include the forces of religious renewal that were particularly active earlier in the century. Although he himself did not use the term to include this earlier phase, reserving it for the period after 1555, Ranke had prepared the way for "Counter Reformation" as a comprehensive term signifying a broad reality beginning well before the Peace of Augsburg. By the end of the nineteenth century, this broader understanding received an important codification in the title of Eberhard Gothein's *Ignatius von Loyola und die Gegenreformation*.[18]

Whatever "Counter Reformation" included or excluded, whenever it began or ended, it was a term used for most of the nineteenth century almost exclusively by German Lutherans. In 1889, a full century after Pütter launched it, Moriz Ritter had already, before Gothein, given the term a new prominence by including it in the title of a volume, *Deutsche Geschichte im Zeitalter der Gegenreformation*.[19] This was an important step in sending *Gegenreformation* on its way into other languages—*Contre-Réforme, Controriforma, Contrarreforma,* and "Counter Reformation."

No matter how *Gegenreformation* was interpreted in these new cultures, it did not altogether replace earlier designations for historical epochs. Scholars in England continued to speak, for instance, of the Age of Elizabeth, in France of the Age of the Religious Wars, in Spain of the Age of Philip II. In its exported versions, therefore, it tended to stand less for a historical epoch, as it had long done for German historians, than for a phenomenon, somewhat elusive and murkily defined. Even in Germany the term was losing its original clarity.

The Germans had coined the term and applied it, and they did so, of course, with the concerns and prejudices consistent with their peculiar religious and political history. Many used it as a cultural battle axe against Catholics as part of the *Kulturkampf*.[20] As the term began to wend its way into other languages, it retained some of the original prejudices and took on new ones, consonant with the different cultures in which it was now employed. In the romance languages, moreover, where, unlike German and English, the same word stands for both reform and reformation, the possibility for confusion was compounded—"anti-Reformation" was the same as "anti-reform."

Meanwhile, a few German Lutheran historians were paying more attention to the early religious and spiritual aspects of Catholicism treated by Gothein. Gothein had himself picked up on von Ranke's thesis that the Catholic phenomenon was propelled in part by such influences, and he was the first to insist on Spain's importance in this regard. Ignatius and the Jesuits were the instrument through which Spain saved the Catholic Church in the *Siglo de Oro*. Two points must be noted: first, that Spain's importance was recognized at a very late date, and second, that Gothein, like Ranke, put the Jesuits at the very center of Counter Reformation.

At about the same time, Wilhelm Maurenbrecher had also pursued the problem of Catholic vitality beyond its political and military aspects to discover the importance of Francisco Jiménez de Cisneros, Savonarola, Erasmus, humanist reformers in Germany, and similar persons and movements. What Maurenbrecher did more than any previous Lutheran historian was indicate the number and variety of the late-medieval efforts that might fall under the rubric "reform." More to the point for our purposes, he bestowed historiographical currency on "Catholic Reformation." Although he did not coin the term, he made it operative in 1880 by enshrining it in the title of the first and only volume of his "History of the Catholic Reformation" *(Geschichte der katholischen Reformation)*.[21]

By his very employment of the term, Maurenbrecher became the first historian to parallel in a broadly influential way *the* Reformation with a "Catholic Reformation." In their virtually unanimous boycott of "Counter Reformation," Catholic handbooks of church history had already been speaking of "a true reformation" and a "Catholic reformation."[22] Constantin R. von Höfler, for his part, had written in 1878 of a "Latin Reformation" (*die romanische Reformation*), by which he wanted to indicate the continuity into the sixteenth century of previous efforts at reform in the Mediterranean world.[23] As early as 1859 Joseph Kerker, a Swiss priest, had drawn attention to steps taken in Italy in the early sixteenth century that he described as "Catholic reform."[24] It was Maurenbrecher, however, who made "Catholic Reformation" a designation to reckon with.

Two important Catholic journals in Germany took immediate and basically favorable notice of Maurenbrecher's book, an unusual occurrence for those days.[25] They recognized that a third designation had joined "Reformation" and "Counter Reformation," the concepts that until that point dominated the field, and their blessing on "Catholic Reformation" helped propagate the new term in Catholic circles.

No sooner had Maurenbrecher published his book, however, than other Lutherans challenged his use of "Reformation" in relationship to the Catholic Church. The term was so laden with theological presuppositions in Protestant circles as to mean that no rival was possible, for *the* Reformation was the *true* reformation, the only authentically Christian reformation, based on the doctrine of justification by faith alone. To speak of a Catholic Reformation was to create confusion. Even Gothein later took issue with Maurenbrecher. What happened in Spain at the time of Queen Isabella, he argued, was a reinstatement of ascetical and religious practices of the Middle Ages, a far cry from the real reformation that Luther later introduced.[26] For Gothein that early "Counter Reformation" in Spain was, despite the sympathy he sometimes manifested for it, basically "the rebirth of the Middle Ages."[27] Against Maurenbrecher, Hermann Baumgarten also argued that what happened in

Catholicism was not a reformation but a restoration.[28] For quite different reasons some Catholic historians also preferred "Restoration" (*Wiederherstellung*) because they, too, recognized the Protestant connotations of "Reformation" and wanted to distance Catholicism from it as far as possible.[29] Neither side could imagine any common ground.

If Catholicism, even a resurgent Catholicism, was nothing more than a reinstatement of the Middle Ages and a continuation of it, what was Protestantism? Protestantism was modern, which was good. Perhaps no one thrust the modernity question into historical awareness as effectively as Jacob Burckhardt in his great masterpiece of 1860, *Die Kultur der Renaissance in Italien*. This was an epoch-making book in the literal sense of contributing mightily to the idea that the Renaissance constituted yet another historical epoch, situated somewhere between the Middle Ages and . . . . . . well, the modern world. In Burckhardt's famous expression, the Italians of the Renaissance were "the first-born among the sons of modern Europe."[30] This was true of them because by their return to the forms and values of classical antiquity they turned their backs on the Middle Ages, which meant in large part that they turned their backs on the Catholic Church.

Thus even from *Kulturgeschichte* came the message that the light and genius characteristic of modernity resulted from breaking with the old church. Several generations later, Gothein would draw the obvious conclusion that the Counter Reformation was a reaction to the great cultural transformation of the Renaissance as well as to the great religious transformation of the Reformation.[31]

Many Catholics were willing to accept that modernity was the result of Renaissance and Reformation, but, unlike most of their contemporaries, they assessed "the modern world" negatively. On a broad front Catholics had begun to claim the Middle Ages as *their* centuries, the "Age of Faith." Riding to some extent on the wings of the Romantic movement, they promoted gothic architecture for their churches and cultivated Gregorian chant as their preferred mode of musical expression. During their liturgies priests wore gothic-style vestments, while Thomas Aquinas meantime refuted the errors of all philosophers since Descartes. Thus by the end of the nineteenth century "Counter Reformation" and "Catholic Reformation" had become categories inseparable from the larger question of the relationship of the Catholic Church to all the bad things (according to Catholics) or to all the good things (according to almost everyone else) that had happened in Europe since the fifteenth century.

Through evidence drawn principally from art and literature, Burckhardt had reinforced the almost axiomatic truth that the church of the fifteenth century was corrupt, the papacy utterly worldly, and religious practice either hypocritical or superstitious. The humanists were essentially pagan. Burckhardt admitted that there were a few sincere and ardent religious figures in Italy, such as Bernardine of Siena and Savonarola, whose sermons moved crowds to frenzied acts of repentance, but he judged their results superficial.

In his "Renaissance," therefore, Burckhardt had constructed an epoch that was not only the chronological equivalent of "Catholic Reformation" but also in a rather backhanded way supported the basic assumption of Catholic Reformation—a few individuals were trying to remedy a seemingly irremediable situation. For Burckhardt, Northern Europe knew what true religion was: "The North produced an *Imitation of Christ,* which . . . worked for the ages; the South produced men who made on their fellows a mighty but passing impression."[32]

In 1893 Gustav Droysen in *Geschichte der Gegenreformation* carried judgments like these a long step further, virtually into caricature.[33] For him, even sixteenth-century Catholic prelates like Gasparo Contarini, Jacopo Sadoleto, and Giovanni Morone were by definition anti-Catholic because they worked for reform. Their triumph would have meant the end of the Catholic Church. By its own inner logic Christianity in sincere inquirers ineluctably led to Protestantism. "Counter Reformation" expressed the quintessence of Catholicism, which was reaction and repression.

✝

Throughout the nineteenth century, then, the discussion and debate about terminology were confined almost exclusively to German-speaking historians, with Lutherans taking the lead and Catholics for the most part reacting. By the beginning of the twentieth century, the categories invented by scholars writing in German were current outside German-speaking lands and were therefore moving into a new phase of their history. Before we turn to that phase, however, a few observations are in order.

As is obvious, in the evolution of the categories several dogmas went virtually unquestioned by both Protestant and secular historians. The first was that the church by the end of the Middle Ages was rotten. Some Catholics like Janssen challenged this assumption by trying to show, through evidence and arguments that sound amazingly similar to some studies published in the last few years, that religious practice among the faithful was vigorous and healthy.[34] Other Catholic historians felt compelled to admit a serious malaise, otherwise the drastic reform measures of the Council of Trent made no sense. Yes, there were some bright lights—Ignatius of Loyola, for instance, and the Oratory of Divine Love—but they served only to call attention to the otherwise unrelieved gloom.

The second dogma was a necessary corollary from the first: every figure of religious importance or intensity was to be defined as a reformer. The assumption behind this dogma was that the shambles of the pre-Reformation church were so great as to be oppressively obvious to the genuinely devout, and therefore the reform of the church had to be the object of their strivings. The devout were perforce reformers. "Reformer" was, moreover, a category peculiarly congenial to Protestant historiography, where the great heroes of the sixteenth century were indeed just that, by definition, and the application of "reformer" to Catholics rested upon an analogy with Protestantism. Catholic reformers were therefore often seen in Lutheran historiography as precursors of Luther.

This leads to a further observation about the state of the evidence available in the nineteenth century. To read these historians today is to be struck by their erudition and by the diligence with which they pursued sources to produce their magnificent works. It is also to be struck by how difficult and limited, in comparison with our own day, was their access to sources, especially for the Catholic subjects about which they wrote. The Vatican Archives, surely the single richest font for such subjects, were not formally opened to researchers until Pope Leo XIII's Regolamento of May 1, 1884.[35]

The great editions of correspondence and other documents prepared according to the increasingly stringent criteria of historical scholarship were yet to be. The Weimar edition of Luther's works was launched in 1883, but critical editions of great Catholic sources were still in the future. The Jesuits, for instance, published the first fascicle of their *Monumenta Historica,* which would grow to some 135 tomes, only in 1894,[36] and not until two years later would Otto Braunsberger begin publishing his eight-volume correspondence of Peter Canisius, the single most important Catholic figure in Germany in the second half of the sixteenth century.[37] Perhaps most significant, the first volume of the critical edition of the documents of the Council of Trent, published by the Görres-Gesellschaft, appeared only in 1901.[38] The history of the council most easily consulted was Paolo Sarpi's brilliant but thoroughly prejudiced *Historia del Concilio Tridentino,* 1619, which argued that Trent was a papal conspiracy to prevent reform.[39]

Finally, we must realize that some historians managed to avoid using any of the terms we have been discussing. Beginning in 1907, for example, Bernhard Duhr published a four-volume history of the Jesuits in Germany until their suppression by the papacy in 1773.[40] In it he divided his material according to centuries or half-centuries, an old device of chroniclers that has its own problems, but that at least enabled him to avoid taking a stand on "Counter Reformation," "Catholic Reformation," and "Catholic Restoration." In speaking of Protestantism, moreover, he not surprisingly also avoided using "Reformation," but neither did he employ the angry terms "Revolution" and "Revolt." He spoke instead of "the religious division" (*die religiöse Spaltung*) and, for the wars of religion, "the fratricidal religious conflicts" (*die religiösen Bruderkämpfe*).

By 1900, in any case, history and church history textbooks in Germany had become standardized and utterly predictable in the basic information they provided and in the sequence of events within which they presented the religious upheavals of the sixteenth century. They had created patterns that even outside Ger-

many would be invariably and unthinkingly repeated almost down
to the present.

✝

C-Ref para

Only at a relatively late date did a Catholic historian achieve the
international stature to make a contribution to the debate that
would have resonances throughout Western culture. That person
was the Austrian Ludwig von Pastor, a student of Janssen's who at
the age of nineteen decided to write a history of the popes beginning with the Renaissance. He meant the enterprise as a vindica-
tion of Catholic historical scholarship and as a challenge to Ranke's
history of the same subject, which still attracted a wide readership.[41]
Although the first volume of his *Geschichte der Päpste seit dem Ausgang des Mittelalters* was published in 1886, most of the subsequent
volumes, including those particularly pertinent to our topic, were
published in the twentieth century, up to 1933.[42] Because of its use
of new sources, especially the Vatican Archives, this undertaking
attracted the attention of scholars of many nations and ideologies.
Despite consisting of sixteen volumes, the work was eventually
translated in full into Italian, French, Spanish, and English (forty
volumes!) and is still consulted today.

Pastor was from the beginning determined to show that even in
the papal court concern for reform of the church antedated the
Reformation, and he carefully assembled and presented documentation to prove it. Although much dependent upon Burckhardt for
his interpretation of the Renaissance, he differed from him most
notably in finding among the Italian humanists some who were
Christian; he "carefully sorted out the sheep from the goats."[43] By
1907, when he had finished his fourth volume (on the two Medici
popes, 1513–1534), he was convinced that he had shown that the

impulses in the Catholic Church toward renewal and reform that culminated in Trent were antecedent to the Reformation and independent of it.

Pastor's fifth volume dealt with the pontificate of Paul III (1534–1549), who convoked the council, approved the Society of Jesus, and established the Roman Inquisition. Pastor in effect retitled his work by giving this and the subsequent six volumes the subtitle "History of the Popes in the Period of the Catholic Reformation and Restoration" *(Geschichte der Päpste im Zeitalter der katholischen Reformation und Restauration).* According to Pastor, "Catholic Reformation" meant the internal regeneration of Catholicism and "Restoration" meant its reestablishment in endangered or lost regions.[44] Volume 12, which begins with Gregory XIII in 1572, he entitled "The Period of the Catholic Restoration and the Thirty Years War."

Even with Pastor's backing, "Catholic Restoration," his alternative to "Counter Reformation," languished in the international marketplace. But as his volumes were gradually translated into other languages, they without doubt gave a new impulse to the idea and term "Catholic Reform/Reformation." Although rooted in the study of individuals, his basic vision was institutional. He wanted, moreover, to avoid any suggestion that true reform might touch doctrine. The result was that, like the Lutherans, he came to define "Catholic Reformation" as effective discipline aimed at changing behavior, thus giving it more of an ecclesiastical than a religious meaning.[45]

Pastor lived many years in Italy, becoming in 1920 the Austrian ambassador to the Holy See, and he emphasized the Italian sources for "the Catholic Reformation and Restoration." Thus he very much influenced younger Italian Catholic historians like Pio

Paschini and Pietro Tacchi Venturi, who especially tended to follow his ideas about what constituted *Riforma cattolica,* even when they chose to use "Counter Reformation" over Pastor's "Catholic Restoration."[46]

In 1929 the *Enciclopedia Italiana* opted for *Controriforma,* giving *Restaurazione cattolica* as its synonym and defining it as the period from Trent until Westphalia.[47] Twenty-five years later the *Enciclopedia Cattolica,* published in Vatican City, opted for *Riforma cattolica* in the sense Jedin gave it in his essay in 1946. Although Jedin himself was the author of the entry, he made no mention of "Counter Reformation" as a name or as a historical reality; nor was there in the encyclopedia another entry under that name.[48]

Paschini and Tacchi Venturi were priests. But it was "lay" *(laici)* scholars—liberals and anticlericals still living the glories and resentments of the Risorgimento—who set the academic pace in Italy. They were happy with "Counter Reformation," interpreting it as a repressive movement responsible in whole or in part for Italy's cultural and political "decline" in the sixteenth century and thus tending to redefine it as an attack not so much on Protestants as on liberal and humane values. For Francesco De Sanctis, the great nineteenth-century historian of Italian literature, Sarpi was a hero whose description of Trent as a "deformation," not reformation, was utterly justified.[49]

From the mid-nineteenth century until today, perhaps nowhere in Europe has scholarship on the sixteenth century been so clearly and consistently divided into two camps—*laici* and *cattolici*—as in Italy and nowhere used so pointedly to argue contemporary political issues.[50] When in the early 1920s, for instance, Fascists held up the Counter Reformation as an ideal epoch of discipline and obedience, Benedetto Croce made the first veiled sign of his turn against "the dominant party" by defining the *Controriforma* as nothing more than the efforts of a besieged institution, destitute of all creative energy, to secure its own survival.[51]

In 1929 Croce, a figure of almost incomparable intellectual prestige in Italy during the first half of the twentieth century, gave *Controriforma* a practical synonym with the title of his "History of the Baroque Age in Italy" *(Storia dell'età barocca in Italia).*[52] Although among art historians "baroque" was well on the road to respectability and moving away from being considered bizarre, vulgar, and manipulative,[53] Croce, philosopher and litterateur, used it to signify the decadence of Counter-Reformation culture and society.[54]

Croce was not the first to indicate reciprocity between Counter Reformation and Baroque. In 1921 with Werner Weisbach's *Der Barock als Kunst der Gegenreformation,* the identification of the one with the other reached an important, though controversial, landmark.[55] Weisbach saw baroque art as a genuine expression of Counter-Reformation spirituality—heroic, mystical, turbulent, ascetic, erotic—and he evaluated it more or less positively. In Italy, however, Croce's negative assessment, itself part of an older and larger Italian tradition, carried the day among the intelligentsia.

"Counter Reformation" *(Contrarreforma)* crept late, obscurely, and almost imperceptibly into Spanish historiography, not becoming established there until several decades into the century.[56] Along with this term, Spanish historians were simultaneously using "Spanish Renaissance," "Catholic Restoration," "Catholic Reformation," and even "Catholic Counter Reformation" more or less as synonyms for a broad, encompassing reality beginning with the reigns of Ferdinand and Isabella and extending into the seventeenth century.

Spanish historians fell into clerical and anticlerical camps, but with an important difference from their Italian counterparts regarding our subject. For Italian "lay" historians the sixteenth century marked a decline in their country's cultural preeminence and an end to political independence for large territories like the Duchy of Milan. It marked, à la Croce, a period of literary decadence. Although well into the next century Italy still produced the largest number of Europe's truly outstanding artists, these historians tended to see the changes in style as a diminishment of the glory achieved by Leonardo da Vinci, Raphael, and Michelangelo. They plunged into a grief about Italy's fate that only the promise of the Risorgimento could assuage.

No Spanish historian or litterateur, however, could or wanted to deny that the sixteenth century was the golden age—*el Siglo de Oro*—of Spanish culture and political hegemony. They could of course point to policies of church or state that sowed the seeds for later decline, but the period itself began with the unification of Aragon and Castille through the royal marriage, with the success of the *reconquista* after seven hundred years of struggle, and with the discovery of America. It resounded with the names of the great *conquistadores,* with the names of great philosophers and theologians like Francisco de Vitoria and Francisco Suarez, with the names of the great religious figures like Ignatius of Loyola, Teresa of Avila, and John of the Cross. With El Greco (an import, of course) and, later, with Velázquez, Murillo, and Zurbarán. With Cervantes and Lope de Vega. Why look further for a name and not rest satisfied, indeed, with *el Siglo de Oro?*

In this regard France was of course much closer to Spain than to Italy or even Germany, where the Thirty Years War had finally wrought devastation on Protestant and Catholic alike. The French Wars of Religion threw the nation into chaos, but *le grand siècle* followed when France attained its political and cultural apogee and also produced some of its most luminous religious and ecclesiastical figures—François de Sales, Jeanne Françoise de Chantal, Cardinal Berulle, to name only a few, and, most important, Vincent de Paul. Whereas in Italy Carlo Borromeo, "the great saint of the Counter Reformation," won harsh assessments from "lay" historians, in France "Monsieur Vincent," the great servant of the poor, held a status analogous to that of Francis of Assisi in Italy, everybody's saint.

The sheer brilliance of this era is one of several factors, but an especially important one, that from the beginning inclined French scholars to an independent path in the naming process. Another factor was a long-standing Gallican tradition that opposed the national genius to the designs of an international "Counter Reformation."[57] Still another was a disinclination to bow too profoundly before the accomplishments of German *Wissenschaft*. In any case, early in the century Augustin Renaudet popularized the term "Pre-Reformation"—*Préréforme*—to denote the religious situation in France before 1517.[58] Although the expression was suggestive of the inevitability of the Reformation, it could be taken in a more neutral sense.

Eventually Evangelism—*l'évangelisme*—utilized in 1914 by the Catholic scholar Pierre Imbart de La Tour for the period between 1521 and 1538, was of more international influence.[59] With Evangelism he believed he had found a concept that united all the lively religious currents of the time, for the one thing they had in common was the evangelical ideal, that is, return to the Gospel. This ideal, Imbart de La Tour thought, later bifurcated into a Protestant (revolutionary) and a Catholic path. Unlike Pastor, who was interested in the ferment only insofar as it represented moral improve-

ment and issued in ecclesiastical discipline, Imbart de La Tour focused on mystical aspirations and religious sentiment, "bringing to
light a world practically ignored" until then, which would increasingly gain attention in French approaches to the period.[60]

This tendency to move away from the ecclesiastical and political
framework characteristic of most earlier scholarship found magnificent expression at about the same time in the eleven volumes of
Abbé Henri Bremond's masterpiece, "Literary History of Religious
Sentiment in France" *(Histoire littéraire du sentiment religieux en
France),* which dealt largely with the seventeenth century.[61] Bremond set as his goal the study of "religion," that is, "the interior
life"—*la vie interière du catholicisme français.* The richness of that life in
the seventeenth century resulted in a "religious renaissance."[62] It
was in the wake of this tradition of Catholic scholarship represented
by Imbart de La Tour and Bremond that Lucien Febvre produced
in 1929 his famous "Question mal posée," in which he besought
historians of the period to stop studying churches and begin studying religion, an essay discussed below in Chapter 4.

Even when French Catholic scholars took a more institutional
approach and professedly wrote histories of the *church,* they still
often avoided the terms commonly used in Germany and ever
more widely appropriated elsewhere. The titles of the four volumes
of the History of the Church inaugurated in 1934 under the editor-
ship of Augustin Fliche and Victor Martin that are pertinent to our
subject are symptomatic of this avoidance: (1) "The Church and the
Renaissance, 1449–1517"; (2) "The Religious Crisis of the Sixteenth Century"; (3) "The Church at the Time of the Council of
Trent"; and (4) "The Catholic Restoration, 1563–1648."[63] Nonetheless, even in France the debate over the respective merits and

demerits of Catholic Reform and Counter Reformation exercised scholars.[64]

When French historians used "Catholic Reform/Reformation," they generally meant the late sixteenth and early seventeenth centuries, precisely the period for which Pastor ceased using it. Martin Phillippson, a Walloon historian antipathetic to Catholicism, tried an altogether different approach. He turned on its head the Catholic designation of the Reformation as Revolution by naming the Catholic phenomenon "The Religious Counter-Revolution" *(la Contre-révolution religieuse),* that is, the church's war against freedom of conscience.[65]

In the early twentieth century, English-language historiography showed inconsistencies similar to those in German, Spanish, and Italian scholarship, but with "Counter Reformation" eventually tending to predominate. English historians, rather than those from former colonies or the outposts of the empire, took the lead. Of all the countries considered so far, England was easily the most thoroughly Protestant, and its history books recognized Catholics, who were now an insignificant and disdained minority, only as perpetrators of armadas and gunpowder plots against the throne and the established church. "Counter Reformation" as a definition of early modern Catholicism fit the bill perfectly. By the turn of the century it was already appearing in texts to mean repression of the Reformation.[66]

The second volume of *The Cambridge Modern History,* 1904, was dedicated to the Reformation. Of some seven hundred pages of text, about ninety treated "the Catholic side," divided between two contributions whose titles indicate how fluid the terminology still was at this date, with "Counter Reformation" notably absent.

W. E. Collins, who dealt almost as much with Protestants and attempts to suppress them as with anything else, entitled his piece "The Catholic South," whereas R. V. Laurence in "The Church and Reform" dealt with the new religious orders and the Council of Trent.[67]

In 1908, with volume 4 of *The Catholic Encyclopedia,* "Counter Reformation" received a reluctant imprimatur in a long and influential article by J. H. Pollen, the English Jesuit historian specializing in the Elizabethan period. There was no entry for Catholic Reform. Pollen accepted "Counter Reformation," "long in use among Protestant historians," for extrinsic reasons only—because it had "recently been introduced into Catholic handbooks."

For Pollen, Counter Reformation meant "the period of Catholic revival" from 1560 to 1648. It seems to be identical with Catholic Reform, a term he also employed. Despite beginning the phenomenon in 1560, Pollen rejected the idea that it followed upon the Reformation, for "Luther was a Catholic Reformer before he became a Protestant." The Counter Reformation was for him more a movement and spontaneous generation of fervor than an organized strategy. The "leaders or best representatives of the movement [were] St. Ignatius, its pioneer . . . St. Philip Neri and St. Vincent de Paul, exemplars of its maturity."

Although Pollen asserted Trent's importance, he was remarkably vague about what the council accomplished, not mentioning even the decree on justification. He singled out, however, "three great reforming popes"—Pius V, because he provided an example of personal austerity and enforced church laws; Gregory XIII, because he was amiable, founded colleges in Rome, established permanent nuntiatures, and held a successful jubilee year in Rome in 1585; and Sixtus V, because he got the papal treasury out of debt and pursued a vigorous program of repair and rebuilding in Rome. This is reform? In any case, Pollen made no mention of inquisitions, or of the St. Bartholomew's Day Massacre, or, for that matter, of Humanism. He gave only slight attention to the religious wars in France and Germany.

Despite the diffuse, apologetic, and sometimes confusing meaning with which Pollen invested "Counter Reformation," his acceptance of the term, howsoever unwillingly, in what was taken as a quasi-official Catholic publication, gave it a significant boost in English-language scholarship as the term to cover many things beginning and ending at many different times. For instance, B. J. Kidd, an Anglican divine, published in 1933 his fair-minded and well-informed *Counter-Reformation, 1550–1600,* one of the few books on the subject by an Anglophone writer.[68] Instead of beginning the book in 1550, however, as his title indicated, he began it in 1520, with what he called "The Revival of Religion in Italy and Spain, 1520–80," that is, he began with what Pastor called "Catholic Reformation." He did not mention why he ended this section in 1580 instead of 1600, with which, according to the title of the book, he brought the "Counter Reformation" to a close, a half-century earlier than Pollen. Perhaps to show himself flexible he dated the last chapter "1555–1618."

In 1930 H. Outram Evennett published *The Cardinal of Lorraine and the Council of Trent,* until then and for several decades afterward the only work of high merit and original scholarship on the Catholic phenomenon by a scholar publishing in English. In this elegantly written and amazingly mature work for a man only twenty-nine years old, Evennett included a paragraph about the "chief insufficiency of the unsatisfactory word 'Counter-Reformation.'" Besides other problems, the term leads us "to misconceive and to underrate what was in fact a most complex movement."[69] But in the Cambridge of the 1930s Evennett seemed resigned to its inevitability.

✟

This was the mess out of which Jedin tried to create order in 1946 with his essay entitled "Catholic Reformation or Counter Reformation?" No one was better qualified than he to do so. He recognized the validity of "Catholic Reformation," by which he meant the impulses toward reform of the church that began in the late Middle Ages and continued even into the eighteenth century. He recognized the validity of "Counter Reformation" in that it designated the defense that the Catholic Church had to mount against the Protestant attack. It is worth noting that in designating Counter Reformation a "defense," Jedin deftly redefined the word almost in defiance of what it originally meant.

Although these two realities were in general related to each other like soul (Catholic Reformation) to body (Counter Reformation), they were sometimes separable. As Jedin pointed out, Saint Bernardine of Siena, who died in 1444, obviously had nothing to do with Counter Reformation, but Bernardine was part of Catholic Reformation. Moreover, both the Council of Trent and the Society of Jesus could be described as now embodying Catholic Reformation, now Counter Reformation. Jedin's solution to the problem, as indicated earlier, was to eliminate the "or" in his title and substitute "and": the correct designation was "Catholic-Reformation-*and*-Counter Reformation."

In the next chapter I will analyze Jedin's essay and his place in scholarship on the issue. In the meantime a few general observations about the essay's fate and impact are in order. If authority won by mastery of a subject has any weight in scholarship, Jedin's solution should have prevailed. But it did not, or only quite imperfectly. Why?

The most fundamental reason, as we shall see, is that with time scholars found his solution either too narrow or too broad. But there were some more immediate problems. For one thing, the name Jedin devised for it was Teutonically long-winded. Such a name could only with great difficulty prevail in a discipline in which its colleagues were snappy designations like the Middle Ages, the Renaissance, the Enlightenment, and the Reformation. More important was the historiographical context in 1946, the year after World War II ended—even scholars' minds were on putting their lives and their countries back together. It was not the most opportune moment to get a hearing, especially on a subject of interest mainly to Catholic apologists.

This helps explain why the book was translated only into Italian, and that not until 1957.[70] As best I can ascertain, it was not reviewed in any English-language journal, not even the *Catholic Historical Review*. Somewhat more surprising, the *Revue d'Histoire Ecclésiastique* gave it a notice of only one paragraph.[71] Some German Catholic journals reviewed it appreciatively but briefly, with more extensive discussions not beginning until a decade later.[72] In Italy it received favorable, mixed, cautious, and neutral reactions from Catholics publishing there. Much more important was the immediate, favorable, and lengthy review from Delio Cantimori, the *laico* historian of Italian heretics.[73] Nonetheless, Jedin's essay, the most considered statement on the issue by a scholar already well on his way to becoming the unquestioned international expert on it, made for the most part a soft impression.

Not surprisingly, therefore, the confusion has persisted for the past fifty years. The latest edition of the authoritative *Oxford Dictionary of the Christian Church* (1997), for instance, has a single entry for our subject, "Counter-Reformation,"[74] whereas the almost simultaneously published *Oxford Encyclopedia of the Reformation* (1996) has two—"Catholic Reformation" and "Roman Catholicism."[75]

In addition to other names that will be discussed in detail in the chapters that follow, "Tridentine Reformation," found at least implicitly in Jedin, has been championed by several scholars, whose sights are set especially on Italy.[76] R. Po-chia Hsia, whose geographical scope is broader, entitled his most recent book *The World of Catholic Renewal, 1540–1770.*[77]

In North America, unlike Britain, "Catholic Reformation" has tended to prevail over its traditional rival. Pierre Janelle, a French scholar writing under American auspices, published in 1949 *The Catholic Reformation,* an informed but apologetic survey from about 1450 to 1650 that fanned life into this alternative.[78] Janelle wrote almost exclusively about piety, religious practice, mysticism and piety, art, doctrine, and literature. He wrote about Catholic Reformation without any Counter Reformation—almost without any Reformation.

In 1969 John C. Olin published *The Catholic Reformation: Savonarola to Ignatius Loyola, Reform in the Church, 1495–1540.*[79] This book, a collection of texts widely used in university courses, has been revised and reissued several times, most recently in 1990 under a new title: *Catholic Reform: From Cardinal Ximenes to the Council of Trent, 1495–1563.*[80] It too has been influential among students and teachers in North America in prompting alternatives to "Counter Reformation."

But that name has had great holding power, as indicated in the fact that *The New Catholic Encyclopedia,* 1967, followed the example of its predecessor in designating the Catholic entry as "Counter Reformation," even though in the now almost ritualistically obligatory disclaimer about it the author, E. L. Lampe, insisted it was "a misnomer." Lampe also maintained, however, that "Catholic Reformation" was as inadequate as "Counter Reformation," because "the essence of the movement is more basic than reform."

Both of the old war-horses are inadequate, perhaps, but, once again, books and chapters must have titles, even if they do not correspond to the contents. The most extreme case of such dissonance that I have run across is the third volume of *The New Cambridge Modern History* (1968). The title consisted in surely one of the most curious of all possible historical couplings: *The Counter-Reformation and the Price Revolution, 1559–1610.* Counter Reformation? Price Revolution? Or, for that matter, 1559? 1610?

Within its seven hundred pages, the volume contained a single chapter on what "Counter Reformation" in the title seemed to promise, "The Papacy, Catholic Reform, and Christian Mission," but the twenty-seven-page chapter was half the length of the chapter on Protestantism, as if volume 2 dedicated wholly to the Reformation were not enough. This volume, entitled *Counter Reformation,* dealt with the Council of Trent in seven pages, the Jesuits in two. "Counter Reformation" seemingly designated a time-frame or epoch, to the underlying reality of which the word bore little relationship. What's in a name?

TWO

✝

Hubert Jedin and
the Classic Position

No scholar of the twentieth century is more important for our subject than Hubert Jedin. He contributed to it through his more theoretical reflections, especially the essay of 1946, but also more generally by providing an impetus to scholarship about Catholicism in the period. In particular, the first two volumes of his *Geschichte des Konzils von Trient,* which appeared in 1949 and 1957, shattered the stereotype of a council going about business as usual. When Jedin showed the sharpness of debate and the differences of opinion at Trent, and thus implicitly indicated how certain aspects of the council had afterward been misinterpreted down to the present, he made the subject interesting. Both directly and indirectly he inspired a generation of students, especially in Germany and Italy, to turn to "the Catholic side" as an important area of research.

Jedin was born on June 17, 1900, the last of ten children of an elementary schoolteacher and sometimes farmer in the small village of Grossbriessen in Upper Silesia, the easternmost part of Germany.[1] His mother was a Jewish convert to Catholicism. He received an excellent secondary education in a classical Gymnasium and also was much influenced by some priests in the *convictus* where he lived. At about age fifteen he joined a morally rigorous youth movement known as the "Quickborn" and took an active part in it. During these years he decided to become a priest for the diocese of Breslau.

After three years of study at the University of Breslau, Jedin was ordained to the priesthood in 1924 at the age of twenty-four. By this time he had decided, with his bishop's approval, on an academic career in history. He was clear from the beginning that the sixteenth century would be his specialty, an option consonant with the singular importance of the Reformation for Germany.[2]

From 1926 until 1929 he worked in Rome on his biography of Seripando, and the next year he successfully presented the first part of it as his *Habilitationsschrift* at the University of Breslau, which won him a teaching post there from 1930 until 1933, when Hitler came to power. Jedin had little interest in politics and did not show much concern over the rise of the National Socialists, although he considered them dangerous.[3] He expressed some sympathy, however, with Hitler's assertions of German needs and German griefs as a result of the Treaty of Versailles. But on September 1, 1933, he was forbidden to carry out his teaching duties because he was, through his mother, a non-Aryan. His teaching career was ended for as long as the Nazis were in power.

Rather than stay in Germany in some pastoral capacity, he decided to return to Rome, where he would be supported by the Görres-Gesellschaft to edit the thirteenth volume of the Acts of the Council of Trent. When he was nearly finished with the volume, published in 1938, he returned to Breslau to take a post in the archives of the diocese, where he discovered that because of the racial laws he could not assume the official title of archivist. On November, 10, 1938, the morning after the *Kristallnacht,* the notorious outbreak of violence against the Jews orchestrated by the Nazis, Jedin was arrested in the archives by the Gestapo to be deported to Buchenwald. When the Gestapo learned he was a Catholic priest, however, they released him—not because of his priestly status but because they thought a mistake must therefore have been made in identifying him as a Jew.

He had gained some time but realized that he had to get out of Germany. Meanwhile, he had conceived the idea of using his biography of Seripando as the cornerstone of a critical history of the Council of Trent. This would be the first comprehensive study of the council since the polemically antipapal work by the Servite friar Paolo Sarpi in the early seventeenth century and the defensive rejoinder to it by the Jesuit Pietro Sforza Pallavicini several decades later.[4] It was a project for which he was by talent and training ideally suited.

For almost a year these plans got nowhere. Finally, Jedin proposed his idea to Cardinal Giovanni Mercati, the highly respected prefect of the Vatican Library, who responded with enthusiasm and agreed to provide financial support, modest but sufficient, for him and the project.[5] In October 1939, just after the outbreak of World War II, Jedin managed to slip out of Germany for Rome, where he would remain until 1949.

Jedin was always politically conservative. During his time in Rome, especially as the Third Reich began to collapse, he had already begun to fear that the Western democracies would never be able to withstand the menace of Communism. The menace became all the more vivid to him by 1946, when he realized that the Allies had allowed his own Silesia to fall behind the Iron Curtain. In the struggle against Communism he, like other Catholics, saw the church as a bulwark.

While suffering these great adversities, Jedin had in any case accumulated ten more years of uninterrupted research at the best depository in the world for documents related to Trent. His circumstances in Rome were of course often difficult, especially during the last years of the war, but he used his time to acquire an incomparable mastery of almost every aspect of the history of the council.

In 1949, the year the first volume of his history of Trent was published, he was finally able to return to Germany to begin teaching church history in the Catholic Theological Faculty of the University of Bonn. He taught at Bonn for fifteen years, until his retirement in 1965 at age sixty-five. During his career there, however, he spent long periods in Rome as a consultant or *peritus* for Vatican Council II, 1962–1965, at which he was much respected but not particularly influential.

While still living in Rome he had been a guiding figure in the founding in 1947 of the important journal *Rivista di Storia della Chiesa in Italia*. He was also instrumental in establishing or administering other professional enterprises in both Germany and Italy. From 1954 until 1966 he was, moreover, in charge of the *Corpus Catholicorum,* the series of critically edited sixteenth-century texts corresponding to the Protestant *Corpus Reformatorum* and Weimar *Ausgabe* of Luther's works. In 1956 he agreed to act as general editor for a new, multivolume history of the church, *Handbuch der Kirchengeschichte,* the first volume of which appeared in 1962 and the last in 1979.[6] Important for its intrinsic merits, the *Handbuch* also rode the crest of Jedin's growing reputation as the most distinguished living historian of the Catholic Church. In 1963 he helped organize an important international conference at Trent in observance of the four-hundredth anniversary of the closing of the council.[7]

After retirement and immediately after the last session of Vatican II in December 1965, Jedin spent nine months at the Institute for Research in the Humanities, University of Wisconsin, Madison. In his *Lebensbericht* he has surprisingly, perhaps ominously, little to say about this, his only extended sojourn outside Germany or Italy. He does mention, however, that he could not believe his eyes when he saw how casually students dressed nor his ears when he heard them address their professors by their first names.[8]

In any case, while Jedin, an excellent speaker, was in North America, he was eagerly recruited for lectures at Stanford, Harvard, and other prestigious universities. The Council of Trent had arrived! This was partly because Jedin was in the course of publishing the first substantive account of the council in three hundred years, but also because another council, Vatican II, had for four or five years been front-page news around the world.

What was the relationship, scholars and others were asking, between these two councils? Was Vatican II really "the end of the Counter Reformation," as the media often reported? Jokes abounded, as when the archconservative Cardinal Alfredo Ottaviani supposedly ordered a taxi driver, "Take me to the council," and was driven to Trent. Jedin, we may be sure, was not particularly amused, but no one seemed better qualified than he to respond to serious questions about the two councils.[9]

At Madison in 1966 Jedin experienced his first "student rebellion," a phenomenon that soon spread to German universities. By the time he returned to Bonn, moreover, he was already concerned that Vatican Council II was being badly misinterpreted by radicals, against whom the bishops seemed afraid to move. Disillusionment set in, as he saw universities under siege and the church in danger of being "democratized." In his persistently cautious or even skeptical attitude toward democracy in both the ecclesiastical and the political sphere, he mirrored the deeply conservative bias of the German historical establishment and its resistance to change that only the upheavals of the 1960s, which Jedin so much feared, began to modify.[10]

Jedin nevertheless continued to write and publish, working especially on completing his history of Trent as well as editing the later volumes of the *Handbuch der Kirchengeschichte*. When he died on July 16, 1980, the number of his publications, including translations into other languages, had reached 717. The quality corresponded to the quantity.

✝

Although Jedin spent many years writing about the Catholic Church in the sixteenth century, he never substantially changed his thinking on the matter. For him there were two aspects to what happened. The first was a renewal that began with the self-reform of church members *(Selbstreform der Glieder)* in the fifteenth century, that received its legal framework at Trent, and that continued in this more orchestrated form into the eighteenth century. This was Catholic Reformation. The second was the defense of the church against its enemies. This was Counter Reformation. These two aspects sometimes were separable from each other, sometimes not. The first was not only antecedent to the second but also its animating and motivating force, as the soul to the body.

Jedin saw four phases for the first aspect, Catholic Reformation. The first phase, "self-reform," was a series of uncoordinated efforts that lasted until about 1540. These efforts consisted of phenomena that historians had been pointing to since the nineteenth century— the Devotio Moderna in the Low Countries and elsewhere, the Oratory of Divine Love in Italy, the measures taken by Francisco

Jiménez de Cisneros in Spain, the Observantist movement in the mendicant orders, and so forth. All who worked for their own salvation or for the salvation of others were, it seems, part of this self-reform.

The second phase began about 1540 and lasted for some twenty years. In 1540 the Society of Jesus was officially approved by Pope Paul III. The event was important for two reasons. It of course marked the appearance of the Jesuits on the scene, but most especially it was a symbol of the resurrection of the papacy from its torpor and timidity regarding the religious crisis. Since his election in 1534 Paul III had been trying to convoke a council, and eleven years later, in 1545, he would finally succeed. By 1545, therefore, Jedin has on the stage the three agents for the Catholic Reformation (*and* for the Counter Reformation): the Jesuits (as well as other religious orders), the beginnings of the "renewed" papacy, and the council.

The third phase was very short, 1562–1563, the two years during which the council hammered out its reform decrees, *de reformatione,* under the brilliant leadership of Cardinal Giovanni Morone. These decrees, which dealt almost exclusively with bishops and pastors, made Trent, according to Jedin, the greatest reform council in the history of the church. They carried the message that the church of the modern era would be a pastoral and missionary church—*Seelsorgs- und Missionskirche*. That was the underlying drive for the reform decrees, expressed in the axiom *Salus animarum suprema lex*— let what is good for the salvation of souls be our only guide.

The final phase was the longest, with the least clear terminal point—from 1563, the end of the council, until the Enlightenment or French Revolution. During this phase the "renewed papacy" took over direction of all aspects of Catholic Reformation and brought them, he implied, to happy fulfillment. That was the Catholic Reformation.

The Counter Reformation began in the 1520s with the Catholic apologists against Luther like Johann Eck and Hieronymus Emser, but efforts to defend the faith were not effectively marshaled until Trent undertook the task with its doctrinal decrees. The founding of the Roman Inquisition in 1542 marked another important development in the church's defense of itself, and, like Trent's condemnation of Protestant doctrine, it was a development in continuity with quite similar defenses in the Middle Ages. Nothing new here, except perhaps better coordination of efforts.

Thus, at about the same time that the papacy began to give shape and impetus to the earlier uncoordinated efforts at self-reform, that is, about 1540, it, too, like the council later, began to fuse together the Catholic Reformation with the Counter Reformation. The "renewed papacy" was the meeting point of both realities and the key to their success.

For Jedin, Catholic-Reformation-and-Counter-Reformation constituted a true epoch of church history and hence showed the inadequacies of the by then standard division into ancient, medieval, and modern. Between medieval and modern lay this "transitional" epoch, still somewhat medieval, not yet fully modern. It ran from the councils of Constance and Basel of the early fifteenth century into the seventeenth or even eighteenth. Jedin thus implicitly seemed to drop the conventional 1648 terminus for the epoch, though later in his *Handbook* he made it clear that in some sense the middle of the seventeenth century marked "the end of the Counter Reformation."[11] No matter what the terminal point, Trent would stand at some distance from both ends of the span and was thus emblematic of its transitional character: Trent reaffirmed the medieval heritage, yet looked to the modern world.

That was Jedin's basic position—lucid, coherent, and persuasive even today. We need to give it a closer look, not least of all because it is for the most part the scenario repeated again and again in textbooks and other publications. It is a given, the still standard account. It is so familiar that, even when in some particular we might know better, we never think to challenge the basic construct.

‡

Jedin, rejecting "Renaissance," "Restoration," and similar designations, accepted "Reformation" as the defining term for Catholicism, whether in the form of "the self-reformation of the members" (Catholic Reformation) or in the form of an orchestrated "self-defense" (Counter Reformation). Making "reform/reformation" the defining term was crucially important.[12] With little question Jedin appropriated the term that defined the other side and that the other side, drawing on its own traditions, had been the first effectively to apply to the Catholic side—*Reformation*.

In 1967 Jedin indicated that for two reasons he had come to prefer "Catholic Reform" to "Catholic Reformation." First, the former avoided using a term "in the sense of 'Protestant Reformation,'" and second, it indicated continuity with the reform impulses of the fifteenth century.[13] In 1946 he used the two expressions almost interchangeably, however, with the latter predominating.

Jedin often maintained that German church historians spent too much time talking about theory and method and not enough actually doing history. He showed himself impatient with what he considered their excessive speculation and penchant for abstractions.

This may help explain why when he himself had recourse to more general concepts they do not always satisfy. The synonym he consistently used here and elsewhere for (true) reform/reformation was "renewal," *Erneuerung,* which as such says little.

At one point in the essay Jedin presented his formal definitions of the two aspects of the Catholic reality. The Catholic Reformation consisted essentially in the church's self-remembrance, or reflection upon its true nature *(Selbstbesinnung).* Delio Cantimori, the great Italian scholar, seems to catch the idea of the difficult word *Selbstbesinnung* in his free translation of it as "examination of conscience."[14] The Counter Reformation was the church's self-assertion *(Selbstbehauptung).* The crucial sentence in Jedin's essay, printed in italics, runs: "The Catholic Reform is the church's remembrance of the Catholic ideal of life through inner renewal, [and] the Counter Reformation is the self-assertion of the church in the struggle against Protestantism."[15]

In these definitions "Catholic Reform" is put in terms almost mercilessly abstract. This vagueness may have been in part tactical, for in 1946 many Catholics, even historians, thought "reform" a bad word, suggestive of the errors of Protestants or, more recently, of the Modernists.[16] More tangible, at any rate, was the redefinition Jedin effected in *Gegenreformation.* Although the term originally meant what the words say, anti-Protestant, Jedin here made it into something positive, self-assertion. He also defined it as the church's rightful defense of its truth and heritage: "In order to defend itself against the enemy the church forged for itself new weapons, with which it eventually turned to a counter offensive in order to win back what was lost."[17]

This was a clever turning of the tables to make Protestantism the aggressor. That is, of course, how Catholics, not without reason,

had always understood what happened. Nonetheless, Jedin's redefinition is another illustration of how slippery the traditional terminology is, of how in our subject the defining words are often
used to mean something quite different from what they seem to say.
Jedin here gives "Counter Reformation" a meaning that is the precise opposite of what Pütter meant when he coined the term.

With this examination of Jedin's language some of his assumptions begin to emerge. In Jedin's understanding of what happened
in the Catholic Church in the sixteenth century, continuity with its
preceding traditions was paramount. He eschewed the word
"change" or its equivalent. We might think change was implicit in
the very words "reform" and "reformation," but, as we have seen,
he did not mention it when he defined them. While he never
spoke of "change" in that regard, he often spoke of "continuity."

Jedin, wittingly or unwittingly echoing von Ranke, singled out
three agents for Catholic-Reformation-and-Counter-Reformation—the papacy, the Jesuits, and the Council of Trent. At a certain
point he virtually identified them with one another, never suggest-
ing that their interests might be different, in some specific ways
even conflicting. What Trent intended the popes carried out, with
the Jesuits "a powerful instrument in their hands."[18] Concomitant
therefore with his assumption of continuity and his emphasis on it
was a vision of all the forces on the Catholic side eventually united
in a seemingly undifferentiated partnership.

Moreover, although the popes, the council, and the Jesuits
(among other orders) were doubtless extremely important, where
was everybody else—like the laity? Only once, in passing, for instance, did Jedin mention even the "House of Habsburg."[19] Jedin
knew better than anybody that the secular and ecclesiastical mag-
nates were intertwined, that pressure from Charles V not Paul III

was the great force originally propelling Trent toward a reform agenda, and that after the council secular rulers collaborated and even took the initiative in implementing Tridentine reforms, yet in this theoretical description of reform he gave the laity no role.

This seeming inconsistency was due at least in part to the way Jedin set boundaries on the subject. Here the word "church" provides the clue. Jedin's métier was, as he repeatedly professed, that of the *church* historian; he was dealing with *church* reform, and with Catholic-Reformation-and-Counter-Reformation he was establishing a new period of *church* history. By "church" it is fairly clear he meant principally the offices of pope, bishops, and pastors (to which he in effect assimilated members of religious orders like the Jesuits). Bishops and pastors were indeed consonant with his subject, for they were a special focus of the Tridentine decrees. But he was also writing out of a framework of Catholic ecclesiology that increasingly since the sixteenth century defined the church in terms of three public offices—pope, bishop, and pastor of parishes. Jedin was aware of the inadequacies of this framework, but even in later years he moved comfortably within it.[20]

This approach correlated with the style of historiography still dominant in 1946 in every Western country, which focused on great men, great events, and great ideas as the real subject of history. This style of history was also by and large consistent with the politically conservative views of many of its practitioners. It implies causality from the top downward.

Jedin's approach was further influenced by the way he defined himself as a church historian. By that designation he did not mean simply that his subject was the history of the church. In the 1970s Jedin took part in a heated debate among Catholic scholars in Germany as to whether church history was a theological discipline, that is, governed in some way by theological principles.[21] Whatever Jedin's reservations about theorizing, as early as 1947 he advocated the affirmative, a position from which he never deviated.[22] That meant that some further and even higher considerations operate in the church historians' method than is true for their secular counterparts.[23] Jedin's theoretical position reflected the institutional reality of German universities, in which church historians are firmly located in the theological faculty, separated from other historians.

In Jedin's actual practice of the discipline of history, he unambiguously identified his approach as inspired by von Ranke's ideal of discovering historical reality "as it really was."[24] The task of the historian, Jedin maintained, was "to seek the truth and nothing but the truth."[25] Nonetheless, he believed that church history, a theological discipline, dealt with so-called salvation history, *Heilsgeschichte*. He made no distinction between church history and what is sometimes called historical theology.[26] The church historian, unlike the historian of Christianity, must be a Christian believer and a member of the church. The church historian's "metahistorical standard excludes relativist writing, but not the writing of true history."[27]

In his essay of 1946 this persuasion occasionally surfaced, as when in reference to Luther's condemnation by Pope Leo X Jedin mentioned the definition of papal infallibility promulgated in 1870 at Vatican Council I.[28] I suspect that his self-identification as a church historian is at least partly responsible for the abstract way in which he defined Catholic Reform *(Selbstbesinnung)* and Counter Reformation *(Selbstbehauptung)*. With those definitions we all at once enter a language that most historians would find foreign to their enterprise.

More revealing of his theological vantage point is the implicit value-judgment on Catholic-Reformation-and-Counter-Reformation, which was positive without qualification. All that happened was for the best. Again and again Jedin spoke of the "renewed" papacy, which seems to mean not just an institution more active in religious issues but one permeated by the spiritual ideals of the earlier "self-reformers" and single-minded in pursuit of spiritual and pastoral goals. In this regard he several times identified Paul IV, Giampietro Carafa, as one of the initiators of the renewal, without a word of qualification for a person who by the time he became pope in 1555 manifested symptoms of an unpredictable fanaticism.

Jedin stood in awe of the renewal that eventually radiated from the papacy to the rest of the church, and he ended the essay with a reflection that went beyond what he calls "historical empiricism." He said: "The renewal of the church in the era of the Council of Trent is a happening so surprising, so wondrous that a purely natural and rational explanation does not do it justice. It is in the final analysis a supernatural mystery whose ultimate causes we cannot altogether attain. One is tempted to call it a miracle."[29]

The first thing to note about this conclusion of an essay dedicated to persuading scholars that Catholic-Reformation-and-Counter-Reformation is the correct designation is that Jedin himself calls it "the era of the Council of Trent." By so doing he at the last moment introduced "Tridentine Era" as another appropriate designation, thereby also raising Trent to an overarching importance as the defining element within the time-frame.

The second point worth noting is his assessment of Trent as a miracle. This designation reveals a mind-set and also warns us, as if we needed it, that historians of almost any persuasion who study the religious issues of the sixteenth century must contend within themselves with values and prejudices they learned at their mother's or father's knee. Did this mind-set affect the "empirical" works in Jedin's corpus? His four volumes on Trent and his many smaller works directly related to the council pass the most stringent tests for academic rigor and for objectivity. But when he ranged more broadly, as in his treatment of the post-Tridentine period in volume 5 of "History of the Church," he showed the effects. In some 150 pages he never mentioned the Roman or Spanish Inquisition, and he made only the most casual references to the Index of Forbidden Books. True, in the final paragraphs of the section he lists some negative aspects of "the post-Tridentine church," such as the fact that liturgy had hardened into performance of rubrics, and even admits that the church became "anti-reform," yet the criticism is brief and muted.[30] This is an example of how naming betrays historians' assumptions and then reinforces them by acting as lenses through which to read the data they encounter in their research.

Jedin's values and prejudices tended to be very much like what many historians would identify as Counter-Reformation values and prejudices—especially the fear of confusion and disorder. Josef Lortz, another Catholic priest-historian, argued in 1939 in his important *Die Reformation in Deutschland* that the un-Catholic Occamism of the late Middle Ages was the nursery out of which came Luther's Reformation.[31] Jedin argued in similar fashion, attributing the situation to the theological uncertainty and abstruseness of the late Middle Ages and to a concomitant failure of the church to exercise its teaching authority. He saw the same confusion afflicting the Catholic Church after Vatican Council II and the same failure of nerve by the bishops.[32]

Throughout his career Jedin drew a firm line of demarcation between reform and revolution. The Protestant Reformation was a revolution, as were certain tendencies within the Catholic Church of his own day, after Vatican Council II.[33] These were bad, incompatible with the true constitution of the church. We know what this constitution is from dogma, *die Dogmatik*.

But on an "empirical" level, how does a historian, according to Jedin, distinguish revolution from reform? A revolution rejects the rights of the status quo or of what "exists"—*das Recht des Bestehenden*.[34] In the concrete Jedin meant by this expression a rejection not only of the papal and episcopal hierarchy of the Catholic Church but even of the Roman Curia.[35] Both of them could be reformed, it seems, but neither abolished.

More specifically, he indicated that in the sixteenth century true reformation or true "renewal" meant, aside from a general reform of people's morals, the remedying of abuses that violated the canonical traditions of the church, especially those regarding pastoral offices. This was precisely the reform Trent undertook.[36] To reform is to remodel the house, not build a new one. It is to revise the book, not write another.[37]

Reform meant, in any case, eliminating abuses. Jedin published his essay in 1946. Already at that point he took little notice of French historiography, a tendency that correlates with a certain antipathy he felt toward French culture, French politics, and what he perceived as undue French influence in the Vatican.[38] He would remain untouched by the *Annales* school and by the methods developed by the Catholic sociologist-historian Gabriel Le Bras. In the essay, though mentioning Imbart de La Tour and a few other French historians, he was symptomatically silent about Lucien Febvre's famous article that almost a generation earlier reformulated the whole approach to the religious crisis of the sixteenth century in a way that shoved to the margin the issues of abuses and decadence, which Jedin assumed as central.

For Jedin eliminating abuses could never be revolution. When in 1968 he was pressed by the Jesuit theologian Karl Rahner on whether revolution might be possible within the Catholic Church, at least on the structural if not the doctrinal level, he denied it.[39] Without any sustained analysis he maintained, moreover, that what Pope John XXIII meant in the early 1960s by *aggiornamento,* the leit-motif of Vatican Council II, was the same as was meant by "reformation" in the sixteenth century.[40] When further pressed by the Lutheran theologian Karl Heinrich Rengstorf and others on his definition of revolution, as distinct from evolution or development, he replied that historical categories are not so sharp as philosophers might wish and he begged indulgence for not providing a more specific definition—"a task generally difficult for historians."[41]

Jedin's emphasis on continuity fits him of course into the tradition of historiography originating in the sixteenth century with Cesare Baronio's *Annales Ecclesiastici,* the Catholic response to the Magdeburg Centuriators, Lutherans.[42] The emphasis corresponds as well, however, to a continuity operative in the historical reality of Catholicism that, for better or worse, almost by definition was not operative in the same way and degree in Protestantism. Jedin's typically Catholic emphasis on continuity cannot be dismissed out of hand, therefore, as just a familiar Catholic ploy. In any case Jedin, for all his "empiricism," was remarkably chary about any up-front admission of change.

When he described reform as pertaining to pope, bishop, and pastor, he accurately reflected the way "reform of the church" was understood by influential Catholic leaders of the sixteenth century. That is important and an achievement. The problem arises when "reform of the church" is taken as standing for everything that was important in Catholicism or determinative of it.

Jedin's emphasis on reform, indeed on a profound and all-pervasive reform, which says change, seems incompatible with his concomitant emphasis on Catholic continuity. Even with that latter emphasis, Jedin saw the Tridentine church as having "modern" characteristics. The "modernity" of the Catholic Church in the period after Trent was for 1946 a bold idea that flew in the face of the convictions of Protestant polemicists, Catholic apologists, and just about everybody else. Asserting it was a sign of Jedin's independence of judgment. But, again, whether Jedin liked it or not, to argue for modernity was to argue for change.

This brings us again to two key concepts—revolution and reformation. Jedin's characterization of the Reformation as a revolution was, as we saw earlier, rooted in nineteenth-century German Catholic historiography, and his refusal to entertain the possibility that revolution, radical discontinuity, might ever be properly applied to Catholicism goes right back to Baronio. He seems to have understood revolution as such a total break with the past that it by definition destroys identity, as if France were no longer France after the French Revolution. It is significant that in Jedin's examples of revolutions and not-revolutions, he never mentioned the Gregorian Reform of the eleventh century, which is difficult to interpret in any other way than as the kind of massive shift in procedures, structures, and self-understanding—or paradigm—that we call revolution.[43] The popes led that revolution.

The correlative terms "reform/reformation" suffer from the same conceptual vagueness when Jedin speaks of them in the abstract. "Renewal" is especially slippery as a synonym, for it is just vague enough to make a reform out of every manifestation of religious fervor and devotion, which is in fact how Jedin interpreted figures like Filippo Neri and Ignatius Loyola.[44] When Jedin gets down to brass tacks, however, that is, when he gets down to the actual reform Trent legislated, he is clear that it consisted in a vast number of decrees dealing with ecclesiastical discipline directed especially toward bishops and pastors of parishes, whose impact would also ultimately be felt by the laity. Discipline, the coercive imposition of standards of behavior, does not necessarily lead to "inner renewal." The outward conformity that discipline imposes can lead, instead, to smoldering resentments.

☦

What, then, did the Tridentine decrees accomplish? Were they simply a grocery list, a slap-dash collection of directives thrown together over an eighteen-year period—an impression they can easily make upon a cursory reading? For all their particularity, Jedin saw them as moving in a single direction and animated by a single motive—"what's good for the salvation of souls." While admitting that they fell short of the reforms of the fiscal and administrative practices of the Roman Curia that so many were demanding, he believed they accomplished "much more . . . In Trent it was decided that the church of the new epoch would be a pastoral and missionary church. That is a turning-point in the history of the church not much less dramatic than are the discoveries of Copernicus and Galileo for our scientific worldview."[45] Strong language, especially for a historian as sober as Jedin.

What led him to conclude that the council had newly created a "pastoral church" *(Seelsorgskirche)?* He proceeded out of three assumptions. The first was that pastoral care before Trent, while not utterly lacking, was woefully inadequate. This was an aspect of his fundamental assumption that pre-Tridentine Catholicism was for the most part in shambles. It was also an aspect of another assumption, that if bishops were not in their sees and pastors not in their parishes, the pastoral mission of the church was by definition unachieved—for church is bishops and priests, and the proper place for ministry is the parish. The third assumption was that once bishops and pastors were in place (and, after Trent, properly trained), pastoral practice was, again almost by definition, better.

How bad was pastoral practice before the Reformation? For that matter, how bad was *anything* before the Reformation? There is really no way to answer questions as global as these, which among other things beg so many assumptions about bad and good. Nonetheless, Jedin assumed what almost all historians of his generation assumed: the situation, despite a few pockets of "reform," was extremely bleak for every aspect of Christian life. Things could only get better.

Many historians today do not accept such a negative assessment of religion in the Renaissance or late Middle Ages.[46] They have, moreover, dug up evidence indicating that at least in certain localities and situations ministry, even as done in parishes by pastors or their vicars, was more vigorous than virtually any historian would have accepted fifty years ago. Even Jedin had to qualify some of his assessment of bishops in light of what he later learned about the Spanish episcopacy before Trent.[47]

Nonetheless, no one could possibly deny that the traditional canons regarding residence, benefices, and other aspects of the discipline of bishops and pastors were either inadequately implemented or flagrantly violated. And according to the canons these were the persons to whom was entrusted "the care of souls" in the technical sense of the term. In that regard Jedin's position is still unassailable.

If ministry in the church could not be effective unless these canons were observed and even strengthened, then ministry surely was not effective.[48]

But maybe the slack in ministry was being picked up in other ways? Jedin seems almost dismissive of the ministry of the friars such as the Dominicans and Franciscans, whom recent research has rescued from the worst slurs of their detractors. He cannot be blamed, however, for not taking account of other recent studies that have almost revolutionized our understanding of the practice of ministry, at least in certain localities. These studies have shown that laymen and laywomen in confraternities were very effective in providing spiritual nourishment for one another. In other words, this research has challenged the received wisdom that just because parishes were not functioning according to a post-Tridentine model the Catholic population was not having its spiritual needs met. It has made it incontestably clear that Christians of the fifteenth and sixteenth century looked to many sources besides the parish for their spiritual well-being—and it is not easy to prove that they were in every case less well served than they were after Trent.[49]

How good was ministry after Trent? Again, no truly satisfactory answer will ever be possible. In any case, the practice of ministry was a subject just beginning to be explored by historians in 1946— through methods in which Jedin later expressed little interest. Today scholars agree that over the course of the decades or even centuries after Trent the parish clergy underwent more formalized programs of education and spiritual formation, and they by and large conformed to new standards of public behavior. Gradually the most shocking patterns of ignorance among them were reduced. For bishops, residency in their dioceses gradually became the rule, though there were still many exceptions, and bishops in many localities took up pastoral duties on a scale uncommon before Trent.[50] These were significant changes, and most of them must be attributed to the Tridentine decrees and to post-Tridentine reformers like Carlo Borromeo in Milan, who through synods and other means further articulated and enforced the standards for clerical life and ministry legislated by Trent.

Even more can be said. Seventeenth-century Catholicism experienced an explosion of ministries and of new pastoral strategies, as books promoting them and witnessing to them poured off the printing presses. The parish clergy was surely part of this phenomenon. Even more of the creativity originated with religious orders of both men and women, however, so that it seems gratuitous to attribute it to the direct influence of the Tridentine decrees, which touched on the ministry of religious primarily in order to restrict it. Perhaps the most striking feature of ministry in seventeenth-century France, for instance, is the amount done by women, who had to contend with the Tridentine decrees as obstacles rather than stimuli.[51]

What all this meant was not that institutions were now finally functioning according to their true nature, but that deeply significant changes were being effected in style, roles, and self-understandings—for ministry and for many other realities as well. To turn the proverb around, the more things seemed to be the same, the more profoundly they had changed. Yes, there was continuity between the reforms of the fifteenth century and the changes that came later, but systemic discontinuities prevailed as well.

"Missionary church" *(Missionskirche)*—Catholic missionary activity outside Europe—began in earnest in the early sixteenth century with the Portuguese and Spanish explorations and conquests and then continued with immense fervor and expenditure through the seventeenth. Few things are more distinctive of Catholicism in this period, for which there is no real Protestant counterpart. Jedin is surely correct in defining Catholicism of the early modern period as incomparably more missionary than before.

In what possible sense, one must ask, are these missions reform or reformation? They pertain to the era not because they relate to reform but because technology, greed, and curiosity coincided at this time, allowing for the great discoveries and opening the way for a massive export of missionaries and for an evangelization often fired by a remarkable religious enthusiasm and, paradoxically, destructive xenophobia. True, the ideology of the missionaries was sometimes strongly millenarian or looked to a reconstruction of "the primitive church," but this is hardly reform in a sense that Jedin seemed to understand it. Is missionary zeal the same thing as Catholic Reformation or Counter Reformation? How, for instance, does the famous debate between Bartolomé de las Casas and Juan Ginés de Sepúlveda over treatment of the Amerindians fit under either of these categories?

There is a further irony in Jedin's position. If Trent initiated the era of the *Missionskirche,* it did so without so much as a syllable about such missions in the many long decrees issued during its eighteen-year history. Jedin acknowledged this omission but forced it to fit his thesis by saying that the Tridentine papacy made up for this lack with the founding of the Congregation for the Promulgation of the Faith in 1622.[52] The problem with this solution is that the congregation is well over a century too late.

Trent's silence is, however, only part of the problem. Not only was the council not concerned with "mission," with "being sent" to unbelievers or heretics, but it bent all its efforts toward stabilizing clergy in the parish church for service to born Catholics. Trent had a remarkably narrow, "local" pastoral focus because it dealt with "reform of the church" precisely in the technical sense that Jedin correctly gives it, that is, reform of bishops and pastors of parishes.

The precondition for the great Catholic missionary activity was a historical contingency: it was the Catholic powers that had the overseas empires. After Trent, true, the popes showed much more concern for this activity than had their predecessors, yet King Philip II of Spain far outdid them in this regard, and not just from worldly considerations. It was the religious orders, moreover, not the bishops and pastors, that provided the start-up personnel and energy for missions outside Europe. They did so on their own initiative, inspired by their own traditions, with no reference to Trent and, generally speaking, with no mandates from the ecclesiastical hierarchy.

‡

For Jedin, historian of the Council of Trent, Trent furnished the defining center for the new era of the history of the Catholic Church to be known as "Catholic-Reformation-and-Counter-Reformation." Much research in the past fifty years has in fact underscored the great and pervasive influence of Trent even on institutions that antedated it by centuries. There can be no doubt: Trent's influence *was* great and pervasive. But was it as defining of the Catholic side as were Luther and Calvin of the Protestant? By accepting the term "Reformation" Jedin implied as much.

In the fifty years since Jedin wrote his essay, historians have continued to waver on what to call the Catholic side. Deliberately or indeliberately they have not always followed Jedin's lead. Their reasons for not doing so vary, as we shall see. Nonetheless, certain problems with Jedin's approach and solution should by now be clear.

The first, not surprisingly, is conceptual. At times Jedin is perfectly clear about what he means by (true) reformation: the restoration of traditional canonical discipline. At other times he means by it simply "renewal," or anything contributing to the salvation of souls.[53] When Jedin defines reform over against revolution, he especially seems to founder.

The second problem is methodological. He was interested in popes, bishops, and pastors. He studied a council that in its reform decrees dealt principally with those same institutions and hoped to change them for the better. This meant that he tended to force into this framework realities that in fact fell outside it, thus attributing to it a more overarchingly determinative force than the evidence warrants.

The third problem concerns the evidence Jedin had at his disposal. Writing when he did, he simply lacked the information we have meanwhile acquired about persons, movements, and institutions other than popes, bishops, pastors, and other phenomena directly related to Trent. But it must be noted that Jedin showed little interest in approaches to religious history that could have mitigated this situation for him.

Finally, Jedin's assumptions and prejudices led him to make questionable judgments and assessments in the essay—and not simply those that were more obviously based on dogma or theology. His understandable preoccupation with Trent and with its accomplishments led him to flatten distinctions among entities, as when he sees papacy, Jesuits, Trent, and presumably all other energies in Catholicism swept up in the same self-conscious reform. In particular he attributed to the post-Tridentine papacy a single-mindedness in the pursuit of reform that hardly seems warranted by many of the popes' actions, which included their continuation of nepotistic practices and their dynastically advantageous maneuvers not dissimilar to their predecessors' in the Renaissance. Yes, the papacy changed, as did all great institutions in the early modern era, but by no means always as a direct result of Trent. Nor is it easy to see the Tridentine reforms, or even the ongoing contest with Protestantism, as the consistent center of the popes' most heartfelt concerns.

From a number of vantage points, therefore, the "renewal of the church in the epoch of the Council of Trent" seems less a miracle than Jedin made out. The status quo before the council was not so dark, and the status quo after not so bright—nor so homogeneous. Both the former and the latter status seem more sprawling than Jedin allowed, spilling out from the categories with which he tried to contain them. Are his categories, even so, the best we can do? Not all historians since 1946 have thought so.

THREE

✝

England and Italy
in Jedin's Wake

Hubert Jedin's masterpiece was his history of the Council of Trent. His interests and training prepared him for it, but he also had the opportunity, coming largely out of the catastrophe of the Holocaust, to be in Rome for long periods of time. There he was encouraged by Cardinal Mercati and others and had at hand the resources he needed for the project. As early as 1937, with the publication of his two-volume biography of Seripando, he might seem to have preempted the subject. But that is a retrospective misreading of the situation. Seven years earlier Cambridge University Press had published *The Cardinal of Lorraine and the Council of Trent,* a book that might similarly seem to have claimed the subject for its author.[1] The book was by H. Outram Evennett, a young scholar at Trinity College, Cambridge, who had expressed the hope of writing the critical history of Trent that Jedin actually produced.

Born in 1901, Evennett was an almost exact contemporary of Jedin.[2] Unlike Jedin, however, he was not in the right place to carry forward such a great project. Rome had the principal sources and community of scholars. Moreover, despite *The Cardinal of Lorraine,* a stunning achievement for a man only twenty-nine years old, this layman, unlike the priest Jedin, did not have the formal training in canon law, theology, and related disciplines that was essential for pursuing in detail the highly technical questions the project entailed at almost every step along the way. The book on Lorraine is ecclesio-political history, virtually devoid of discussion of theological and canonical issues. Evennett also suffered from bad or precarious health and, perhaps more important, lacked Jedin's robust self-confidence. When Jedin's first volume appeared in 1949, Evennett was far from having anything comparable ready and possibly had already given up on the idea. With that volume Jedin definitively claimed the field.

Two years later Evennett was invited to deliver the Birkbeck Lectures in Ecclesiastical History at Trinity College. It is not surprising that he chose to speak on "the Counter Reformation," his specialty. Within that specialty he was far and away the person in England best qualified to address it—indeed, to address the Council of Trent, which is probably what most people expected of him. Yet, as John Bossy said in his postscript to the published lectures, "Evennett found it possible to construct a convincing and at least reasonably comprehensive plan of the Counter-Reformation almost without mentioning the Council of Trent."[3]

We can only speculate as to why Evennett chose to develop his lectures the way he did. Perhaps he was intimidated by Jedin's work, or did not want to compete, or simply wanted to signal—to himself as well as to others—that he was yielding the field. He began, in any case, almost deprecating the lectures to follow by saying that he had "no startling discoveries to announce, hot-foot from the archive-room" and that the subject was so large and complex that there had ever more been borne in upon him "an unhappy consciousness of amateur status."[4] That these expressions of inadequacy were not a perfunctory *captatio benevolentiae* is indicated by Evennett's later insisting that he would never publish his script.

Nonetheless, the book was published by Cambridge University Press in 1968, four years after his death, edited by his student, John Bossy. "The first serious attempt at a general understanding of the subject ever made by an English historian," it is still in print, over thirty years later.[5] That printing history is an achievement for any book, especially for one that so professedly presents itself as an interpretation, a genre often with brief life expectancy in academia.

The phenomenon can be explained in part by the dearth of good studies on the subject in English, *faute de mieux,* and to Catholics' desire to keep available a generally appreciative view of their side of things. The book also has two intrinsic and closely related qualities that make it attractive—the originality of Evennett's approach, at least for English-speaking readers of the time, and his judicious, non-churchy, non-polemical, non-apologetic framing of issues. These qualities resulted in Evennett's anticipating, at least by subtle suggestion, some interpretations that are being validated today by new research and more precise categories of analysis.

The most profoundly original aspect of the lectures was Evennett's postulating that the task ahead was (1) the incorporation into church history of the history of spirituality or piety and (2) a similar coordination of church history with secular history—that is, not treating church history in an ecclesiastical/doctrinal vacuum. With an expression wittingly or unwittingly reminiscent of Jedin, he saw the two sides of both aspects as "representing a kind of mysterious body-soul relationship within the Church."[6]

In the lectures he led the way toward the goal he proposed,

addressing first one, then the other, task. The earlier lectures dealt with spirituality, the latter with institutional developments, seen especially as manifestations of more general cultural phenomena over which the church had no control—as, indeed, manifestations of certain aspects of "modernity."

In 1951 for a professional historian to lecture on spirituality was startling. As Evennett pointed out, on the Continent the study was somewhat advanced, well exemplified in Bremond's *L'histoire littéraire du sentiment religieux,* the first three volumes of which had been translated into English by 1936.[7] But the breadth and accessibility of Bremond's approach to "religious sentiment" were exceptions in a field dominated by narrow specialists from religious orders, most of whom were incapable of placing their subject in a cultural or historiographical context, uninterested in relating it even to ecclesiastical history. Joseph de Guibert was one of the founders in 1937 of the magnificent *Dictionnaire de spiritualité.*[8] His history of Jesuit spirituality, published posthumously in French in 1953, was a landmark in certain aspects of its reinterpretation of Loyola and in other ways as well.[9] For all its merits, however, it betrays many of the defects of the genre. Ecclesiastical historians like Jedin (to say nothing of other historians) by definition excluded religious sentiment and devotion from their purview, sometimes with only slightly concealed disdain for it.

Evennett actually undertook to discuss what Jedin abstractly postulated when he defined "Catholic Reform" as the soul of the Catholic side. To some extent Evennett was doing for Catholics what scholars like Karl Holl and others had done decades earlier for Protestants in discovering the "religious" Luther. Evennett enunciated with a boldness striking for the times a thesis implicit or explicit in other historians but hedged with thousands of confessional qualifications, that is, that both the Reformation and the "Counter Reformation" were two different outcomes of the same general aspiration toward "religious regeneration" that pervaded the late fifteenth and early sixteenth centuries.[10] Moreover, he implied the conclusion, which only later historians would develop, that with the hindsight of four hundred years the two movements were more significant for the ways of thinking, feeling, and behaving that they shared than for what divided them. When he criticized Pastor for simplified dichotomies and for nowhere attempting "a serious analysis of either the exact nature or the true historical significance of his subject matter," Evennett communicated his own intention to take the opposite course.

Even in spirituality Evennett saw manifestations of broader cultural movements, as when he analyzed the individualism and activism of Jesuit spirituality. But it was especially when he dealt with institutional issues—the emergence of a stronger, centralizing papacy, the development of permanent nuntiatures, and similar features—that he expressed the "modernity" thesis with clarity. Whereas Jedin described the popes, for instance, as spiritually or morally "renewed," Evennett saw them as "vigorous sixteenth-century executives" typical of the era.[11] The "modernity" thesis was not exclusive to him (Jedin espoused a version of it), but the kind of training he had undergone allowed him to express it in a concrete and particularly illuminating way, without ever minimizing how medieval the sixteenth- and seventeenth-century church was in any number of regards.

As is so often true in life, the very weaknesses of Evennett's training and of his academic situation in comparison with Jedin's turned out to be his greatest strength. Not a professional church historian, Evennett had interests that happened to be religious and ecclesiastical. This accounts not only for his desire to break down barriers between church history and general history, but also for his ability to show how it could be done. Furthermore, he was not trained by a Catholic faculty nor located in one. He taught in a secular university that had a confessional tradition inimical to Roman Catholicism. This accounts for his being able to convey in just a few words his awareness of the dark side of his subject, while meanwhile avoiding partisan insinuations about better and worse that the very term "reform" sometimes connotes. His presentation never suggests anything but an honest attempt to get at the heart of the matter, without apology or polemic.

Nor is there evidence that Evennett was engaging in crypto-polemics with Jedin, for whom he seemed to have the greatest respect. Yet, even as these two Catholic historians dealt with ostensibly the same subject matter, they came up with presentations whose contrast exemplifies how slippery and elusive their subject was. Jedin, for instance, pinpoints three great agents of Catholic-Reformation/Counter-Reformation: Trent, the Jesuits, and the papacy. He has most to say about Trent, least about the Jesuits (and other orders). Evennett has least to say about Trent, most about the Jesuits.

The difference was, however, more in how the Jesuits were interpreted than in how much coverage they were accorded. For Jedin the Jesuits were the instrument of the papacy, whereas for Evennett they were about something altogether different—heartfelt conversion. For Jedin the "renewed" popes were the result and the agent of Catholic Reform, but Evennett was interested in how they resembled their secular counterparts—the other European princes, who were in the process of redefining themselves along more "modern" (indeed, absolutist) lines.

☦

Until the first volume of Jedin's *Trent* appeared in English in 1957, Evennett was one of the few people in the English-speaking world to take notice of his work. The direct influence of Jedin's essay in Spain and France at this time seems to have been felt only slightly more. Outside Germany the one country where it had an important impact from the beginning, 1946, was Italy. This is due in part to Jedin's long sojourns there and to his accessibility to young scholars who sooner or later came to Rome to work in the Vatican Library or Archives.

But Jedin's debut into Italian academia that reached beyond Catholic circles happened through the review article about his essay written by Delio Cantimori, already the *doyen* of Italian "lay" historians of religious issues in the Cinquecento.[12] The article, published in *Società,* a "lay" journal of opinion, caught the attention of the educated public. From that day until the present nowhere has the debate over naming been more heated or persistent than in Italy.

Cantimori and Jedin had become friends in Rome during the war. Jedin spent evenings as a guest of Cantimori and his wife at their home there at about the time the Cantimoris joined the Communist Party.[13] Cantimori, four years younger than Jedin, had had an excellent education in philosophy and history in Pisa at the university and at the Scuola Normale Superiore, and he later spent six months studying at the Protestant faculty of theology at Basel, where he knew Karl Barth.[14] In 1939 he was appointed to the prestigious *cathedra* of modern history at the Normale. That was also the year in which his *Eretici italiani del Cinquecento* was published, the work that established his reputation.

Among intellectuals in Latin countries anticlerical and anti-Catholic sentiment received brilliant articulation in the Enlightenment and unleashed its fury in the turmoil and aftermaths of the French Revolution. In Italy, however, it has been particularly bitter since the mid-nineteenth century because of the papacy's resistance to Italian unification during the Risorgimento. Catholic boycott of modern Italy was not officially lifted until the Lateran treaties of 1929, which made the Vatican a sovereign state. This stand-off from 1870 until 1929 is the most dramatic symbol of the two cultures in Italy—"lay" and "Catholic." The clash between them has fired the naming debate.[15] It was altogether typical that Cantimori would write about Italian heretics, not about the overwhelmingly Catholic tradition of his country.[16] On the Catholic side, "church history" was taught in seminaries, culturally isolated institutions, and it comprised little more than the history of popes, bishops, and priests.

Although the institutional stand-off ended in 1929 with the agreement between the Holy See and the Fascist state, the ideological stand-off continued and in some ways intensified as World War II drew to a close.[17] By 1945 the Italian Communist Party was emerging as a powerful political force. Into what ideological camp would postwar Italy fall? The Holy See became more vigilant than ever in inhibiting any sign of compromise with the "lay" enemy in any aspect of life. That enemy constituted by and large the intelligentsia—surely left-leaning, increasingly Communist.

The year 1945 marked not only the end of the war and the crisis about Italy's future but also the four-hundredth anniversary of the opening of the Council of Trent. Some "lay" scholars in Italy or-

ganized a conference on the subject and invited Catholic and "ecclesiastical" peers. The principal participants were by and large
young scholars but already men of some distinction—Eugenio
Garin, for instance, as well as Giorgio Spini, Luigi Firpo, and, indeed, Delio Cantimori. Included in the group was Arturo Carlo
Jemolo, a Catholic layman. None of the "ecclesiastics," that is,
priest-historians, accepted the invitation to join in the proceedings.

According to Luigi Rosso, who later edited the proceedings,
several priests expressed their support for the meeting, but said they
feared to participate because of the difficulties the hierarchy would
create. They could not afford to be seen side-by-side with Protestants and *laici*. Rosso excoriated the "Catholic conformists," who
preferred their own security and even bank accounts to rigorous
scholarship. "Once again," he commented, "we come to the bitter
conclusion that the Catholic Church neither can nor wants to engage in historical scholarship."[18] The Jesuit Pedro de Leturia, in his
review of the volume in *Civiltà Cattolica,* replied to the impassioned
salvo by insinuating that the project was ideologically inspired.[19]
Jedin made no mention of the affair in his autobiography.

Cantimori's generous review of Jedin's essay, appearing shortly
after its publication in 1946, was thus a hand extended across a
blood-drenched war zone in which, as Cantimori commented, the
controversies of the present were fought through the controversies
of the past. He saw in Jedin's acceptance of the legitimacy of the
term "Counter Reformation" a sign intimating the end of a blindly
apologetic historiography in the Catholic camp, just as the reality of
"Catholic Reform" required the abandonment by the other side of
the viewpoint that persons like Savonarola and the other usual
suspects were "precursors" of the Reformation. He not only accepted Jedin's distinction and the utility of his two-term solution

but maintained that it applied far beyond church history to political history, to intellectual and cultural history—to every aspect of the era.[20] More important, he edged slightly away from the traditional "lay" interpretation of the Counter Reformation as representing nothing but repression and regression and as the cause of Italy's loss of cultural hegemony.

Cantimori's article could not blot out generations of distrust on both sides, but it opened a thin channel of communication. Later, in 1958 at the first congress of Italian church historians, Jedin and Cantimori played off each other in formal and informal dialogue that was something unheard of.[21] This respectful relationship was by now a spur especially to young Catholic intellectuals, who were ignited afresh to pursue the history of the religiously turbulent Cinquecento freed from mandated apologetics. One of them, Paolo Prodi, who considered Jedin his *maestro,* wrote his dissertation on Gabriele Paleotti, the archbishop of Bologna and the most important "implementer" of Trent in Italy after his contemporary, Carlo Borromeo of Milan. When in 1959 Prodi had completed the first volume, Cantimori almost literally took him by the hand in Rome and led him to the office of Giuseppe De Luca, the founder and guiding spirit of the publishing house Edizioni di Storia e Letteratura, a man intent on breaking down the lay-Catholic barriers in Italian culture. Relying to a large extent on Cantimori's recommendation, Father De Luca accepted the volume for publication.[22]

This new atmosphere helps account for the appearance of significant studies of "the Catholic side" in which it became difficult to detect the ideology or religious beliefs of the authors—studies like Giuseppe Alberigo's on the Italian bishops at the Council of Trent, 1959,[23] and Adriano Prosperi's ten years later on Giammateo Giberti, the bishop of Verona.[24] Expressive of this atmosphere was the international congress held at Trent in September 1963, the four-hundredth anniversary of the closing of the Council, which I had the privilege of attending. Although dominated by "Catholic" historians, especially by Jedin himself, it was also attended by some "lay" and Protestant scholars, and, during those heady days of Vatican Council II, the congress received a greeting from the newly elected Pope Paul VI conveyed in person by the cardinal of the Ecumenical movement, Augustin Bea.[25]

Prodi correctly assessed the situation when he wrote that, in retrospect, the congress at Trent marked the crest of the new atmosphere, after which a regression began in Italy among both Catholic and lay historians that became ever more manifest following the recent death of De Luca and of Cantimori three years later.[26] Meanwhile, Cantimori himself had begun to express misgivings about certain interpretations of "Catholic Reform" that seemed, among other things, almost to obliterate "Counter Reformation."[27]

In 1984, on the occasion of the four-hundredth anniversary of the death of Carlo Borromeo, the fearfully austere and uncompromising reformer of Milan after the Council of Trent, Prodi called attention to the polemics in the press that the anniversary occasioned. He remarked, echoing Cantimori twenty years earlier, "They indicate that we are really not talking about something from the past but about our situation today."[28] He added that the polemics were "a manifestation of a crude anticlericalism that we thought had definitively departed but in fact was only napping."[29]

In any case, the atmosphere of the 1950s that held out the promise of a rapprochement or at least easier communication between Catholic and lay historians in Italy never fulfilled its promise. Many of the policies of John Paul II, the pope since 1978, did not help matters, but the antagonisms transcend any current irritants.

Worthy of note among lay historians in the past twenty years has been a certain focus on the so-called *spirituali* or "Catholic Evangelicals," that is, first, on persons like Cardinal Gasparo Contarini, Cardinal Reginald Pole, Cardinal Giovanni Morone, Vittoria Colonna, Marcantonio Flaminio, Pietro Carnesecchi, and the text entitled *Beneficio di Cristo,* and, then, on the persons (and institutions) that opposed and persecuted them—especially Cardinals Giampietro Carafa (later Pope Paul IV) and Cardinal Michele Ghislieri (later Pope Pius V), operating especially through the Roman Inquisition, established in 1542.[30]

As early as 1948 Cantimori influenced the direction these studies would take by proposing that some highly placed Italians, including some cardinals, adhered to *evangelismo,* a nondogmatic, conciliatory, and Christocentric piety, which, because of their orthodox enemies, they were forced to practice through dissimulation, which he called *Nicodemismo.*[31] The conflict, or at least contrast, between these two parties soon came to be seen as a sorting-out point between "heresy" (found in Pole, Morone, and others) and "Catholicism" (defended by "intransigents" like Carafa and Ghislieri).

The thesis has excited considerable debate and provoked massive research, as the six-volume critical edition of the minutes from the inquisitorial process against Morone, edited by Massimo Firpo and Dario Marcatto, testifies.[32] Some scholars have challenged the verifiability of a sharp distinction between *spirituali* and *intransigenti,*[33] while others, like Firpo himself, continue wholeheartedly to subscribe to it and in so doing dismiss Jedin and the very idea of "Catholic Reform."[34]

Paolo Simoncelli subscribes to the distinction and has written extensively on the *spirituali.*[35] In 1988 he published a sharply polemical attack on Jedin's definitions of "Catholic Reform" and

"Counter Reformation." For Simoncelli "Catholic Reform" is not much more than a deceitful euphemism.[36] He recalled that Jedin in his 1946 essay said that Catholic Reform took organizational shape in 1555 with the beginning of the pontificate of Paul IV, Carafa. But, Simoncelli asserts, inquisition and repression were the only instruments that pope knew to accomplish doctrinal purification and ecclesiastical discipline. What Jedin failed to state, indeed, tried to hide, was the intrinsic relationship between the Roman Inquisition and Catholic Reform. When Jedin and Alberigo dealt with Carlo Borromeo in their volume on the "ideal type" of bishop according to Tridentine specification, they conveniently failed to mention the severely repressive aspects of his episcopacy.[37]

As Simoncelli understands it, after 1555 the popes funneled all so-called Catholic Reform into "Counter Reformation." Simoncelli thus rejects the definition of "Catholic Reform" as Jedin proposed it and, insofar as he admits it at all, makes it virtually indistinguishable from older definitions of "Counter Reformation"—that is, the repressive and regressive actions after 1542 or 1555 that turned the church into an essentially repressive, regressive, and retrograde institution.

Simoncelli is far from being alone in rejecting Jedin's "Catholic Reformation." Sergio Zoli in *La Controriforma,* 1979, argued that to postulate a Catholic Reformation as the genetic epicenter of the Counter Reformation one would have to demonstrate that the Catholic Church had undergone a profound renewal before the Council of Trent and that in Trent it gave birth to a truly new structure. Neither of these things happened. "Counter Reformation" says all that need be said.[38]

We seem to be back where we started from. One point in Simoncelli's position needs especially to be noted: although he differs from Jedin in his conclusions, he argues within the same institutional framework as Jedin did, that is, he deals directly and head-on with church institutions like the inquisitions and with churchmen like the popes and cardinals. His is, like Jedin's, an ecclesiastical approach—by somebody who is not himself an ecclesiastic. This helps keep him within the categories Jedin used to deal with the problem.

‡

Paolo Prodi testified in several publications that Jedin's categories were helpful to him and his generation in their early years, but by 1980, the year Jedin died, Prodi seemed ready to question their adequacy in the presence of the master himself.[39] Two years later he published his important book whose English-language title is *The Papal Prince: One Body and Two Souls, the Papal Monarchy in Early Modern Europe*.[40] For Jedin the "renewed" papacy was the driving force behind both Catholic Reform and Counter Reformation. For him what was characteristic of the papacy after 1555, what was most important about it, was that it was more in accord with ideals of Catholic Reform or traditional ecclesiastical discipline. Gone, we might therefore assume, were the long-standing abuses like nepotism and fiscal irregularities. Barbara Hallman's book on the church as property disabused us of that misconception, even though she studied no further than 1563.[41] But Prodi, who acknowledges his debt to Evennett, goes a step further in seeing the papacy of the latter part of the sixteenth and early part of the seventeenth centuries as evolving and acting as a creature of the new social, political, and cultural situation. It was the impact of this situation on the papacy that gave it its new character—that gave it, indeed, a distinctly modern character.

Prodi's thesis is that the papacy in the early modern era was not a relic of medieval universalism but a protagonist in the new political reality of Europe that began to look and act like a modern bureaucratic state. The new Roman tribunals and congregations were not "Tridentine," but the result of something bigger. The Holy See's new structures and new centralizing tendencies reflected and promoted the similar transformations taking place in modern states, as they moved "on the way to exalting the personal power of the princes."[42] For all intents and purposes, the faithful became "subjects" of the church, as the medieval sense of corporatism receded ever more from memory.

Prodi largely eviscerates the papacy of the significance Jedin attributed to it with the denomination "renewed," a synonym for "reformed." He of course recognizes that the popes at home and abroad tried to support and see implemented specific disciplinary decrees of Trent, but he also points out that within the Papal State even the great "Tridentine reformer" Pius V thwarted implementation when papal interests were at stake.[43] Moreover, in the papal court and curia the old "abuses" of nepotism, the sale of ecclesiastical offices and other forms of simony, rather than disappearing, simply took somewhat different forms.[44] Papal diplomacy in the courts of Europe, portrayed by Catholic historians as motivated solely by the desire to further the Tridentine discipline, sometimes obstructed it for reasons of state.[45]

For Jedin the papacy was the central axis of Catholic Reform and Counter Reformation, as it was also the central axis around which both Trent and the Jesuits revolved—in the triad of the three agents Trent-Papacy-Jesuits. Prodi's perspective on the papacy could hardly be further from Jedin's: "The efforts towards reform *in capite et membris,* proclaimed and continuously restated during the whole of this period, one after another came to nothing because of these underlying institutional tendencies, and certainly not through individual moral weakness nor the abuses on which so much of traditional historiography still dwells."[46]

Prodi again explicitly addressed the naming issue in 1989 in an article entitled in Italian "Counter Reformation and/or Catholic Reform: Resolving Old Dilemmas with New Historiographical Purviews."[47] This time Prodi did not mince words. Jedin formulated a distinction helpful at a particular historiographical juncture, but today "Catholic Reform" and "Catholic Reformation" are of only modest utility as instruments of analysis. It was time to move on to others. Prodi, who frequently acknowledged his profound debt to Jedin, has like many other Italian scholars moved on especially to "confessionalization" and "social disciplining" as more adequate categories of interpretation, about which more will be said in Chapter 4.[48]

In 1989 Prodi made another observation that, wittingly or unwittingly, paid tribute to Evennett, while being more immediately dependent upon Ernst Walter Zeeden, Wolfgang Reinhard, and Heinz Schilling. According to Prodi, we now see that what happened up to the Peace of Westphalia in 1648 represents not only the religious fracture of the West but even more important the "confessionalization" of the West—that is, a regrouping of states and other communities on new bases of ecclesiastical structures. This is of course obvious in the new bases of the Protestant churches, but it is just as true of the Roman Catholic Church, with its new juridical institutions, its new religious discipline, new catechesis, and new models of deportment.

Prodi insisted that we are now far beyond the point where ecclesiastical history and the history of the Christian community, where history from above and history from below, can continue to be separated. What he called for—and here is where we again hear a tune from Evennett, to whom Prodi paid explicit tribute—is exploration of the dynamic interaction of ecclesiastical organization, religious practice, spirituality, and theology.[49]

In this regard Evennett early on had had a counterpart in Italy—Don Giuseppe De Luca. De Luca, born in 1898, was fortunate, amid a mediocre education in Roman seminaries, to have Father Pio Paschini as one of his teachers of church history.[50] The aftereffects of the harsh purge of "Modernists" launched by Pope Pius X in 1907 were still keenly felt when De Luca was a theological student, and they would be partly responsible for the intellectual stultification of Catholic clergy and laity that persisted in Italy and that De Luca would later try to combat.

Decades after the Modernist crisis was over, Paschini himself was a victim of the censorship that continued. In 1944, at that delicate moment in Italian history, he submitted to the Papal Academy of Science (Pontificia Accademia delle Scienze) the manuscript of his life of Galileo that the academy had itself commissioned. The manuscript somehow found its way to the Inquisition or Holy Office, which held it for two years before pronouncing publication "inopportune." Paschini died in 1962. Only then, in 1964, was permission granted to publish a posthumously revised "official version."[51]

In the postwar years De Luca was one of the very few "ecclesiastics" respected by persons from all parties, as he tried to promote a fruitful encounter between "lay" and ecclesiastical scholarship. His integrity and vast erudition made him ideal for the task. Besides seemingly hundreds of younger persons, he enjoyed cordial relations with Giovanni Gentile, Delio Cantimori, Hubert Jedin, Federico Chabod, Werner Jaeger, Berthold Ullman, Paul Oskar Kristeller, Arnaldo Momigliano, Carlo Dionisotti, and other scholars of equally high repute. He corresponded with Croce.[52] In the winter of 1961–62 he was elected a Corresponding Fellow of the Medieval Academy of America.[53]

De Luca was also known and respected by some of the great political figures of the epoch, including Alcide De Gasperi, the head of the Christian Democratic Party, and Palmiro Togliati, the head of the Communist Party. His relationship with the Vatican was complicated and his stance regarding it often bitterly critical. He had long known and generally respected Giovanni Battista Montini, the future Pope Paul VI.[54] During the pontificate of John XXIII he played a role in the easing of tension between the Kremlin and the Holy See.[55] Pope John, in a gesture of esteem that was then a departure from papal protocol, visited him in the hospital a few days before his death. The pope was himself mortally ill at the time and died the next year.

Given the intellectual stagnation among Italian Catholics, De Luca had had to look elsewhere for inspiration and stimulation. As a young priest he discovered John Henry Newman, for instance, and translated some of his works into Italian.[56] His special predilection was, however, for French scholarship. He was in close intellectual contact with the historians André Wilmart, de Guibert, and Bremond.[57] More interesting still, he read Lucien Febvre's famous essay on the causes of the French Reformation the very year it was published, 1929, and his approach to religious history showed affinities with Febvre's.[58]

De Luca wanted to produce for Italy a history of *pietà*, but he did not envisage simply an Italian version of Bremond's *Histoire littéraire*, about which he had reservations. He had in mind something broader and more inclusive in its scope, reaching down to the religious practices of the most ordinary, even the most "rustic," folk.[59] It would be a history not of ideas about piety but of lived reality *(pietà vissuta)*. It would examine, for instance, hagiography, liturgical texts, poetry, painting and architecture, pilgrimage sites, superstitions, and folkloric practices.[60]

In view of his goal he assembled a huge personal library of many thousands of volumes before he died in 1963. He never wrote his history but, besides founding the publishing house Edizioni di Storia e Letteratura, which produced impressive publications, he also began in 1951 the serial entitled *Archivio italiano per la storia della pietà*. Embodying the highest standards of scholarship, the *Archivio,* which languished for some years, has recently taken on new life,[61] in tandem with renewed interest in De Luca and the kind of scholarship he advocated.[62]

In his famous introduction to the first volume of the *Archivio,* De Luca described what he meant by *pietà*—"the loved presence of God in human life."[63] This history would get at the center of the religious reality by dealing with love—not an abstraction but the propelling force in every genuinely religious person. It would also perforce have to deal with impiety—"the hated presence of God." In this rambling essay that betrays De Luca as an autodidact, he surely underestimated the methodological problems of such a radical approach, but, believing love to be a reality in human life as much as greed, hate, and the will to power, which historians had not hesitated to address, he thought the difficulties could be overcome. To bolster his case, he quoted Febvre, "Nous n'avons pas l'histoire de l'amour, qu'on y pense."[64]

Although De Luca's approach was very much his own, it helped engender among a few young Catholics in Italy empathy for social history and for the methods and issues developed in France particularly, but not exclusively, by the *Annales* school, of which of course Febvre was a founder. In this development Gabriele De Rosa, a younger colleague of De Luca, took the lead. More influenced by Gabriel Le Bras than by Febvre, Bloch, or Braudel, he in 1971 published his *Vescovi, popolo e magia nel Sud,* the first work in Italy to approach "Catholic Reform" as social history. It was a landmark, a work of impressive scholarship but, like most Italian historical writing, not without implicit polemics related to the contemporary situation in its refutation of Italian Marxist interpretations of De Rosa's subject.[65]

The next year was in any case a great turning point, when under De Rosa's leadership a *convegno di studi di storia sociale e religiosa* was held at Cappaccio-Paestum with some French participants, and when, in tandem with the conference, De Rosa launched publication of the journal *Ricerche di storia sociale e religiosa.*[66] The journal was published by De Luca's Edizioni di Storia e Letteratura. Two years later another group of scholars initiated a similar journal, *Ricerche per la storia sociale e religiosa di Roma.* All at once, it seemed, the social history of religion came crashing upon the scene in Italy, with the early modern period to a large extent its target. The enterprise, soon detached from the French developments that at first partially inspired it, has only gained momentum up to the present. It is characterized by a meticulous examination of data and a painstaking exactitude in reporting the results. It has produced a large number of impressive studies.[67]

FOUR

✝

France, Germany, and Beyond

The relatively small but influential Protestant minority that lived in northeastern France was fluent in both French and German, and scholars from this milieu were much taken by German universities and their research seminars. It was to emulate this German model that the French state in 1868 created the École Pratique des Hautes Études.[1] Nonetheless, the overwhelmingly Catholic majority in the country had considerably less interest in the Reformation than did Germans. Moreover, as mentioned, the seventeenth century marked not tragedy as in Germany, not real or supposed decline as in Italy and Spain, but the brilliant culmination of French culture and civilization. When dealing with literary, academic, or cultural subjects, French scholars without qualm extend the term "Renaissance" into the seventeenth century, whereas German and Italian scholars generally put the end much earlier, at 1517 or 1527.[2]

In such a context it is not surprising that the French took relatively little notice of Jedin's essay. It is also not surprising that when in 1977 Marc Venard reviewed the terms current for our subject in French historiography, he found the situation "highly confusing," a judgment Alain Tallon echoed twenty years later.[3]

France was also special in that, even though many of the intelligentsia and of the academic establishment nursed a tradition of anticlericalism and anti-Catholicism dating back to the Enlightenment and the Revolution, many others did not, and Catholics maintained a vigorous presence in the intellectual and cultural mainstream. Since the nineteenth century there had even been a number of well-publicized conversions to Catholicism and, especially after World War I, a general reconciliation of Catholics to the Third Republic.[4]

Péguy, Claudel, Bernanos, Mauriac—such eminent literary figures were therefore symptomatic of a much broader reality in French life. In the world of learning Catholics, both laymen and clerics played important and respected roles, including historians like Henri Bremond, Michel de Certeau, Jean Delumeau, and numerous others. Like these scholars, many took the sixteenth and seventeenth centuries as the focus of their research.

France was special, finally, in its development of new, or almost new, approaches to history that have had a significant impact on the historical study of Christianity, particularly in the medieval and early modern period. This has in turn resulted in some new attempts at more adequate naming of the latter period. It would be difficult to disagree with Peter Burke's assessment that "a remarkable amount of the most innovative, the most memorable and the most significant historical writing of the twentieth century has been produced in France."[5] The so-called *Annales* school is the best-known proponent of new approaches, and it is with it that we must begin.[6]

Nineteenth-century France for a long time lacked the strong university tradition characteristic of Germany. Nonetheless, by 1876 it had a sufficient number of scholars influenced by the meth-

ods established by von Ranke at the University of Berlin to found
La Revue Historique, which fast became the leading and normative
journal of the discipline in France. While the journal professed
neutrality on all questions of religion and doctrine, its editorial
team, typically enough for the times, contained many Protestants
and Masons, a few Jews, and virtually no Catholics. Especially in its
early years it betrayed a particular animus against every aspect of the
Contre-Réforme.

The team subscribed to the proposition that the historical enterprise was fundamentally political and military, although we must
bear in mind that many distinguished French historians practiced
the discipline differently.[7] In the main, however, the establishment
believed that the proper subject of history was politics, great men,
and important events, and in France it was members of this establishment who occupied the chairs in the newly refounded universities, who fashioned the historical programs in primary and secondary schools, and who directed the great historical series so
characteristic of French scholarship.

The challenge came from Strasbourg, where at the university in
the 1920s the historians Lucien Febvre and Marc Bloch and their
colleagues from other disciplines met and found common ground
in their desire to create an approach to the past that differed in
almost every respect from what then held sway. This new approach
would be multidisciplinary—economics, sociology, geography, and
psychology would all be brought into play. As we see in retrospect,
it would dethrone, or at least demote, politics-centered, event-
centered, great-men-centered history. The crucial turning-point
came in 1929. That year Febvre and Bloch founded the journal
Annales d'histoire économique et sociale. In its pages a new kind of
geographical, economic, and social history came into being, in

which were studied human communities and their collective mentalities as they responded to their ever-so-slowly changing material
and social environments.

That same year Febvre published one of the most famous articles
ever written about historical approaches to the Reformation and to
its Catholic counterpart—"Une question mal posée."[8] The full title
rendered into English is "A Badly Put Question: The Origins of the
French Reformation and the Problem of the Causes of the Reformation."[9] This passionate article dismissed as ridiculous the then
standard thesis that revulsion at ecclesiastical abuses caused the Reformation.

For Febvre, who had a remarkably positive appreciation of the
doctrines and ethos of early Protestantism, the Reformation was
spiritually too powerful to have been caused simply by a reaction to
a bad state of affairs. To understand what happened we must, according to him, set aside our preoccupation with such institutional
factors and turn our attention to the thoughts, aspirations, and de-
sires, indeed to the "religious sentiments," of the men and women
of the time. To this end we must especially study sermons, books of
devotion, and practices of piety in the context of the new economic and social situation. The Reformation succeeded not because it dealt with abuses but because "it was the outward sign and
the work of a profound revolution in religious sentiment."[10] On the
eve of the Reformation "there was a tremendous appetite for all
that was divine, which satisfied itself as best it could on chance
encounters and on adulterated, miserable fare."[11]

Historians must therefore study religion, not churches, if they
hope to understand the sixteenth century. As Dermot Fenlon put it,
"The real question [for Febvre] about the origins of the Reformation, the question as it were, *bien posée,* was one which turned upon

the history of men's emotions, *l'histoire des sentiments.*"[12] In his appeal to "religious sentiment," Febvre both showed his debt to Bremond and at the same time adumbrated the history of collective mentalities that would characterize much of the later scholarship of the *Annales*. Febvre was also advocating the integration of "theology into history and history into theology" as "a method for the future."[13] The essay opened Febvre to the criticism that he was promoting a "history without institutions."[14]

Febvre published his manifesto not, as we might expect, in the newly launched *Annales* but in the very citadel of the enemy, *La Revue Historique*. This ensured a wide audience, much wider than Jedin's essay some fifteen years later, which took no notice of Febvre's *question*. Yet Febvre's point that "abuses" do not explain what happened stands out as especially important for Jedin's essay and our subject. Febvre did not deny that abuses existed, or that both Luther and Trent tried to deal with them, but he displaced them from center to periphery.[15] If what he postulated was true, then "reform" in the traditional sense of elimination of abuses loses validity as the defining term for the phenomenon, although Febvre did not draw this conclusion.

The movement founded by Febvre and Bloch rapidly gained disciples and produced works of landmark significance, such as Febvre's *The Problem of Unbelief in the Sixteenth Century: The Religion of Rabelais*[16] and Bloch's masterpiece *Feudal Society,* published just at the outbreak of World War II.[17] By the end of the war the *Annales,* now in Paris, had itself become the establishment in France, a position secured tightly in 1947 when Febvre became the founding president of the Sixth Section of the École Pratique des Hautes Études, concerned with social sciences, and the director of the

Centre des Recherches Historiques within it. This is a tale often told, and we need not tarry over it here.

For our subject none of Febvre's other writings come close to equaling the importance of the "Question mal posée." To the degree Febvre was correct, he shot the foundation out from under standard church history of the sixteenth century and, hence, out from under the standard categories of interpretations—like Catholic Reform and Counter Reformation.

Although the article was much discussed, its immediate impact on research is difficult to assess. The least that can be said is that it signaled scholarship's shift away from predominantly politico-ecclesiastical history to other approaches, which the *Annales* and scholars from other "schools" were beginning to promote. For whatever reason, historians associated with *Annales* have consistently shown keen interest in the period 1500–1800 but have sometimes taken surprisingly little account of church and religion, as in the "total histories" of Fernand Braudel.[18]

But *Annales* is far from being the whole story.[19] We must return to 1929. That year Étienne Delaruelle published his first article.[20] Although Delaruelle was never directly associated with Febvre and Bloch and spent virtually his whole life and career in Toulouse, far from the powerhouse of influence that was Paris, in his research he nonetheless showed the same desire to move away from the traditional focus on great men, especially great churchmen, and on ecclesiastical politics.

Delaruelle was ordained a priest in 1934 and after 1945 taught at the Institut Catholique in the Faculté des Lettres, where he developed an approach to the history of medieval Catholicism that would stress the importance of the laity and of popular practices like

crusades and pilgrimages, as well as of common cults like those of
the cross and the saints. Indeed, almost every article he wrote contained the word "popular" in its title, indicating an approach to
"church history" in which he was a pioneer. Delaruelle also believed that as the centuries moved on, this piety became more
interiorized, with deeper personal appropriation. Although often
not credited for the influence he exerted on scholarship, he was,
André Vauchez said, "one of the principal artisans of the renewal of
the religious history of the medieval West."[21]

The importance of Gabriel Le Bras is much more widely recognized. In that very same year of 1929 Le Bras, a colleague of Febvre
and Bloch at Strasbourg but unlike either of them a Catholic, was
called to a chair on the Faculté de Droit of the University of Paris,
where he would serve for thirty-five years, while also directing
research at the École des Hautes Études.[22] Two years later he issued
a call for a statistical and quantitative study of French Catholicism
that, though less well known, was perhaps more immediately
efficacious than Febvre's "Question mal posée" in recruiting scholars for a new approach to religious history.[23]

In his travel throughout France Le Bras had been struck by the
great diversity in religious practice and attitudes in the different
regions of the country. He was especially concerned that large sec-
tions of the country were "dechristianized," to use a term that
would later become fashionable in French historiography. The explanation for this situation, he believed, was to be found in the past.
In his appeal in 1931, he therefore encouraged every diocese to
appoint at least one priest to study these remote causes because he
believed it would be helpful for understanding the present situation
and dealing with it.

Le Bras was a medievalist. His first specialty was the history of canon law, which he pursued with striking originality, for as an outgrowth of it he became a leader in the application of sociological methods to the historical study of religion, especially of religious practice, as revealed, for instance, in visitation records. He explained that this aspect of his intellectual development was due to a greater interest in human beings than in texts, to a greater interest in *religion vécue* than in *religion légale*.[24] He proposed to study "the structure and life of organized groups for which the sacred was their beginning and end."[25] Such study cast a glaring light on the discrepancy between the ideal and the reality, between Christian teaching and popular practice.

Perhaps more than any other person of his generation he nudged scholarship away from "church history" to the history of practicing Christians—to the study not of great bishops but of communities of ordinary persons, to history "from below," to the social history of Christianity in the various guises in which it flourishes today. This puts him, like Delaruelle, at the other end of the historiographical spectrum from the more traditional Jedin. Although Le Bras did not promote the study of heretics, Jews, and other marginalized groups as a way to help define the "ordinary Christian" through definition of "the other," by the 1970s such research, some of which was catalyzed by Michel Foucault's theories, gained ground.[26]

Le Bras, like his old colleagues from Strasbourg, with whom he always maintained a cordial relationship, worked toward a *histoire totale* that would encompass as many disciplines as possible and that would see a whole society behind every institution. He was not of the *équipe* of the *Annales,* but he led scholarship in directions congenial to it.[27] At some points he, Febvre, and Bloch seem to speak with one voice, and in their disciples influence was reciprocal.

Le Bras's starting point, nonetheless, was the institution known as canon law, which at first glance looks like a stunning example of an institution "from above." But for Le Bras behind every law lay a passion and a "mentality" of which the law was but an expression. Laws were not timeless ethical prescriptions or abstract traffic regulations but mechanisms of human interaction. Le Bras's objective was "to show the *social* origin of laws and then the effect of laws on *society.*"[28]

Le Bras's influence was further institutionalized when in 1943 he, a layman, succeeded Cardinal Baudrillart as the president of the Société d'histoire ecclésiastique de France, the learned society that publishes the *Revue d'Histoire de l'Église de France*. He retained that position for more than twenty-five years. In 1956 he was the prime mover in the founding of the journal *Archives de sociologie des religions,* which he also continued to guide for a decade and a half.[29]

Although Le Bras worked exclusively in medieval history, by the time he died in 1970 the methods and vision he proposed had already profoundly influenced scholars working especially in the period 1500–1800.[30] When in 1971 Jean Delumeau said, "From now on every religious history is necessarily sociological and as far as possible serial and quantitative," he almost certainly exceeded what Le Bras himself would have subscribed to, but he accurately reflected the enthusiasm of the moment and the decisive turn those years marked.[31]

Recall that it was Le Bras who especially influenced Gabriele De Rosa, the disciple of Giuseppe De Luca and the "founder" of the social history of Christianity in Italy just at the time of Le Bras's death in 1970. Within a year Delumeau would publish in Paris *Le Catholicisme entre Luther et Voltaire,*[32] John Bossy in *Past and Present* "The Counter-Reformation and the People of Catholic Europe,"[33] and Brian Pullan with Harvard University Press *Rich and Poor in Renaissance Venice: The Social Institutions of a Catholic State.*[34] Both Delumeau and Bossy have been especially powerful voices of the past thirty years in their respective cultures and beyond, influencing how we think about the Catholic side of things in the early modern period.

Jean Delumeau launched his scholarly career in 1957–1959 with the publication of two volumes that, characteristically for an *Annales* disciple, analyzed the economic and social situation in Rome in the second half of the sixteenth century.[35] When in 1965, just as the Ecumenical movement was gaining momentum, he published in the Nouvelle Clio series a book on the Protestant Reformation, he moved into a field for which his Catholic upbringing had little prepared him and which forced him to examine the sixteenth century from new perspectives.[36] In 1971 in the same series he produced *Catholicisme,* the Catholic counterpart to the volume on the Reformation.

These books led him away from economic and social history and toward religious history, especially the history of religious mentalities as persisting over long periods, *la longue durée*. They also moved him to deep appreciation for Le Bras's call for the history of religious practices. The title of *Catholicisme entre Luther et Voltaire* is significant. Not "Catholic Reformation," not "Counter Reformation," not even "Catholic Church," but "Catholicism," which of course points to a history of mentalities, practices, and collectivities, and away from a history of *the* ecclesiastical institution, the church as such. In so pointing it renders less pertinent the classic terminology for a book covering this period. As noted, "Catholic Reform" and "Counter Reformation" almost demand "church" as a correlate. When "church" is displaced from its commanding position, these other categories suffer a proportionate diminution of importance, and some alternative seems called for—such as "Catholicism." How ironical that the editors of the English-language edition found it necessary to add a clarifying subtitle: "A New View of the Counter-Reformation"! "Between Luther and Voltaire" extends the chronological scope all the way to the French Revolution, far beyond 1648, the time-honored terminus for the "Counter Reformation."

From his chair for the "History of Religious Mentalities in the Modern West" at the Collège de France, Delumeau has subsequently published many volumes, some of prodigious size, on topics appropriate to his position.[37] The best known are the three dealing with the history of fear, guilt, and the pursuit of reassurance.[38] A professed and practicing Catholic, Delumeau has, like Le Bras, sought to understand the present "dechristianized" situation of the church in France by placing it in historical perspective—and to offer a word of hope.[39] The attention and praise his grand theses receive from admirers must be balanced by the many reservations of his critics.[40]

In the best known of these publications Delumeau, without denying the critical importance of the early sixteenth century, located his theses in a much larger chronological framework by reaching far back—into the thirteenth or fourteenth century—so as to move on to the late eighteenth. For him this is the broader sweep in which to place both the Reformation and the Catholicism of the early modern period, which he sees as not much more than intensifications of realities already operative in the late Middle Ages. Among the most impressive of those realities was the sense of fear, guilt, and sin that

pervaded Western Christianity, fostered by forms of pastoral intimi-
dation *(pastorale de la peur)* that portrayed God as the exacting judge
of the Last Day. Like a true *Annales* disciple, Delumeau wants to
understand a "civilization" at the deepest psychological level, for
which a privileged entry is through its fears.

Delumeau sees the later centuries in this long continuum as special in that, for the first time in the West, both Protestant and
Catholic areas—urban and rural alike—were fully evangelized or
Christianized. Because of the almost terroristic tactics of the evan-
gelizers, however, the victory was pyrrhic, won at the cost of almost certain defection in the future. In such a purview, Delumeau
obviously joins forces with the scholars who maintain that the Middle Ages were only partially or superficially Christian.[41] He also
provides comfort for the scholars who can see little good in early
modern Christianity. Louis Châtellier, a distinguished French historian who also deals with religious phenomena in that period,
arrives at an assessment of pastoral strategies almost diametrically
opposed to such negative ones: "the rural missionaries, who were in
daily contact with the immense mass of the poor, were led to
emphasize whatever might help and console them best, while leav-
ing in shadow, and eventually in oblivion, that which worried,
troubled or conduced to despair."[42]

John Bossy's article of 1970, in which he paid explicit tribute to
Le Bras, appeared just two years after his edition of Evennett's
lectures.[43] He was obviously moving into the social history of
Christianity, a field unknown to Evennett, who had been his super-
visor at Cambridge University. Bossy has continued to write on
various aspects of religious practice in the early modern period.[44]
Even the title of his most important work, *The English Catholic*

Community, 1570–1850, might suggest the influence of French social history—"community" not church—over a span of three hundred years.[45]

Unlike Evennett's neutral or even appreciative judgment on "the Counter Reformation," Bossy's has been negative. What he finds bad about the Catholicism—and about the Protestantism—of that period is the enforcement of codes of behavior. What Bossy finds particularly bad for Catholics is precisely what Jedin found good, that is, the ultimately successful implementation of the decrees of Trent intended to strengthen the parish and its pastors. This resulted in a situation of "parochial conformity." For Bossy, when the implementation of the council drove Catholics to locate their religion ever more exclusively in the parish, it deprived them of the spontaneity and life-giving "kinships" of medieval Christianity. Bossy's view of the Christianity of the Middle Ages tends to be as positive as Delumeau's is negative: " . . . the medieval Church made for life and the Counter-Reformation Church against it."[46]

In 1985 Bossy published *Christianity in the West, 1400–1700,* his most comprehensive presentation of his viewpoint.[47] He wrote a history of Christianity, not a history of the church. One of his major aims was to show that in the sixteenth century Christianity underwent significant changes that had both Catholic and Protestant modes. He explicitly eschewed in this regard words like "abuses," "reforms," and "reformed," as well as names that he had earlier used freely—"Counter Reformation" and even "Tridentine Catholicism." In this book he called the status quo before the Reformation simply "traditional Christianity" and the status quo afterward "translated Christianity." More names!

Bossy had three major theses about "traditional Christianity" that separate him from some other social historians who have written about it, especially Delumeau: (1) traditional Christianity was Christian; (2) this traditional Christianity was not a burden most people were wittingly or unwittingly resisting or wanted to shake off, nor were they reduced to nervous wrecks by a pervasive sense of sin and guilt; (3) traditional Christianity was not radically divided between an elite and popular culture, especially if the latter is axiomatically taken to be non–Christian.

Why call the second phase "translated Christianity"? So as to use "Reformation" (in both its Protestant and its Catholic forms) as sparingly as possible. "Reformed" implies that a bad form of Christianity was replaced by a good form; moreover, it is a term derived "from the vocabulary of ecclesiastical discipline," meaning a restoration to some ideal state by the action of superiors—it is "too high-flown to cope with actual social behavior . . . and it sits awkwardly across the subject without directing one's attention anywhere in particular."[48]

What does "translated" mean? Bossy invokes Foucault to help explain the term.[49] It suggests, for one thing, changes in the meaning of words that reflect changes in social structures, attitudes, and mentalities. More specifically, it indicates movement from more natural, spontaneous, fraternal realities to things more rationalized, impersonal, individualistic, and bureaucratic. With such an understanding, Bossy manifests a certain affinity with historiographical and hermeneutical categories like "social disciplining," which were developing in Germany at just about the same time.

In his most recent book Bossy has abandoned "translated Christianity" in favor of the less opaque "Post-Reformation." He does not explain or justify the term, although he in passing notes, as we might expect, "that I shall be using words like 'reform' sparingly, if at all." In "Post-Reformation" he includes Protestantism, which means he subscribes to the idea first clearly articulated by von Ranke that by sometime in the mid-sixteenth century the Reformation was over.

‡

As mentioned, even in German journals Jedin's essay received relatively little attention when first published. Three years later, after the appearance of the first two volumes of his *Trent,* Jedin returned to Germany almost in triumph. His essay now began to be widely read and discussed by Catholic historians, especially after it was partially reprinted in 1973.[50] Even earlier the categories had begun to impose themselves on a much wider audience through another and more effective medium, Jedin's *Handbuch der Kirchengeschichte.* The title of the fourth volume (volume 5 in the English-language edition) enshrined the familiar categories—*Reformation, katholische Reform und Gegenreformation*—and the pertinent section opened with a résumé of the arguments for the designation that Jedin had developed in 1946. The *Handbuch* was, moreover, translated into Spanish, Italian, and English, and it long remained the most extensive and, for Catholics, most authoritative "church history" in those languages. Although far too detailed to be assigned to students as a textbook, it worked on them through their teachers.

Catholic historians in Germany learned little from the new work in the social history of the Reformation that began after the publication of Bernd Moeller's *Reichstadt und Reformation* in 1962.[51] They were still culturally insulated, despite the new political prominence, almost predominance, of Catholics during the Adenauer years, a dramatically new phenomenon for modern Germany. They were also caught in the paradigm of Catholic-Reform-Counter-Reformation, which did little to spark interest in the daily lives of ordinary folk in the cities. Many Catholic Church historians in Germany continue to this day to show disdain for the social history of Christianity.[52]

Contrariwise, for two decades Protestant historians of the Reformation in Germany paid no attention to Jedin's essay, an indication that in Germany, as in Italy, there were lines of demarcation across which no one passed, even though the origins and character of those lines were quite different in the two countries. Finally in 1975 the Lutheran Kurt Dietrich Schmidt briefly acknowledged both the merits and the demerits of the essay, while paying it the implicit compliment of adopting "Catholic Reform and Counter Reformation" as the title of the fascicle he wrote on the subject for another *Handbuch*.[53]

In 1976, however, Gottfried Maron in his *Antrittsvorlesung* criticized it severely upon acceding to his chair of history at the University of Kiel.[54] By a dozen years he anticipated some of Simoncelli's objections. Maron saw Jedin as engaging in that typical Catholic ploy, an emphasis on the continuities of the Catholic Church, which meant he failed to reckon with the profound changes that had taken place within Catholicism in the sixteenth century. The concept of "Catholic Reform" helped blind Jedin to the changes, for it seemed to indicate that the earlier reforms, that is, those before the Reformation, continued unchanged in the latter part of the century except for being better coordinated and mobilized owing to the guiding hand of the papacy.

Maron zeroed in quite specifically on the establishment of the Roman Inquisition in 1542 and on the pontificate of Paul IV (1555–1559), the great promoter of the Inquisition and the promulgator of the first papal Index of Prohibited Books. Jedin did not, according to Maron, give due emphasis to the drastic character of realities like these, but, more important, he failed to indicate how they were symptomatic of across-the-board changes in the old church, changes that affected the character and operations even of long-standing institutions. Catholic Reform and Counter Reformation are not two distinct, though interactive, realities. After a certain point the character of Catholic Reform was determined by the Counter Reformation.

Even as Maron attacked Jedin's nomenclature, important alternatives to it were already in the making in Germany. Years before Maron—and, to a limited extent, the Protestant academic establishment—began to take notice of Jedin, Ernst Walter Zeeden had proposed a new category of interpretation that was destined to have a long trajectory. In 1958, the year after he assumed the chair for medieval and modern history at the University of Tübingen, Zeeden published an article on the development of religious (or ecclesiastical) confessions in the era of the religious conflicts— "Konfessionsbildung im Zeitalter der Glaubenskämpfe."[55] In German as in English the word "confession" indicates both a confession of faith, that is, a doctrinal statement like the Augsburg Confession of the Lutherans, and the community that subscribes to it. Zeeden, a convert to Catholicism, had studied under the great Lutheran scholar Gerhard Ritter, from whom he took the designation "Age of Religious Strife" (Zeitalter der Glaubenskämpfe), yet another name, to denote the period after 1555.

It was understandable but nonetheless brilliant that in this article Zeeden, a convert, should call for a comparative study of the process that in the wake of the Reformation eventually led to the formation of the principal Christian confessions, Konfessionsbildung, which took from 50 to 150 years to achieve completion. Konfessionsbildung implied that processes in the several churches were similar and that, with hundreds of years of hindsight, the similarities appeared more important than the differences. Zeeden had thus created a category that, finally, had the potential to integrate Calvinists and German Catholics on an equal footing with Lutherans into the larger history of Germany, and he had directed attention to the relatively neglected period of German history between the Peace of Augsburg and the outbreak of the Thirty Years War, 1555–1618, as critical for the formation of the confessions.

It was no accident that a German formulated a design for a comparative approach sooner than scholars in other countries. In Germany there were two (even three) churches, each with clearly defined territories of influence. After four hundred years it occurred to somebody to set them side-by-side—not in order to judge which was better or more Christian, that is, more authentically "reformed," but in order to analyze them according to less exalted, more precisely formulated criteria.

Zeeden continued to write about *Konfessionsbildung*[56] and to encourage others to pursue it, especially through the examination of visitation records from parishes and similar institutions.[57] Among the scholars who paid him heed, two would be by far the most influential—Wolfgang Reinhard, a Catholic,[58] and Heinz Schilling, a Protestant.[59] In the early 1980s, at about the time of Jedin's death, they each recast the category and substituted "confessionalization" *(Konfessionalisierung)* for "confessional formation" *(Konfessionsbildung)*.

The original term indicated the intellectual and organizational hardening of the diverging Christian confessions into more or less stable church structures with their own doctrines, constitutions, and religious and moral styles, a process that, although under way earlier, gained impetus in Germany after 1555. The character of the development was formed and expressed through the churches' active interventions in culture, their self-defense against threats from outside, and the influence exercised on them by non-ecclesiastical elements, especially the state.

With the introduction of the new term, Reinhard and Schilling wanted to move the category out of the narrow framework of church history and have it indicate a fundamental process in the social history of early modern Europe by providing "a historically accurate conception of the social effects of religion and the churches."[60] Their interest in social history was by that time typical of many younger German historians, who through contact with social historians in France and especially in the English-speaking world were seeking alternatives to the conservative tradition of political historiography that remained dominant in Germany in the 1950s and 1960s.

The publication in 1962 of Moeller's little book broke the hold of that tradition on many historians of the Reformation. Despite Reinhard and Schilling's desire some fifteen years later to put confessionalization into the realm of social-history discourse, their focus was still on the two institutions traditional in German historiography, the church and the state—precisely "the two very dry elements" that Febvre wanted historians to transcend.[61]

Both Reinhard and Schilling stressed the symbiosis of the churches and the territorial states, the chief long-range political development in Germany in the sixteenth and seventeenth centuries, through the reciprocity of influence, the interlocking mechanisms of organization, and the general codependency of these two institutions.[62] Just as the churches became confessionalized, so did the states. Religious intolerance, for instance, served the purposes of the states as much as it did the purposes of the churches, and for the states it was almost a necessary condition for survival. Focusing first on Germany, these historians believed that they had found a paradigm analogously applicable on the pan-European level.

Both historians place developments within the churches in the broad perspective of the different cultures and societies in which they were forced to play a role. They see the formation of the major confessions as creative responses of rival siblings to the radical and wide-ranging changes in European civilization that occurred in the early modern period. According to Schilling, "Confessionalization modernized, above all, the churches themselves."[63] With a nod to Evennett, Reinhard as early as 1977 argued that Catholicism as well as Protestantism contributed to the "modern world" through its rationalization of procedures, its growing bureaucratization, and its social disciplining.[64] Not surprisingly, he and others often adduce the Jesuits' ways of proceeding as examples to support this argument. This "modernization thesis" *(Modernisierung)* in Catholic hands amounts, moreover, to a frontal attack on the old Weber thesis about "the Protestant ethic."[65] It largely assumes, as well, that the rise of the modern state is the most important development of the early modern period.

In the early 1980s Reinhard proposed seven common procedures involved in the formation of confessional identity, and he has continued to develop and refine them.[66] They are the elaboration of clear dogmatic or theological positions, often in the form of "Confessions" or "Professions of Faith"; the promotion and safeguarding of such professions through institutional forms such as synods, right-thinking jurists, and examinations of candidates for ordination; their internalization, especially through schools and seminaries; the use of means of communication, especially the printing press, to propagandize, and the use of censorship to hinder the propaganda of others; disciplinary measures, such as inquisitions, the visitation of parishes, and fines and other penalties; control of the nature of rites and of access to them, for example, by keeping careful records about the reception of the sacraments, with disabilities for delinquents; and the development of a peculiar confessional language, as in the predilection for certain given names—Mary in Catholic Bavaria, for instance, and Fredrich in Lutheran Prussia.

Early on Reinhard described "Counter Reformation" as a hindrance to clear thinking, whereas "the Confessional Age" bypasses the landmines buried in the traditional category of "reform" in all its variations.[67] If one must speak of Counter Reformation, then, according to Reinhard, one must redefine its relationship to the Reformation as not so much a reaction to an action as two "slightly dislocated parallel processes." To the degree it was reaction, it was "still not simply reactionary."[68]

This approach also means that, when speaking of a (Catholic) Counter Reformation, one must in the same breath mention a Protestant Counter Reformation—not only in the sense that, when the Protestants were able, they were by and large just as repressive of Catholics as the Catholics of Protestants, but, even more literally, in the sense that the magisterial Protestants acted against the left-wing, and later generations acted against important principles of the founding generation.

Schilling has been no less diligent or effective than Reinhard in promoting the confessionalization thesis. In 1986, for instance, he edited the acts of the symposium on the subject sponsored by the Protestant Verein für Reformationsgeschichte.[69] In 1993 he and Reinhard organized in Augsburg another such symposium entitled "Catholic Confessionalization" under the joint auspices (first time ever!) of the Verein and its Catholic counterpart.[70] The Ecumenical movement and the drive toward the political, cultural, and economic integration of Europe have obviously provided the larger matrix for these developments to happen and for the confessionalization thesis to prosper.[71]

For the specific issue with which we are dealing, Schilling could not be clearer: "I have drawn a conclusion regarding terminology from the concept of confessionalization: instead of the Counter-Reformation, Lutheran Orthodoxy, and the 'Second Reformation,' we should speak of 'Catholic confessionalization,' 'Lutheran confessionalization,' and 'Reformed or Calvinist confessionalization.' By using linguistically parallel terminology it becomes clearer that these are three processes running parallel to each other and that the concept of confessionalization includes an over-arching political, social, and cultural change."[72]

Schilling's moral judgment on the ultimate consequences of the confessionalization process is harsh: confessionalization was a path "toward a surrender to the pressures of religious and ideological systems, and thus toward a collective failure that led to the catastrophe of self-mutilating civil war and international war, which remained unsurpassed in its ferocity and destructiveness until the wars of the twentieth century."[73] His negative assessment of confessionalization is the polar opposite of Jedin's "miracle" for Catholic-Reformation-and-Counter-Reformation. For Schilling and Reinhard "modernization" is rife with postmodern ambivalence.[74] Both democracy and totalitarianism are the result of that same process.[75]

The creation and refinement of the confessionalization thesis have been an extraordinarily important historiographical event. This event has had its most immediate impact in Germany, of course, but it has also been especially influential in Italy, where it was early mediated into scholarship through the Istituto Storico Italo-Germanico in Trento, of which, ironically, Jedin was a key founding figure.[76] From Germany and Italy it has gained disciples in North America, especially under the rubric of "social disciplining."

Among the merits with which Reinhard, Schilling, and now many others have endowed the thesis is the combination of sharp categories of analysis along with insistence that these categories respond to the results of ongoing research and, if necessary, be reshaped by them. As the thesis has gained disciples, it has in some of them further assimilated methods, for example, of cultural anthropology and, particularly in its social-disciplining aspect, the history of crime, confinement, and policing. Its advocates have been criticized for overemphasizing the uniformity of developments in Catholic Germany, for getting the chronology wrong, and even for misrepresenting "religion."[77] For Reinhard, in any case, the thesis, almost breathtaking in the scope it claims for itself, has a modest side: "The concept of confessionalization cannot and will not throw light on every aspect of church history of the era but only on a certain piece of it, on a process and its results."[78]

For both Reinhard and Schilling "social disciplining" *(Sozialdisziplinierung),* like "modernization," is almost the equivalent of confessionalization because what both the churches and the states sought to ensure and enforce were confessionally correct belief and behavior.[79] Confessionalization led to social disciplining. The concept of "social disciplining" derives ultimately from Max Weber, but Gerhard Oestreich reformulated it and introduced it into historical discourse in the late 1960s as characterizing the state in the Age of Absolutism.[80] Reinhard and Schilling adopted it from Oestreich and modified it so as to emphasize the role of religion in the process to a greater degree than he did.

Oestreich defined it as "the disciplining of individuals to achieve corporate order."[81] For him *disciplina,* whose relationship to the revival of Neo-Stoicism in the sixteenth and seventeenth centuries he particularly emphasized, was a pervasive mode that began to gain momentum in the middle of the sixteenth century. "Bureaucracy, militarism, and mercantilism [for instance] were all manifestations of social discipline in particular spheres, different ways of serving the state." *Disciplina,* imposed by oneself or others, an expression of the *Zeitgeist,* reached down to the most inward and intimate aspects of one's life.[82] The process of social disciplining entailed a radical, often unconscious transformation of personal and societal values and of institutional dynamics. For Oestreich the process was essentially directed to state-building. For Reinhard and Schilling it was directed more to confession-building, but it was also a manifestation of the impact of religion on society at large, with special reference to the state.

"Social disciplining" has meanwhile caught on among some historians of the early modern period as the preferred category of analysis, so that one could almost begin speaking of those times as the "Age of Social Disciplining." Critics have pointed out limitations of the category and argued about its precise relationship to confessionalization, to "self-disciplining," and to the Absolutist State.[83] In its transmission from historian to historian, it has undergone subtle modifications and assimilated new assumptions. In this regard it has sometimes silently (or not so silently) been modified by theories of Michel Foucault, particularly as expounded in his *Surveiller et punir* (1975).[84]

Foucault was formed in a philosophical milieu altogether different from that of our German scholars, did not assign as principal a role to church and state in the emergence of the "disciplinary society" in modern Europe, and located that society in a later period. Fascinated by the role of the Christian pastorate in this development and regarding it as very important, he saw it as eventually symptomatic of more generalized, pervasive mechanisms and forces leading to the same result.[85] For Foucault discipline is, in the last analysis, "a type of power," a specification not explicit in Reinhard and Schilling.[86] In Foucault, furthermore, the onslaught of the disciplinary modality is more relentlessly all-conquering; as a modality of power, it infiltrated all others, undermining or transforming them.[87] Despite these and other divergences from the confessionalization thesis as originally articulated, Foucault's ideas have sometimes affected how the thesis is understood and applied.

In any case, the category of "social disciplining" has proved itself a powerful tool of analysis and has drastically refashioned discourse on the religious issues of the sixteenth and seventeenth centuries. Sometimes implicitly taken as a synonym for the older and more venerable term "reform," it occasionally seems poised almost to supplant it.

Even more impressive, perhaps, has been the growing use of "the Confessional Age" to denote what von Ranke and hosts of historians after him called "the Age of the Counter Reformation." While it is true that "Confessional Age" antedates Zeeden, Reinhart, and Schilling, it has come into prominent usage largely as a result of their work.[88] There could hardly be a more telling indication of their influence than the choice of *Temps des confessions (1530–1620)* as the title for volume 8 (Paris, 1992) of the new *Histoire du Christianisme,* surely the most worthy of such series on library shelves today.[89] Not 1517 or 1555, but 1530, the year of the Augsburg Confession, is the line of demarcation for the new age. In his introduction to the volume, Marc Venard observes that at about 1530 two logically distinct realities set off on their course: doctrinal schism *(Glaubensspaltung)* and the formation of confessional identity *(Konfessionsbildung)*. These two categories borrowed from German historiography indicate, according to him, phenomena not manifest in the traditional French *Réforme* or *Réformation*.[90]

In this volume of more than a thousand pages, with contributions by a dozen historians, *Réforme catholique* is sometimes an operative category, but *Contre-Réforme* makes little more than a cameo appearance. Venard, citing Jedin's essay, insists at one point on the validity of the latter term and on the reality of what it denotes.[91] But except in passing reference, the word "Counter Reformation" has otherwise vanished, or been banished, into the night.

CONCLUSION

✝

There's Much
in a Name

Fifty years ago Hubert Jedin had reason to believe that he had settled the problem of naming "the Catholic side." His publications were already establishing him as the most authoritative voice for the history of sixteenth-century Catholicism, and his solution, building on the two names by then most widely used, seemed to reconcile the opposing viewpoints they represented. He must have been gratified by the attention and largely favorable response his solution received from scholars in Italy, which is where he was then living and where the acrimony between "lay" and Catholic interpretations was especially bitter.

His solution did not, however, put an end to controversy. At least as many names circulate today to designate the Catholic side as when Jedin took the matter in hand. The two terms Jedin declared inseparable continue to appear separately—either casually, without sharp definition, or deliberately, with polemical intent. Other terms current in Jedin's day have persisted to the present—le Grand Siècle, el Siglo de Oro, Age of the Baroque. Others have since appeared—Renaissance Christianity, Tridentine Era, Post-Tridentine Era, Translated Christianity, Post-Reformation, Catholic Renewal, Catholicism between Luther and Voltaire, Confessional Catholicism, (in effect) Age of Social Disciplining—and some of them enjoy ardent support.

Moreover, chronological demarcations have proliferated. "Counter Reformation" traditionally meant, and in textbooks still means, 1555–1648. Jedin framed his Catholic-Reform-Counter-Reformation between about 1415 and 1648, though he allowed it to extend in some sense through the seventeenth and even into the eighteenth century. R. Po-chia Hsia frames "the world of Catholic renewal" between 1540 and 1770.[1] Jean Delumeau wrote of "Catholicism between Luther and Voltaire," that is, from 1517 almost to the Revolution, but his larger vision of the religious psychology of Europe begins much further back, in the thirteenth or fourteenth century, and extends just as far forward. Other historians have, by contrast, tended to slice the chronology into ever smaller units, as for instance sometimes distinguishing in Italy between the severity of Tridentine implementation lasting until the end of the sixteenth century and a milder piety and discipline afterward; in that latter period, indeed, a "Christian optimism" manifested itself in art and devotional literature.[2] Baroque artists painted more visions of heaven than of hell.

Although the Reformation has not been insulated from this proliferation of names and chronologies, Catholicism has suffered it longer and more notably by far. Why?

The answer lies to a large extent in the history of the naming process. The first names for the epoch were devised by Protestants. The model and standard for understanding Catholicism was what happened in Protestantism. Thus "Counter Reformation" and "Catholic Reformation." The resistance some Catholic historians originally had to "Catholic Reformation" stemmed from anti-Protestant animus, surely, but it suggests the hermeneutical gap between outsiders and insiders investigating any historical phenomenon.

Since at least the early nineteenth century until recently, the question historians of all persuasions asked was, "What caused the Reformation?" This is the larger context for the naming problem. For our subject the question was modified somewhat: "What in the Catholic Church caused the Reformation?" The answer, from all sides, was "abuses." The next question, when one bothered to ask it, was, "What impact did the Reformation have on the Catholic Church?" No matter how this question was answered, its starting point was the Reformation. Lately, different questions have begun to be asked, such as, "What was Catholicism like?" or "How was modern Catholicism formed?"[3] Questions like these put the subject and the problem of naming on a different footing and are less prejudicial for the outcome.

The inferiority in quantity and quality of scholarship about Catholicism in the early modern period is also partly responsible for the proliferation of names for the Catholic side. Labels easily multiplied or were variously understood because there was no accumulated and critically examined mass of scholarship against which to test them. The proliferation happened even though, paradoxically, the received truth for all parties was that Catholicism was in essence monolithic. When scholars recently began to give more attention to Catholicism, its diversity and complexity came to the fore, a development that, not so paradoxically, caused further labels to proliferate.

The problem thus derives not only from the vagaries of historiography but also from the diversity and complexity of the subject under examination. Scholars have long agreed on the diversity and complexity of the Reformation phenomenon—Henry VIII was no Martin Luther—but they are now coming to see the diversity and complexity, sometimes the incoherence, of Catholicism as well.

To be sure, Catholicism is diffuse, complex, and incoherent in ways different from early modern Protestantism. It was, for instance, doctrinally diffuse in that it did not have a single, clearly formulated teaching like justification by faith alone or, perhaps more significantly, "Scripture alone," to give it center, and it rather gloried in the fact. The doctrinal assertions at Trent covered a wide range of teachings with seemingly even hand. Those assertions found expression, moreover, in subtle and technical "committee documents" that represented compromises and were thus incapable of packing the wallop of Luther's tracts and polemics or even of Calvin's *Institutes*.

With both doctrine and discipline Trent sent out the difficult message: you must stand pat—yet things are not going to be the same. The continuity/discontinuity issue thereby assumed a different form from that of the Protestant churches and sects, where at least in theory a sharp and clean break with the immediate past defined, with one or two exceptions, every group's identity. Of course, Catholic institutions changed sometimes drastically during the early modern period, but their *longue durée* must be reckoned with differently from analogous Protestant continuities with earlier traditions.

No council had ever insisted so explicitly, so repeatedly, and so forcefully on the continuity of the present with the apostolic past as did Trent.[4] This defensive rhetoric signaled a recognition that the break Trent's own reforms instituted would somehow have to build on the old ways or at least live side-by-side with them. Thus "Reformation" and "Counter-Catholicism" were more defining and encompassing of the Protestant side than "Reform" and "Counter Reformation" of the Catholic.

Catholic leadership was, consequently, notably diffuse. Few of the popes, for instance, took "Catholic Reform" as the emotional center of their lives. The ambivalent politics and nepotistic practices of Urban VIII (1623–1642) manifest tendencies present but not so obvious in most pontiffs. With the exceptions of Paul IV and Pius V, the all-consuming passion for reform was to be found in officers outside the papacy, in prelates like Archbishop Carlo Borromeo in Milan, whose assumption of authority to reform clashed with Roman claims to rule. As the example of Borromeo suggests, often no one knew precisely who was in charge in a given situation. No one knew where the rights and duties of one entity began and where another's ended. The accumulated tangle of papal bulls and briefs, canons of councils and synods, royal and ducal prerogatives, and the claims to autonomous action of cathedral chapters, local traditions, and similar titles was impossible to sort out.

Catholic bishops, including the bishop of Rome, had to contend, as did their Protestant equivalents, with a strong and more clearly articulated role for secular monarchs in church polity, but they also contended with other medieval institutions that Protestantism had by and large eliminated, many of which vaunted their independence of episcopal control and supervision. The confraternities were important among these, as the flood of publications in the past two decades has shown.

Even more important were the religious orders, which operated as a separate corps of organized ministers alongside and often in conflict with bishops and the parochial clergy. No Protestant church had anything like them. The members of these orders, old and new, were both before and after the Reformation much better trained and more effectively organized than the clergy of any diocese, and they operated by and large in institutions other than parishes. They had their own traditions of theology and piety. By reason of their international character and their traditions of ministry, many of them stood ready to undertake overseas missions on a grand scale.

Established women's orders continued and new ones were founded; in France and New France they began to run schools and hospitals. Yet at the same time the medieval mystical tradition continued and found perhaps its most sublime expression in Teresa of Avila, who was largely responsible for what Bremond called the *invasion mystique* into France in the seventeenth century.[5]

Catholicism continued to sprawl across Europe, where it had to deal with many diverse cultures. That is to say, it managed, without always predominating, to remain strong or regain strength in virtually every culture where it had been present before the Reformation, with the exception of England, Scotland, and Scandinavia. Within a given nation strikingly diverse Catholic cultures existed, as for instance with the Jesuits and Jansenists in France, whose differences were far more profound than their respective theological positions suggest.[6] With the exception of music, in these many cultures Catholicism generally had a livelier and more complex engagement with the arts than did Protestant churches.

Riding with the sails of the Spanish, Portuguese, and French galleons, Catholicism spread to "the Indies" of the Americas, where, aside from the relatively threadbare English colonies, it established itself as the dominant religion. It did the same in the Philippines, and it penetrated, sometimes with bold cultural accommodations into India, Japan, and China.[7]

‡

There are thus many reasons that the names have proliferated, not least of which is both the analytical and the imaginative character of the historian's enterprise. At this point, however, what we need to know is not how the proliferation happened but how to deal with it. I have three basic suggestions to make in this regard.

First, we need to accept that, given the history of the problem, many of these names are here to stay, and even more might well appear in the future. Accepting this reality does not mean making the best of a bad situation; rather, it means recognizing the fundamental hermeneutical principle that our categories, for all their relationship to the historical sources, are constructs. They reduce the radical particularities of history to generalizations and thus distort them. The multiplicity of names is thus consonant with the imperfection of the epistemological process. That multiplicity reveals and vindicates the myriad perspectives from which the past might legitimately be viewed. We must accept the multiplicity not as a postmodern celebration of diversity but as a recognition of the futility of the quest for the perfect name.

That brings me to my second suggestion. Many of the names, especially "Catholic Reformation" and "Counter Reformation," have traditionally been taken as precisely such perfect or exhaustive definitions. Too much has, at least implicitly, been claimed for them. The same is true for "Tridentine Era." "Confessional Catholicism" and "Social Disciplining" sometimes seem to be hurtling down the same proud path. We must strive to avoid taking a part for the whole.

It is incumbent upon historians, therefore, to be more self-conscious in their choice among such terms, to say what they mean and mean what they say. They need to be aware of the lenses that every designation puts over their eyes and realize that those lenses are also blinders. "Counter-Reformation Rome," again, is not "early modern Rome." Sometimes the former term, sometimes the latter, is appropriate, even for church and religion.

My final suggestion is that "Early Modern Catholicism" be added to the categories of interpretation.

‡

What are some of the merits and demerits of the names that have appeared in the course of this book? I will limit my summary to the four that have international currency and that historians of almost all disciplines most frequently employ. Even with these four I will hold myself to a few basic issues.

Counter Reformation. This name has the longest pedigree. It is among the most controversial, yet it is still perhaps the most commonly found in both academic and popular media, sometimes with no more thought to what the words say than is commonly given to "Middle Ages." Hotly advocated even today by some scholars who take it as expressing the very essence of Catholicism after the middle of the sixteenth century, the term evokes disclaimers from many others who use it, they imply, for lack of a better one. It has had great staying power. We could probably not get rid of it even if we wanted to.

But why would we want to? When Pütter put the term into circulation, he used it in a precise sense that then as now captures crucially important aspects of early modern history and of early modern Catholicism—the political, diplomatic, and military measures Catholics undertook against Protestants. This happened, no matter which side we consider the aggressor and which the victim. The Catholics in the German and French Wars of Religion mounted arms in order to wipe Protestantism from the face of the earth. The Armada had precisely the same purpose.

We can move beyond such brutalities. Even though no reformers were mentioned by name at Trent, the doctrinal canons of the council cannot be interpreted in anything but an anti-Reformation sense; doctrines that the best-known Reformers did not challenge, such as the Trinity, Trent did not address. More broadly, anti-Protestant militancy and polemic seeped to a greater or lesser degree into almost all aspects of Catholic life, including institutions of long standing such as the older religious orders. Chairs of "controversialist theology" were founded for the first time. Catholic campaigns of sermons and lectures were launched to win back the heretics.

But beyond certain limits the term begins to be a distortion. The Jesuits are a case in point. Founded in 1540, they were defined in the older historiography as a religious order of the Counter Reformation, even though opposing Protestantism was peripheral and occasional to them for their first ten or fifteen years. With the passage of time, however, anti-Protestantism became an intrinsic part of their self-definition, and it sometimes took fiercely aggressive forms. Nonetheless, the degree to which it was operative varied from place to place, from ministry to ministry, from period to period. England, for instance, can be considered the epicenter of anti-Reformation density in a series of concentric circles, with Poland, France, the Low Countries, and Germany in the next circle, with the rest of Europe in the next, the Americas after that, and so forth until India, Japan, and China find their places in the outermost, least dense circle.[8]

The Spanish Inquisition antedated the Reformation yet became an anti-Protestant force. The Roman Inquisition was founded in 1542 precisely to counter the Protestant threat, but, like its Spanish counterpart, it went considerably beyond the anti-Protestant remit. Given that these two institutions changed in this way, "social disciplining" would appear to express their scope better than "Counter Reformation."

Does either "Catholicization" or "re-Catholicization" rather than "Counter Reformation" more precisely capture the campaigns of sermons and lectures to win back heretics? In some cases, but it seems sufficient simply to grant the obvious: that anti-Protestant sentiment and activities constituted a defining trait of Catholicism after the middle of the sixteenth century. Did they characterize it enough and did they affect the whole age enough to justify following von Ranke and calling the period after 1555 the "Age of the Counter Reformation?" Yes, on condition that we allow other names to coexist with it.

"Counter Reformation" deserves to survive, moreover, if only because it intimates, as none of the other names do, the dread and rage that underlay the religious controversies and imbued them with such ferocious energy. If we lose sight of that *Sturm und Drang,* we blind ourselves to the high stakes and intense drama that bestirred the age.

Counter Reformation is a good name, therefore, for many aspects of the Catholic reality after about mid-century, particularly for those decisions, institutions, and mind-sets that Catholic officialdom, lay and clerical, deliberately set into motion in order either to oppose Protestantism or to fence Catholics off from it. It is not, however, a synonym for Catholicism.

Among its other liabilities, the term suggests that whatever happened in Catholicism—or in Europe—was a direct result of decisions by "the church." It thus attributes too much to top-down causality and, in addition, isolates "the church" from culture, as if churchmen stood outside or altogether against their times, always imposing their will on reluctant and resentful others, as if the decisions they took were not often manifestations of the changes in values and taste occurring in the larger society of their day. The "church" was an agent of change, of course, but also its subject.

Much has been written, for instance, about "Counter-Reformation art." By this expression historians mean that the decree of the Council of Trent that encouraged bishops to promote the veneration of sacred images and urged them to ensure that the images were appropriate to that end initiated a series of significant changes in content, style, the relationship between artists and "the church," and even in the definition of "sacred art." The term has been applied, in my opinion, in far too comprehensive and uncritical a way and has led to a number of contrived interpretations. Yet there can be no doubt about its essential validity, especially if "Counter Reformation" is taken in a somewhat broad sense. It is illuminating to note, however, that in decreeing that "all superstition be removed . . . and all lasciviousness avoided," the bishops at Trent were echoing, but in much milder terms, sentiments that Erasmus, the great Renaissance humanist, had been tirelessly, sometimes tiresomely, hammering into the consciousness of the educated classes of Europe for two generations.[9] In this instance Counter Reformation is a direct offspring of Renaissance.

Thus "Counter Reformation" did not come into being from

nowhere or exist in a cultural vacuum. Nor should it be singled out as the sole culprit for whatever historians might find repressive, artificial, impersonal, centralizing, or bureaucratic about later Catholicism. These characteristics, undoubtedly more prominent than earlier, undoubtedly promoted by certain actions of "the church," undoubtedly generated as a defensive reaction, were riding the crest of larger cultural movements. Something as religiously neutral as the invention of printing, for instance, gave newly powerful impetus to the conviction that human behavior could be made to conform to norms set forth in written documents.

Catholic Reform or Catholic Reformation. These names also have venerable pedigrees, and they are still today fervently espoused. In English-language usage they are commonly taken as synonyms, and in some languages, such as Italian and Spanish, no distinction between them is possible, since the same word stands for both reform and reformation. Jedin, as we saw, came to prefer "Reform" because "Reformation" suggests strict parity with the Protestant counterpart. Although as Catholicism and Protestantism developed after about 1530 they exhibited many of the same patterns, the radicalness of Protestant "changes for the better" *(reformatio in melius)* makes questionable the use of "Reformation" for the Catholic side.[10] "Reform" has, we might concede, a slight edge as the better term.

Some historians of course deny that there was such a thing as Catholic Reform by the middle of the sixteenth century, for by then reform was identical with repression, indistinguishable from the assault on culture that they identify with "Counter Reformation." According to them, "Catholic Reform" prettifies that irredeemably ugly reality. Other historians have virtually stopped using the word "reform" by equating it with social disciplining. Moreover, in its historiographical genesis "Catholic Reform" implied that before 1517 the Christian fabric was rotten, an assessment much questioned today. Is the term still useful?

A major difficulty with eliminating "Catholic Reform" is that *reformatio* appears so insistently in ecclesiastical sources from the eleventh century forward, with special intensity beginning with the Council of Constance, 1414–1418, and reaching a kind of culmination at Trent with its well over one hundred canons *de reformatione*. Whatever their philosophical or hermeneutical persuasions, historians need to take such a phenomenon into account. Much of the murky confusion about "Renaissance Humanism," for instance, has been dispelled through analysis during the past fifty years of *umanista,* in all its cultural manifestations and ramifications.[11]

Reformatio is perhaps not susceptible to such a satisfying resolution, but the mainline tradition of the term from Constance forward focused on trying to get the clergy to do their jobs, as the ancient canons described and prescribed them, and to live in a manner appropriate to their state, with the presupposition that, with these goals accomplished, the laity would then follow suit. In Trent that focus was as sharp as it could possibly be—on the papacy, the episcopacy, and the local pastors of parishes (as well as on others who like pastors had *cura animarum* in the strict canonical sense of the term). "Reform" meant change self-consciously introduced by ecclesiastical officials in order to improve the functioning in the first instance of other ecclesiastical officials.

That is what Trent was all about, even though it handled, but almost in passing, other disciplinary issues. The greatest irony of the council was the utter frustration of the hope of many of its participants to reform the papacy. Thus Trent in its decrees only indirectly and minimally dealt with perhaps the most burning reform issue of the day for Catholics and Protestants alike, the one issue that, within limits, they all agreed had to be addressed.

But the bishops were eminently successful in issuing more than one hundred canons for the reform of themselves and those over whom they claimed the most direct supervision, the local, that is, the diocesan, clergy. Those ordinances taken cumulatively amounted to a program, which in its comprehensiveness and in the detail and sharp clarity of its provisions resulted in something new. The fundamental ideas had long been on the books, however, and some had even before Trent found a certain implementation, with Spain in that regard perhaps in the forefront. The outcome was discontinuity, therefore, but with recognizable continuity.

To be sure, *reformatio* appeared in other contexts. Even within clerical confines *reformatio* had for generations been a rhetorical and practical engine of change beyond bishops and pastors, most strikingly in the Observantist movement in the mendicant orders.[12] Instead of the ancient canons, the mendicants called upon the "primitive" statutes of their respective institutions, so that in accepting traditional ordinances as normative they subscribed to the same premises of *reformatio* as that proposed at Trent. The Observantist movement was correlative, analogous, and related to "reform of the church," but it was not quite the same thing. While broader meanings of *reformatio*—and of close approximations to it like *renovatio* when they referred to politics, education, art, or even apocalyptic fantasies and ravings—cannot be excluded altogether from "Catholic Reform," they are not what "the church," both before and after Trent, meant by the term.

There are, then, a number of considerations to be kept in mind. First, *reformatio* had a continuous, though tumultuous, history from at least the eleventh century forward, and the *disciplina* it entailed must be understood within this long continuum, not just in its manifestations in the sixteenth and seventeenth centuries. Second, though the meaning of *reformatio* was later surely influenced by the Neo-Stoic revival and other factors, the "philosophical roots" of the term lay in the Bible, in the canonical tradition, and in other medieval sources. This means that *reformatio* often retained, despite its legalistic expressions, a connection with Biblical and medieval ideas of a conversion of attitude and affect. It was a canonical term but with religious implications. By correcting behavior the canons looked in some fashion to setting the heart on the right path.

Third, although by the sixteenth century *reformatio* had a diffuse meaning, it also had a technical and relatively precise one relating to the proper functioning of three offices—those held by the pope, the bishops, and the pastors of parishes. Thus *reformatio* is a crucially important aspect of what happened in Catholicism from the fifteenth century forward.

Extending the expression "church reformer" beyond such clear limits to everyone serious about religion in early modern Catholicism has distorted our vision. Jiménez de Cisneros, the archbishop of Toledo, was surely a church reformer before Trent, as later, after Trent, was Carlo Borromeo, the archbishop of Milan. The former strove to implement ancient canons regarding the clergy, whereas the latter did the same as they were amplified and modified according to the *reformatio* of Trent. But Filippo Neri, Ignatius of Loyola, and many other seriously religious persons moved on different planes. If *reformatio* in its best form was intended to work from the outside to the inside, that is, if its proponents assumed that by modifying behavior a step had been taken that might later touch affect, persons like Neri and Loyola had as their focus and starting point interiority itself.[13] *Reformatio* is not the same thing as heightened religious inspiration and commitment.

Finally, though "better" and "worse" are tricky concepts in historical discourse, the intent of *reformatio* to improve the functioning of ecclesiastical offices in view of the common good needs to be taken seriously. *Reformatio* from the fifteenth century forward was an attempt to deal with what was perceived by most thinking people as a long-standing, seemingly intractable, profoundly disturbing problem. The results and procedures of *reformatio* were, as with every human endeavor, ambivalent and pursued by imperfect human beings; they had unforeseen consequences, and sometimes caused as many problems as they solved. Nonetheless, insofar as *reformatio* aimed at regularizing the functioning of the Catholic bishops and pastors and at holding them to the performance of their traditional duties, it more or less, sooner or later, had some success, with results that in some respects can be called an improvement—if not quite Jedin's *Wunder*.[14]

"Catholic Reform" seems to capture this important reality fairly well, though it must take account of the fact that later changes in religious sensibilities imbued *reformatio* with modalities it did not earlier have. Like "Counter Reformation," moreover, it should not be taken as synonymous with Catholicism in the early modern period—even in combination with "Counter Reformation," as in Jedin's solution.

Tridentine Reform and Tridentine Age. To a large degree these terms manifest the same strengths and weaknesses as "Catholic Reform." They differ from it most notably by, first, being much more specific in pinpointing a single event as determining the character of subsequent history, and, second, by indicating a break and shift that are missing in "Catholic Reform."

The Council of Trent without a doubt had a direct and long-term impact on modern Catholicism that in its pervasiveness transcended the immediate influence of any single person or any other happening in the period. If for force of impact we must find a Catholic counterpart to Luther, it is the council—and by council I here mean Trent as it was interpreted and implemented, which was not necessarily or always the same thing as what the council intended.

There is thus every justification for speaking of a Tridentine Age in Catholicism that extended from the mid-sixteenth through the seventeenth century and in certain palpable ways even into the mid-twentieth. Trent's emphasis on the parish as the privileged locus where Catholics would practice their faith, for instance, gradually eclipsed the preeminent role confraternities played in this regard in the late Middle Ages; in many parts of the world the emphasis eventually eliminated that role altogether. This is but one of hundreds of important changes that in straight or crooked lines lead back to the council.

There is also justification, as mentioned, for speaking of a Tridentine Period in Italian history in a restricted chronological span, to extend to about 1600. Further, there is justification for seeing sixteenth- and seventeenth-century France as less Tridentine in certain respects than Italy. And so forth.

The major problem with the term, however, is that, when used in an unreflective way, it attributes too much to the council. I point again to three almost defining characteristics of modern Catholicism for which, in my opinion, the council cannot be held respon-

sible. The first is the much stronger profile of the papacy, manifested in many institutional ways, such as the development of the
modern nuntiatures, but perhaps most dramatically in an extraordinarily significant change in mentality among Catholics. The papacy, from not being mentioned in medieval catechisms—how
many Christians in the Middle Ages knew there was such an institution?—became almost the essence of Catholic self-definition.
Yes, Trent in minor and unintended ways played accompanist to
this thundering crescendo, as when in its last session it commended
to the Holy See the completion or undertaking of certain tasks, like
the Index of Forbidden Books and the revision of the breviary and
missal. Taken in the large, however, Trent wanted to assert episcopal prerogatives and to contain or even reduce those of the papacy.

The second problem with "Tridentine Age" is that it ignores the
strong missionary character of early modern Catholicism. As earlier
indicated, over the course of its eighteen years Trent had not a
word to say about this subject. The third problem is that the emergence of the active congregations of "nuns," first notable in seventeenth-century France, almost seems to contravene Tridentine leg-
islation requiring the strict cloister of such women. By the end of
the seventeenth century the Ursulines alone—and they were only
one among many—were running more schools for girls in France
than the Jesuits for boys.

The Confessional Age or Confessional Catholicism. Unlike the three
categories discussed above, this one is more recent, and its authors
are still practicing historians, applying it and modifying it in conver-
sation with colleagues. Unlike the others, moreover, it expands the
conventionally narrow focus on a single confession to delineate
characteristics common among at least three of them; at the same

time, it refuses to treat the history of the churches as something apart from developments in political and social history. It thus opens "church history" to broader vistas.

Perhaps the most striking difference is that, as expressive of the "confessionalization thesis," the term brings with it a coherent and elaborated set of subcategories that make it by far the most precisely defined of all the names we have seen. When we hear historians speak of confessionalization, we know what they are talking about. Given the history of attempts to name the Catholic side, that is no small achievement.

The most incisive of the subcategories and now certainly the most frequently invoked is "social disciplining." The high tide of enthusiasm for the term has sometimes caused it to drift from its mooring in the larger thesis and take on philosophical colorings not found in the original construct. In any case, its popularity with historians today is deserved. It has exposed on a grand scale patterns of maneuvering for control and of subtle applications of coercion of which we were earlier little aware. It has revealed a side of "reform" to which we were blind.

The merits of the confessionalization thesis are therefore many and obvious. It has brilliantly captured and called our attention to the obsession gripping Western culture to define "who's in, who's out." In so doing it has provided a map for helping us find our way through one aspect of a significantly intensified stage in the Western quest for order, system, and conceptual clarity that surged powerfully in the twelfth and thirteenth centuries and continued thereafter to gain force in every aspect of society and culture. In the seventeenth century the confessionalizing impulse was to the social, political, and ecclesiastical order what Descartes' "clear and distinct ideas" were to philosophy.

Sometimes the confessionalization thesis seems to be sweeping all before it. As mentioned, it is to the credit of Wolfgang Reinhart to admit, however, that the thesis "cannot and will not throw light on every aspect of church history." It labors, furthermore, under some problems. The thesis has, for instance, a top–down bias. While it unmistakably indicates the changes Catholicism underwent after the middle of the sixteenth century, it obscures the continuities. By dwelling on Catholicism's parallels with the Lutheran and Re-formed confessions, it minimizes the considerable differences be-tween them. "Social disciplining," intrinsic to the thesis, sometimes bears in its train a dour, reductionist view of human motivation open to challenge on several scores.

Those are more general criticisms, but others apply specifically to Germany, where the category has been most extensively tested. By emphasizing the period leading up to the Thirty Years War, it does not correlate well with recent findings that Catholic identity in Germany crystallized most notably after 1650. With the symbiosis between state-building and the development of confessional iden-tity as fundamental to it, the thesis leaves unexplained the vast regions of Catholic Germany without centralizing states.[15]

More basic is the problem raised by the application of any such "model" to historical data. The results the model yields conform to the grid the model imposes. The model becomes a self-fulfilling prophecy. It puts a net on the sources that will capture only what the net will hold, letting everything else slip through. As we have repeatedly seen, this is the fundamental problem raised by any cate-gory of interpretation, but it is particularly acute when the category is as sharply yet comprehensively defined as this one.

One aspect of the historical reality that escapes the net deserves special mention. The confessionalization thesis wants especially to show the social and political effects of religion; that is, more specifically, to show the codependency of church and state, with each influencing the other as well as society at large according to similar patterns. The thesis has had considerable success in this respect. It also has thereby manifested a curious similarity to traditional "church history," with its tendency to reduce everything to ecclesiastical politics.

But what about religion in and of itself—religion not as a political or social force but as a yearning for the transcendent or an experience of it? Whether historians believe such yearning can be genuine and such experience possible is irrelevant if they define their task as in some measure to deal with what people in the past felt and believed and to enter into that mental and emotional set, as far as possible, in its fullness.

In other words, this is the problem of what to do with François de Sales's *Introduction to the Devout Life,* what to do with Jesuit (and Protestant) emblem books, what to do with Rubens's *Holy Family with Saint Anne.* It is the problem of what to do with Filippo Neri and his seeming freedom of spirit, of what to do with Teresa of Avila as mystic and transmitter of spiritual wisdom rather than as entrepreneur or proto-feminist.

These individuals and phenomena can be studied from many perspectives, but is it not incumbent upon us to study them for what they head-on purported to be about, the sacred? "Confessionalization" catches the "confessional" aspects of Bremond's and Febvre's "religious sentiment," of Evennett's "spirituality," and of De Luca's "history of love," but the issue that they tried to make central with these expressions gets sidelined, redefined, or dismissed.

For the specific question addressed by this book, all four of the aforementioned categories, traditional though some of them are, are affected by this problem to a greater or lesser extent. They handle the bleakness of the moral codes, the brutality of the religious wars, and the self-promotion of the patrons of art, but they leave little room for the playfulness of baroque angels and for the ardor of the mystic's poetry. They often seem to leave little room even for simple human kindness and compassion.

I call attention specifically to this problem because it goes to the core of our subject and also because it is symptomatic of a larger current in academia today that holds suspect—or seems wholly unskilled in dealing with—the sublime, the self-transcending, the wondrous.[16]

‡

The last thing that seems to be needed is another name for the already long list of those purporting to define "the Catholic side." Yet in writing and lecturing I have found that the other names do not always say what needs to be said, whereas Early Modern Catholicism, or some version of it, does. Despite what a few critics have assumed, since first proposing it I have always insisted that it was meant not to replace the other names but to complement them.[17]

There is no perfect name. Early Modern Catholicism is not perfect—it is bland and faceless, lacking the stern countenance of Counter Reformation and missing the carefully crafted features of Confessionalization. It has, nonetheless, many advantages, most of which are the obverse side of its weaknesses. Although bland and less specific than the four names we have discussed, it welcomes them under its umbrella, where they can, when properly defined, provide more precision on certain issues. In the same way it makes room for other names we have encountered—Renaissance, Baroque Era, Siglo de Oro, for instance—that do not deserve to sink out of view. It is in the same way open to categories and perspectives that historians might devise in the future.

Early Modern Catholicism suggests both change and continuity without pronouncing on which predominates. It leaves the chronological question open at both ends, thereby allowing different determinations to be made according to different cultures and different issues. It meanwhile indicates a span that has some determinacy, a span of two hundred to four hundred years, somewhere between the fifteenth and the late eighteenth centuries, far less extensive than the thousand years we call the Middle Ages. Chronologically it is no less indeterminate than Renaissance, which according to current conventions ended in Italy virtually before it began in England. It is neutral on whether all forces before 1517 were tending, inevitably and ineluctably, toward the Reformation (or something similarly cataclysmic) and on the extent to which Catholicism after that period was a reaction to it.

This term seems more amenable to the results of "history from below" than the four just discussed, all of which indicate more directly the concerns and actions of ecclesiastical, political, or politico-ecclesiastical officialdom. Early Modern Catholicism more easily allows consideration of the resistance to control attempted by any social, ecclesiastical, or intellectual elite. It allows for the negotiation that seems to have occurred at all levels—between bishops and Rome, between pastors and bishops on the one hand and pastors and their flock on the other, between accused and inquisitors—with even illiterate villagers emerging as effective negotiators when their interests were at stake.

On a more positive note, it allows that even after Trent Catholic

religious identity might have found its genesis more in the traditional practices and the close-knit kinships of local communities
than in passive acceptance of hierarchy and of ecclesiastical disciplining, increasingly important though these were. It allows that
popular attachment to Catholicism might sometimes be explained
by the comfort people found in everyday experience of it and not
always by a grudging conformity to a grid imposed from above.[18]

"Early Modern" looks, of course, to early modern Europe, and it
can therefore be criticized for being as Eurocentric as the other
names. Yet Early Modern History has traditionally included the
great voyages of discovery and exploration that in fact very much
help mark the end of the Middle Ages. The Early Modern Age has
been understood as indistinguishable from the Age of Discovery—
or now, from the perspective of the discovered peoples, the "Age of
European Discoveries," with all the radical reevaluations that perspective entails. Early Modern Catholicism thus provides room to
move back a step from Europe to include in our purview Marie de
l'Incarnation in Quebec, José de Acosta in Peru, and Matteo Ricci
in Beijing. It thereby provides room for postcolonial perspectives.
Some scholars argue, moreover, that in non-European cultures
analogous "early modernities" manifested themselves at roughly the
same time.[19]

"Early Modern Catholicism," as a more open term, has space for
the new roles played by Catholic women, lay and religious. Because it is not as susceptible to reductionism as the others, it more
easily allows that important influences on religious institutions and
mentalities were at work in early modern culture that did not originate with religion and church as such but that nonetheless helped
refashion them. "Confessional Catholicism" of course also takes
good account of forces other than ecclesiastical, but it does so with

a bias toward the state. Early Modern Catholicism breaks out of that traditional church-state framework in a way that permits consideration of claims to the sacred and the transcendent on their own terms. It can, moreover, don or doff the robes of the hanging judge.

Yet it is problematic. In its chronological indeterminacy, for instance, it leaves us dangling about the significance of 1517, 1555, and 1648, even of 1492. It builds on the construct Early Modern History, which has long been in use in English-language historiography but whose equivalent is not always found in the historiography of other language groups. Even though it has been traditional in anglophone scholarship, it can be taken as favoring recent approaches to the period, especially by literary scholars, that see little use in other traditional categories like "Renaissance," approaches whose philosophical premises are surely not shared by everybody.[20] The litany could continue.

I believe, nonetheless, that "Early Modern Catholicism" deserves a place among the many names for "the Catholic side" that have appeared in the last two hundred years because its strengths and weaknesses complement and balance those of the alternatives. It has a scope and a flexibility the others lack. Catholicism with its sluggish continuities as well as its new realities was bigger than what the other names intimate. Particularly to be said in its favor is that "Early Modern Catholicism" indicates more straightforwardly than they that what happened in Catholicism in the sixteenth century was an aspect of Early Modern History, which it strongly influenced and by which it was itself in large measure determined.

Bibliography

Notes

Acknowledgments

Index

BIBLIOGRAPHY

✠

Alberigo, Giuseppe. *I vescovi italiani al Concilio di Trento (1545–1547)*. Florence: G. C. Sansoni, 1959.

————. "Il Cinquecento religioso italiano nell'opera storica di Pio Paschini." *Rivista di Storia della Chiesa in Italia* 17 (1963), 234–247.

————"La 'riforma' come criterio della Storia della Chiesa." *Annali dell'Istituto storico italo-germanico in Trento* 6 (1980), 25–33.

————. "Dinamiche religiose del Cinquecento italiano tra Riforma, Riforma cattolica, Controriforma." *Cristianesimo nella storia* 6 (1985), 543–560.

Antonazzi, Giovanni. *Don Giuseppe De Luca, uomo cristiano e prete (1898–1962)*. Brescia: Morcelliana, 1992.

Aubenas, Roger, and Robert Ricard. *l'Église et la Renaissance (1449–1517)*. Vol. 15 of *Histoire de l'Église depuis les origins jusqu'à nos jours*, edited by Augustin Fliche and Victor Martin. Paris: Bloud and Gay, 1951.

Bailey, Gauvin Alexander. *Art on the Jesuit Missions in Asia and Latin America* (Toronto: University of Toronto Press, 1999).

————. "'Le style jésuite n'existe pas': Jesuit Corporate Culture and the Visual Arts." In *The Jesuits: Cultures, Sciences, and the Arts, 1540–1773*, edited by John W. O'Malley et al. Toronto: University of Toronto Press, 1999, pp. 38–89.

Baron, Hans. *Calvins Staatsanschauung und das konfessionelle Zeitalter*. Berlin: R. Oldenbourg, 1924.

Barraclough, Geoffrey. *Main Trends in History,* revised by Michael Burns. New York: Holmes and Meier, 1991.

Baumgarten, H. Review of *Geschichte der katholischen Reformation* by Wilhelm Maurenbrecher. *Historische Zeitschrift* 46 (1881), 154–165.

Bellesheim, Alfons. "Professor Maurenbrecher über die katholischer Reformation." *Historisch-politische Blätter für das katholische Deutschland* 88 (1881), 608–622.

Benedict, Philip. "Between Whig Traditions and New Histories: American Historical Writing about Reformation and Early Modern Europe." In *Imagined Histories: American Historians Interpret the Past,* edited by Anthony Molho and Gordon S. Wood. Princeton: Princeton University Press, 1998, pp. 295–323.

Bergin, Joseph. *The Making of the French Episcopate, 1589–1661.* New Haven: Yale University Press, 1996.

———. "L'Europe des évêques au temps de la Réforme catholique." *Bibliothèque de l'École des Chartes* 154 (1996), 509–531.

Bernauer, James W. "Michel Foucault's Ecstatic Thinking," *Philosophy and Criticism* 12 (1987), 156–193.

Bertelli, Sergio. "Il Cinquecento." In *La storiografia italiana degli ultimi vent'anni,* 3 vols, edited by Luigi De Rosa. Bari: Laterza, 1989, vol. 2, pp. 3–62.

Bireley, Robert. "Early Modern Germany." In *Catholicism in Early Modern History: A Guide to Research,* edited by John W. O'Malley. St. Louis: Center for Reformation Research, 1988, pp. 11–30.

———. "Two Works by Jean Delumeau." *Catholic Historical Review* 77 (1991), 78–88.

Blet, Pierre. "France." In *Catholicism in Early Modern History: A Guide to Research,* edited by John W. O'Malley. St. Louis: Center for Reformation Research, 1988, pp. 49–67.

Bloch, Marc. *La société féodale,* 2 vols. Paris: A. Michel, 1939–1940. English translation: *Feudal Society,* translated by L. A. Manyon, 2 vols. Chicago: University of Chicago Press, 1961.

Borromeo, Agostino. "The Inquisition and Inquisitorial Censorship." In *Ca-*

tholicism in Early Modern History: A Guide to Research, edited by John W. O'Malley. St. Louis: Center for Reformation Research, 1988, pp. 253–272.

———. "I vescovi italiani e l'applicazione del concilio di Trento." In *I Tempi del concilio: Religione, cultura e società nell'Europa tridentina,* edited by Cesare Mozzarelli and Danilo Zardin. Rome: Bulzoni Editore, 1997, pp. 27–105.

Bossy, John. "Postscript." In *The Spirit of the Counter-Reformation: The Birkbeck Lectures in Ecclesiastical History Given in the University of Cambridge in May 1951,* by H. Outram Evennett, edited by John Bossy. Cambridge: Cambridge University Press, 1968, pp. 126–145.

———. "The Counter-Reformation and the People of Catholic Europe," *Past and Present* 47 (May 1970), 51–70.

———. "The Counter-Reformation and the People of Catholic Ireland, 1596–1641." In *Historical Studies: Papers Read before the Irish Conference of Historians,* edited by T. D. Williams, VIII, May 17—30, 1969. Dublin: Gill and MacMillan, 1971, pp. 155–169.

———. "The Social History of Confession in the Age of the Reformation." *Transactions of the Royal Historical Society,* 5th series, 25 (1975), 21–38.

———. *The English Catholic Community, 1570–1850.* New York: Oxford University Press, 1976.

———. "The Mass as a Social Institution, 1200–1700." *Past and Present* 100 (1983), 29–61.

———. *Christianity in the West, 1400–1700.* Oxford: Oxford University Press, 1985.

———. "Christian Life in the Later Middle Ages: Prayers." *Transactions of the Royal Historical Society,* 6th series, 1 (1991), 137–148, with Virginia Reinburg's commentary, 148–150.

———. *Peace in the Post-Reformation* (Cambridge: Cambridge University Press, 1998).

Bourdé, Guy, and Hervé Martin. *Les écoles historiques.* Paris: Éditions du Seuil, 1983.

Bouwsma, William J. "Eclipse of the Renaissance." *American Historical Review* 103 (1998), 115–117.

Bremond, Henri. *Histoire littéraire du sentiment religieux en France depuis la fin des guerres de religion jusqu'à nos jours,* 11 vols. Paris: Bloud and Gay, 1916–1933. English translation: *A Literary History of Religious Thought in France from the Wars of Religion Down to Our Own Times,* translated by K. L. Montgomery, 3 vols. London: Society for Promoting Christian Knowledge, 1928–1936.

Breuer, Stefan. "Die Formierung der Disziplinargesellschaft: Michel Foucault und die Probleme einer Theorie der Sozialdisziplinierung." *Sozialwissenschaftliche Informationen für Unterricht und Studium* 4 (1983), 257–264.

———. "Sozialdisziplinierung: Probleme und Problemverlangerungen eines Konzeps bei Max Weber, Gerhard Oestreich und Michel Foucault." In *Soziale Sicherheit und soziale Disziplinierung: Beiträge zu einer historischen Theorie der Sozialpolitik,* edited by Christoph Sachsse and Florian Tennstedt. Frankfurt a/M: Suhrkamp Verlag, 1986, pp. 45–69.

Burckhardt, Jacob. *The Civilization of the Renaissance in Italy,* translated by S. G. C. Middlemore. New York: Harper and Brothers, 1958.

Burke, Peter. *The French Historical Revolution: The Annales School, 1929–89.* Stanford: Stanford University Press, 1990.

Bynum, Caroline Walker. "Wonder." *American Historical Review* 102 (1997), 1–26.

Camaiani, Pier Giorgio. "Interpretazioni della Riforma cattolica e della Controriforma." In *Grande Antologia Filosofica,* edited by Umberto Antonio Padovani et al., 21 vols. Milan: Marzorati, 1954–1971, 6:329–386, with illustrative texts, pp. 387–490.

———. "Cinquecento religioso italiano e concilio di Trento." *Critica Storica* 3 (1964), 432–465.

Canisius, Peter. *Beati Petri Canisii Societatis Iesu Epistulae et Acta,* edited by Otto Braunsberger, 8 vols. Freiburg i/Br.: Herder, 1896–1923.

Cantimori, Delio. "'Nicodemismo' e speranze conciliari nel Cinquecento italiano." In Cantimori, *Studi di storia.* Turin: Giulio Einaudi, 1959, pp. 518–536.

———. "Riforma cattolica." *Società* 2 (1946), 820–834. Reprinted in Cantimori, *Studi di storia.* Turin: Giulio Einaudi, 1959, pp. 537–553.

————. "Il dibattito sul Barocco." *Rivista Storica Italiana* 72 (1960), 489–500.

Cantor, Norman F. *Inventing the Middle Ages: The Lives, Works, and Ideas of the Great Medievalists of the Twentieth Century.* New York: William Morrow, 1991.

Cassese, Michele. "Giuseppe De Luca e John H. Newman." *Ricerche di storia sociale e religiosa,* n.s. 28 (1985), 131–146.

Certeau, Michel de. "Henri Bremond et 'la Métaphysique des Saints': Une interpretation de l'expérience religieuse moderne." *Recherches de science religieuse* 54 (1966), 23–60.

Chadwick, Owen. *Catholicism and History: The Opening of the Vatican Archives.* Cambridge: Cambridge University Press, 1978.

Châtellier, Louis. *La religion des pauvres: Les missions rurales en Europe et la formation du Catholicisme moderne XVIe-XIXe siècle.* Paris: Aubier, 1993. English translation: *The Religion of the Poor: Rural Missions in Europe and the Formation of Modern Catholicism, c.1500–c.1800,* translated by Brian Pearce. Cambridge, New York: Cambridge University Press, 1997.

Clark, Michael. *Michel Foucault: An Annotated Bibliography—Tool Kit for a New Age.* New York: Garland Publishing, Inc., 1983.

Cochrane, Eric W. "The Transition from Renaissance to Baroque: The Case of Italian Historiography." *History and Theory* 19 (1980), 21–38.

————. "Counter Reformation or Tridentine Reformation? Italy in the Age of Carlo Borromeo." In *San Carlo Borromeo: Catholic Reform and Ecclesiastical Politics in the Second Half of the Sixteenth Century,* edited by John M. Headley and John B. Tomaro. Washington: Folger Books, The Folger Shakespeare Library, 1988, pp. 31–46.

Collins, W. E. "The Catholic South." In *The Cambridge Modern History.* Planned by Lord Acton, edited by A. W. Ward et al., 13 vols. plus atlas. New York: The Macmillan Company, 1902–1912, vol. 2, pp. 377–415.

Il concilio di Trento e la riforma tridentina. 2 vols. Rome and Freiburg i/Br.: Herder, 1965.

Concilium Tridentinum: Diariorum, actorum, epistolarum, tractatuum nova collectio, 13 vols. in 18 to date. Freiburg i/Br.: Herder, 1901–.

Congar, Yves. *Vraie et fausse réforme dans l'Église,* rev. ed. Paris: Éditions du Cerf, 1968.

Conway, Martin. *Catholic Politics in Europe, 1918–1945.* New York: Routledge, 1997.

"Counter-Reformation." In *The Oxford Dictionary of the Christian Church,* edited by F. L. Cross, 3rd ed. edited by E. A. Livingstone. Oxford: Oxford University Press, 1997, pp. 423–424.

Craveri, Piero. "Cantimori, Delio." In *Dizionario biografico degli Italiani.* Rome: Istituto della Enciclopedia Italiana, 1960–, vol. 18, pp. 283–290.

Crises et réformes dans l'Église, de la Réforme grégorienne à la Préréforme. Paris: Editions du CTHS, 1991.

Cristiani, Léon. "Réforme catholique ou Contre-Réforme." *Dictionnaire de théologie catholique,* 15 vols. in 30. Paris: Letouzey and Ane, 1903–1950, 13:2097–2098.

———. *L'Église à l'époque du concile de Trente.* Vol. 17 of *Histoire de l'Église depuis les origins jusqu'à nos jours,* edited by Augustin Fliche and Victor Martin. Paris: Bloud and Gay, 1948.

Croce, Benedetto. "Controriforma." *La Critica* 22 (1924), 325–333.

———. *Storia dell'età barocca in Italia: Pensiero, poesia e letteratura, vita morale.* Vol. 23 of *Scritti di storia letteraria e politica.* Bari: G. Laterza, 1929.

———. "La crisi italiana del Cinquecento e il legame del Rinascimento col Risorgimento." *La Critica* 37 (1939), 401–411.

Dejob, Charles. *De l'influence du Concile de Trente sur la littérature et les beaux arts chez les peuples catholiques: Essai d'introduction à l'histoire littéraire du siècle de Louis XIV.* 1884. Reprint ed., Geneva: Slatkine Reprints, 1969.

Delaruelle, Etienne. *La piété populaire au Moyen Âge.* Turin: Bottega d'Erasmo, 1975.

Delcorno, Carlo. "Don Giuseppe De Luca e gli studi recenti sulla letteratura religiosa medievale." *Archivio italiano per la storia della pietà* 9 (1996), 323–337.

De Luca, Giuseppe. "Introduzione." *Archivio italiano per la storia della pietà* 1 (1951), xiii–lxxvi.

De Luca, Giuseppe, and Giovanni Battista Montini. *Carteggio, 1930–1962.* Rome: Edizioni di Storia e Letteratura, 1993.

Delumeau, Jean. *Vie économique et sociale de Rome dans la seconde moitié du XVIe siècle,* 2 vols. Paris: De Boccard, 1957–1959.

———. *L'Alun de Rome, XVe–XIXe siècle.* Paris: S.E.V.P.E.N., 1962.

———. *Naissance et affirmation de la Réforme.* Paris: Presses Universitaires de France, 1965.

———. *La Civilisation de la Renaissance.* Paris: Arthaud, 1967.

———. *Le Catholicisme entre Luther et Voltaire.* Paris: Presses Universitaires de France, 1971. English translation: *Catholicism between Luther and Voltaire: A New View of the Counter-Reformation,* with an introduction by John Bossy, translated by Jeremy Moiser. Philadelphia: Westminster Press, 1977.

———. *Rome au XVIe siècle.* Paris: Hachette, 1975.

———. *Le christianisme va-t-il mourir?* Paris: Hachette, 1977.

———. *La peur en Occident (XIVe–XVIIIe siècles): Une cité assiégée.* Paris: Fayard, 1978.

———. *Un chemin d'histoire: Chrétienté et christianisation.* Paris: Fayard, 1981.

———. *Le cas Luther.* Paris: Desclée de Brouwer, 1983.

———. *Le Péché et la peur: La culpabilisation en Occident (XIIIe–XVIIIe siècles).* Paris: Fayard, 1983. English translation: *Sin and Fear: The Emergence of a Western Guilt Culture, 13th–18th Centuries,* translated by Eric Nicholson. New York: St. Martin's Press, 1990.

———. *Ce que je crois.* Paris: B. Grasset, 1985.

———. *Rassurer et protéger: Le sentiment de sécurité dans l'Occident d'autrefois.* Paris: Fayard, 1989.

———. *Une histoire du paradis,* 2 vols. to date. Paris: Fayard, 1992–. English translation of volume 1: *History of Paradise: The Garden of Eden in Myth and Tradition,* translated by Matthew O'Connell. New York: Continuum, 1995.

———, ed. *L'historien et la foi.* Paris: Fayard, 1996.

De Maio, Romeo. "La storia religiosa: Il Rinascimento." In *La storiografia italiana degli ultimi vent'anni,* edited by Luigi De Rosa. 3 vols. Bari: Laterza, 1989, vol. 2, pp. 85–95.

De Maio, Romeo, et al., eds. *Baronio storico e la Controriforma: Atti del convegno internazionale di studi, Sora, 6–10 ottobre, 1979.* Sora: Centro di Studi Sorani "Vincenzo Patriarca," 1982.

De Rosa, Gabriele. "De Luca, Giuseppe." In *Dizionario biografico degli italiani.* Rome: Istituto della Enciclopedia Italiana, 1960–, vol. 38, pp. 353–359.

———. *Vescovi, popolo e magia nel Sud: Ricerche di storia socio-religiosa dal XVII al XIX secolo* (Naples: Guida, 1971).

De Rosa, Luigi, ed. *La storiografia italiana degli ultimi vent'anni,* 3 vols. Bari: Laterza, 1989.

De Sanctis, Francesco. *Storia della letteratura italiana,* edited by Niccolò Gallo, 2 vols. *Opere di Francesco De Sanctis,* 8 and 9. Turin: G. Einaudi, 1958.

Despland, Michel. "How Close Are We to Having a Full History of Christianity? The Work of Jean Delumeau." *Religious Studies Review* 9 (1983), 24–33.

Dickens, A. G., and John Tonkin, with Kenneth Powell. *The Reformation in Historical Thought.* Cambridge, Mass.: Harvard University Press, 1985.

Dittrich, Franz. Review of *Geschichte der katholischen Reformation* by Wilhelm Maurenbrecher. *Historisches Jahrbuch* 2 (1881), 602–617.

Dosse, François. *New History in France: The Triumph of the "Annales,"* translated by Peter V. Conroy, Jr. Urbana: University of Illinois Press, 1994.

Droysen, Gustav. *Geschichte der Gegenreformation.* Berlin: G. Grote, 1893.

Duffy, Eamon. *The Stripping of the Altars: Traditional Religion in England, c.1400–c.1580.* New Haven: Yale University Press, 1992.

Duggan, Lawrence G. "The Unresponsiveness of the Late Medieval Church: A Reconsideration." *Sixteenth Century Journal* 9 (1978), 3–26.

Duhr, Bernhard. *Geschichte der Jesuiten in den Ländern deutscher Zunge.* 4 vols. Freiburg i/Br.: Herder, 1907–1913; Munich-Regensburg: G. J. Manz, 1921–1928.

Dürrwächter, A. "Konstantin von Höfler und die fränkische Geschichtsforschung: Zu seinem 100. Geburtstage." *Historisches Jahrbuch* 33 (1912), 1–53.

"Early Modernities." *Daedalus* 127 (Summer 1998).

Elkan, Albert. "Enstehung und Entwicklung des Begriffs 'Gegenreformation.'" *Historische Zeitschrift* 112 (1914), 473–493.

Elm, Kaspar, ed. *Reformbemühungen und Observanzbestrebungen im spätmittelalterlichen Ordenswesen.* Berlin: Duncker and Humblot, 1989.

Engen, John Van. "The Christian Middle Ages as an Historiographical Problem." *American Historical Review* 91 (1986), 519–552.

Evennett, H. Outram. *The Cardinal of Lorraine and the Council of Trent: A Study in the Counter-Reformation.* Cambridge: Cambridge University Press, 1930.

———. *The Spirit of the Counter-Reformation: The Birkbeck Lectures in Ecclesiastical History Given in the University of Cambridge in May 1951,* edited by John Bossy. Cambridge: Cambridge University Press, 1968.

Farago, Claire, ed. *Reframing the Renaissance: Visual Culture in Europe and Latin America, 1450–1650.* New Haven: Yale University Press, 1995.

Febvre, Lucien. "Une question mal posée: Les origines de la Réforme française et le problème des causes de la Réforme." *La Revue Historique* 159 (1929), pp. 1–73. Reprinted in Lucien Febvre, *Au coeur religieux du XVIe siècle.* Paris: Sevpen, 1957, pp. 1–70. English translation: "The Origins of the French Reformation: A Badly-Put Question?" In Lucien Febvre, *A New Kind of History: From the Writings of Febvre,* edited by Peter Burke, translated by K. Folca. New York: Harper and Row, 1973, pp. 44–107.

———. *Le problème de l'incroyance au XVIe siècle: La religion de Rabelais.* Paris: A. Michel, 1942. English translation: *The Problem of Unbelief in the Sixteenth Century: The Religion of Rabelais,* translated by Beatrice Gottlieb. Cambridge, Mass.: Harvard University Press, 1982.

———. "La pratique religieuse et l'histoire de la France." *Mélanges d'histoire sociale* 4 (1943), 31–35.

Fenlon, Dermot. "*Encore une question:* Lucien Febvre, the Reformation and the School of Annales." In *Historical Studies: Papers Read before the Irish Conference of Historians,* IX, May 29–31, 1971. Belfast: Blackstaff Press, 1974, pp. 65–81.

Ferguson, Wallace K. *The Renaissance in Historical Thought: Five Centuries of Interpretation*. Boston: Houghton Mifflin Company, 1948.

Findlen, Paula, and Kenneth Gouwens. "Introduction: The Persistence of the Renaissance." *American Historical Review* 103 (1998), 51–54.

Fiorenza, Francis Schüssler. *Foundational Theology: Jesus and the Church*. New York: Crossroad, 1992.

Firpo, Massimo. *Inquisizione romana e Controriforma: Studi sul cardinal Giovanni Morone e il suo processo d'eresia*. Bologna: Il Mulino, 1992.

Firpo, Massimo, and Dario Marcatto, eds. *Il processo inquisitoriale del Cardinal Giovanni Morone*, 6 vols. Rome: Istituto storico italiano per l'età moderna e contemporanea, 1981–1995.

Flynn, Thomas. "Foucault's Mapping of History." In *The Cambridge Companion to Foucault*, edited by Gary Gutting. Cambridge: Cambridge University Press, 1994, pp. 28–46.

Forster, Marc R. "Kirchenreform, katholische Konfessionalisierung und dörfliche Religion um Kloster Salem, 1650–1750." *Rottenburger Jahrbuch für Kirchengeschichte* 16 (1997), 93–110.

———. "Clericalism and Communalism in German Catholicism." In *Infinite Boundaries: Order, Disorder, and Reorder in Early Modern German Culture*, edited by Max Reinhart. Kirksville, Mo.: Sixteenth Century Journal Publishers, 1998.

———. "With and Without Confessionalization: Varieties of Early Modern German Catholicism." *Journal of Early Modern History* 1 (1998), 315–343.

Foucault, Michel. *Surveiller et punir: Naissance de la prison*. Paris: Gallimard, 1975. English translation: *Discipline and Punish: The Birth of the Prison*, translated by Alan Sheridan. New York: Pantheon Books, 1977.

Fueter, Eduard. *Geschichte der neueren Historiographie*. Handbuch der mittelalterlichen und neueren Geschichte, Abt. 1, edited by G. Von Below et al. Munich: R. Oldenbourg, 1936.

Fumaroli, Marc. *L'âge de l'éloquence: Rhétorique et "res literaria" de la Renaissance au seuil de l'époque classique*. Geneva: Droz, 1980.

————. "Baroque et classicisme: L'Imago Primi Saeculi Societatis Jesu (1640) et ses adversaires." In Marc Fumaroli, *L'école du silence: Le sentiment des images au XVIIe siècle*. Paris: Flammarion, 1994, pp. 343–365.

————. "The Fertility and Shortcomings of Renaissance Rhetoric: The Jesuit Case." In *The Jesuits: Cultures, Sciences, and the Arts, 1540–1773*, edited by John W. O'Malley et al. Toronto: University of Toronto Press, 1999, pp. 90–106.

Gentilcore, David. "Methods and Approaches in the Social History of the Counter-Reformation in Italy." *Social History* 17 (1992), 73–98.

Giard, Luce. "S'il faut conclure, ou comment l'histoire intellectuelle de la Renaissance est encore à écrire." In *Sciences et religions, de Copernic à Galilée (1540–1610)*. Rome: École Française de Rome, 1999, pp. 493–524.

————, ed. *Les jésuites à la Renaissance: Système éducatif et production de savoir*. Paris: Presses Universitaires de France, 1995.

Giarrizzo, Giuseppe. "Il Seicento." In *La storiografia italiana degli ultimi vent'anni*, edited by Luigi De Rosa, 3 vols. Bari: Laterza, 1989, vol. 2, pp. 63–84.

Gleason, Elisabeth G. *Gasparo Contarini: Venice, Rome and Reform*. Berkeley: University of California Press, 1993.

Goichot, Émile. *Henri Bremond, historien du sentiment religieux: Genèse et stratégie d'une entreprise littéraire*. Paris: Éditions Ophrys, [1982].

————. "Don Giuseppe De Luca et l'histoire de la piété." *Ricerche di storia sociale e religiosa* n.s. 48 (1995), 91–111.

Goodheart, Eugene. "Reflections on the Culture Wars." *Daedalus* 126 (Fall 1997), pp. 153–175.

Gothein, Eberhard. *Ignatius von Loyola und die Gegenreformation*. Halle: Max Niemeyer, 1895.

————. "Staat und Gesellschaft des Zeitalters der Gegenreformation." In *Staat und Gesellschaft der neueren Zeit (bis zur französischen Revolution)*. In the series *Die Kultur der Gegenwart*. Teil II, Abt. V, 1. Berlin, Leipzig: B. G. Teubner, 1908, pp. 137–230.

Gouwens, Kenneth. "Perceiving the Past: Renaissance Humanism after the 'Cognitive Turn.'" *American Historical Review* 103 (1998), 55–82.

Gritsch, Eric W. "Joseph Lortz's Luther: Appreciation and Critique." *Archive for Reformation History* 81 (1990), 32–49.

Le Groupe de Sociologie des Religions. "Quinze ans de vie et de travail (1954–1969)." *Archives de Sociologie des Religions* 28 (1969), 3–92.

Guarnieri, Romana. "Tra storia della pietà e sensibilità religiosa: Don Giuseppe De Luca e Lucien Febvre." In *Società e religione in Basilicata nell'età moderna: Atti del Convegno di Potenza-Matera (25–28 settembre 1975),* 2 vols. n.p.: D'Elia, 1977, vol. 1, pp. 81–129.

———. *Don Giuseppe De Luca: Tra cronica e storia.* Milan: Edizioni Paoline, 1991.

Gugelot, Frédéric. *La conversion des intellectuels au catholicisme en France, 1885–1935.* Paris: CNRS, 1998.

Guibert, Joseph de. *La spiritualité de la Compagnie de Jésus: Esquisse historique.* Rome: Institutum Historicum Societatis Iesu, 1953. English translation: *The Jesuits, Their Spiritual Doctrine and Practice: A Historical Study,* translated by William J. Young. Chicago: The Institute of Jesuit Sources / Loyola University Press, 1964.

Halkin, Léon E., and L. Willaert. *La Restauration catholique, 1563–1648.* Namur: Facultés Universitaires, 1960.

Hallman, Barbara McClung. *Italian Cardinals, Reform, and the Church as Property, 1492–1563.* Berkeley: University of California Press, 1985.

Harline, Craig. "Official Religion—Popular Religion in Recent Historiography of the Catholic Reformation." *Archive for Reformation History* 81 (1990), 239–62.

Hergenröther, Joseph. *Handbuch der allgemeinen Kirchengeschichte,* edited by Johann Peter Kirsch, 5th ed., 4 vols. Freiburg i/Br.: Herder, 1911–17.

Heussi, Karl. *Altertum, Mittelalter und Neuzeit in der Kirchengeschichte: Ein Beitrag zum Problem der historischen Periodisierung.* 1921. Reprint ed., Darmstadt: Wissenschaftliche Buchgesellschaft, 1969.

Höfler, Constantin R. von. "Die romanische Welt und ihr Verhältnis zu den Reformideen des Mittelalters." In *Sitzungsberichte der kaiserlichen Akademie der Wissenschaften* (Vienna) phil.-hist. Classe, 91 (1878), 257–538.

Hsia, R. Po-chia. *The World of Catholic Renewal, 1540–1770.* Cambridge: Cambridge University Press, 1998.

Hudon, William V. *Marcello Cervini and Ecclesiastical Government in Tridentine Italy.* DeKalb: Northern Illinois University Press, 1992.

———. "Religion and Society in Early Modern Italy: Old Questions, New Insights." *American Historical Review* 101 (1996), 783–804.

Iggers, Georg G. *New Directions in European Historiography,* rev. ed. London: Methuen, 1985.

Imbart de La Tour, Pierre. *L'Évangelisme (1521–1538).* Paris: Librairie Hachette, 1914, vol. 3 of his series, *Les origines de la Réforme* (1905–35).

"Les intellectuels catholiques: Histoire et débats." Special issue of *Mil neuf cent: Revue d'histoire intellectuelle (Cahiers Georges Sorel)* 13 (1995).

Iserloh, Erwin. "Kirchengeschichte als Geschichte und Theologie in der Sicht Hubert Jedins." *Annali dell'Istituto storico italo-germanico in Trento* 6 (1980), 35–39.

Janelle, Pierre. *The Catholic Reformation.* Milwaukee: The Bruce Publishing Company, 1949.

Janssen, Johannes. *Geschichte des deutschen Volkes seit dem Ausgang des Mittelalters,* 8 vols. Freiburg i/Br.: Herder, 1876–94. English translation by M. A. Mitchell and A. M. Christie, 17 vols. London: K. Paul, Trench, Trübner, 1896–1910.

Jedin, Hubert. *Die Erforschung der kirchlichen Reformationsgeschichte seit 1876: Leistungen und Aufgaben der deutschen Katholiken.* Münster: Aschendorff, 1931.

———. *Girolamo Seripando: Sein Leben und Denken im Geisteskampf des 16. Jahrhunderts,* 2 vols. Würzburg: Rita-Verlag, 1937, translated into English as *Papal Legate at the Council of Trent: Cardinal Seripando,* translated by Frederic C. Eckhoff. St. Louis and London: Herder, 1947.

———. "Il significato del Concilio di Trento nella storia della Chiesa." *Gregorianum,* 26 (1945), 117–36.

———. *Katholische Reformation oder Gegenreformation? Ein Versuch zur Klärung der Begriffe nebst einer Jubiläumsbetrachtung über das Trienter Konzil.* Lucerne: Josef Stocker, 1946.

———. "Il regime hitleriano fino allo scoppio della Seconda Guerra Mondiale," *Enciclopedia Italiana di scienze, lettere ed arti, Seconda Appendice,* 2 vols. Rome: Istituto della Enciclopedia Italiana, 1948, 1:1035–1042.

———. "Riforma cattolica." In *Enciclopedia Cattolica.* 12 vols. Vatican City: Ente per L'Enciclopedia Cattolica e per il Libro Cattolico, 1948–54, vol. 10, cols. 904–7.

———. *Geschichte des Konzils von Trient,* 4 vols. in 5. Freiburg i/Br: Herder, 1949–75. Only the first two volumes have been translated into English: *A History of the Council of Trent,* translated by Ernest Graf. London: Thomas Nelson and Sons, 1957–61.

———. "General Introduction to Church History." In *Handbook of Church History,* 10 vols. New York: Herder and Herder, Crossroad, 1965–81, vol. 1, pp. 1–56.

———. "Kardinal Giovanni Mercati 80 Jahre alt." In *Kirche des Glaubens, Kirche der Geschichte: Ausgewählte Aufsätze und Verträge,* 2 vols. Freiburg i/Br.: Herder, 1966.

———. "Gewissenerforschung eines Historikers." In *Kirche des Glaubens,* vol. 1, pp. 13–22.

———. "Zur Aufgabe des Kirchengeschichtsschreibers." In *Kirche des Glaubens,* vol. 1, pp. 23–35.

———"Das II. Vatikanische Konzil in historischer Sicht." In *Kirche des Glaubens,* vol. 2, 589–603.

———. "Vaticanum II und Tridentinum: Tradition und Fortschritt in der Kirchengeschichte," *Arbeitsgemeinschaft für Forschung des Landes Nordrhein-Westfalen,* no. 146. Cologne: Westdeutscher Verlag, 1968.

———. "Kirchengeschichte als Theologie und Geschichte," *Internationale katholische Zeitschrift,* 8 (1979), 496–507.

————. *Lebensbericht,* edited by Konrad Repgen. Mainz: Matthias-Grüne-wald Verlag, 1984.

————, ed. *Handbuch der Kirchengeschichte,* 7 vols. in 10. Freiburg im/Br.: Herder, 1962–79. English translation: *Handbook of Church History* (after vol. 4 *History of the Church*), 10 vols. New York: Herder and Herder, Crossroad, 1965–1981.

Jedin, Hubert, and Giuseppe Alberigo. *Il tipo ideale di vescovo secondo la Riforma cattolica.* Brescia: Morcelliana, 1985.

Jemolo, Arturo Carlo. "Controriforma." In *Enciclopedia Italiana di scienze, lettere ed arti.* 35 vols. [Rome]: Istituto della Enciclopedia Italiana, 1931–39, vol.11, 260–263.

Jones, Pamela M. *Federico Borromeo and the Ambrosiana: Art and Patronage in Seventeenth-Century Milan.* Cambridge: Cambridge University Press, 1993.

Kaegi, Werner. "La Spagna e la Controriforma nel pensiero di J. Burck-hardt." *Annali della Scuola Normale Superiore di Pisa,* series II, 21 (1952), 158–173.

Kerker, Joseph. "Die kirchliche Reform in Italien unmittelbar vor dem Tri-dentinum." *Tübinger theologische Quartalschrift* 41 (1859), 3–56.

Kidd, B. J. *The Counter-Reformation, 1550–1600.* London: Society for Promoting Christian Knowledge, 1933.

Kieckhefer, Richard. "Reform, Idea of." In *Dictionary of the Middle Ages,* ed. Joseph R. Strayer. 12 vols. plus index New York: Charles Scribner's Sons, 1982–1989), 10:281–1288.

Knowles, David. "Foreword." In H. Outram Evennett, *The Spirit of the Counter-Reformation,* edited by John Bossy. Cambridge: Cambridge University Press, 1968, pp. vii–xi.

Kristeller, Paul Oskar. *Renaissance Thought: The Classic, Scholastic, and Humanistic Strains.* New York: Harper, 1961.

Kurz, Otto. "Barocco: Storia di una parola." *Lettere italiane* 12 (1960), 414–444.

Ladner, Gerhart B. "Die mittelalterliche Reform-Idee und ihr Verhältnis zur

Idee der Renaissance." *Mitteilungen des Instituts für österreichische Geschichtsforschung* 60 (1952), 31–59.

―――. "Two Gregorian Letters: On the Sources and Nature of Gregory VII's Reform Ideology." *Studi Gregoriani* 5 (1956), 221–242.

―――. *The Idea of Reform: Its Impact on Christian Thought and Action in the Age of the Fathers.* Cambridge, Mass.: Harvard University Press, 1959.

Lampe, E. L. "Counter Reformation." In *New Catholic Encyclopedia,* 14 vols. plus index. New York: McGraw-Hill, 1967, vol. 4, pp. 384–389.

Lang, Peter Thaddäus. "Konfessionsbildung als Forschungsfeld." *Historisches Jahrbuch* 100 (1980), 479–493.

Laurence, R. V. "The Church and Reform." In *The Cambridge Modern History.* Planned by Lord Acton, edited by A. W. Ward et al., 13 vols plus atlas. New York: The Macmillan Company, 1902–1912, vol. 2, pp. 639–689.

Le Bras, Gabriel. "Statistique et histoire religieuses: Pour un examen détaillé et pour une explication historique de l'état du catholicisme dans les diverses régions de la France." *Revue d'Histoire de l'Église de France* 17 (1931), 425–449.

―――. *Introduction à l'histoire de la pratique religieuse en France,* 2 vols. Paris: Presses Universitaires de France, 1942–1945.

―――. *Études de sociologie religieuse,* 2 vols. Paris: Presses Universitaires de France, 1955–1956.

―――. "Sociologie religieuse et science des religions." *Archives de sociologie des religions* 1 (1956), 3–17.

―――. "L'historiographie contemporaine du catholicisme en France." In *Mélanges Pierre Renouvin: Études d'histoire des relations internationales.* Paris: Presses Universitaires de France, 1966, pp. 23–32.

―――. "'Discourse synthétique' d'un récipiendaire." *Archives de sociologies des religions* 29 (1970), 7–14.

―――. "Religion légale et religion vécue: Entretien avec Gabriel Le Bras." *Archives de sociologie des religions* 29 (1970), 15–20.

Lehmann, Hartmut. "Zur Bedeutung von Religion und Religiosität im

Barockzeitalter," In *Religion und Religiosität im Zeitalter des Barock* ,edited by Dieter Breuer, 2 vols. Wiesbaden: Harrassowitz, 1995, 1:3–22.

Lemarignier, J.-F. "Gabriel Le Bras (1891–1970)." *Aevum* 46 (1972), 146–153.

Le Roy Ladurie, Emmanuel. *The Territory of the Historian*, translated by Ben and Siân Reynolds. Chicago: The University of Chicago Press, 1979.

Leturia, Pedro de. "Il Concilio di Trento nel Quaderno Primo di 'Belfagor.'" *Civiltà Cattolica* 100/2 (1949), 82–98.

Logan, Oliver. *The Venetian Upper Clergy in the 16th and Early 17th Centuries: A Study of Religious Culture.* Lewiston, N.Y.: Edwin Mellen Press, 1996.

Lortz, Josef. Review of Hubert Jedin, *Geschichte des Konzils von Trient*, vol. 1. *Theologische Revue* 47 (1951), 157–170.

———. *Die Reformation in Deutschland*, 4th ed., 2 vols. Freiburg i/Br.: Herder, 1962. English translation: *The Reformation in Germany*, translated by Ronald Walls, 2 vols. New York: Herder and Herder, 1968.

Lukens, Michael B. "Lortz's View of the Reformation and the Crisis of the True Church." *Archive for Reformation History* 81 (1990), 20–31.

Maccarrone, Michele. "Mons. Pio Paschini (1878–1962)." *Rivista di Storia della Chiesa in Italia* 17 (1963), 181–221.

Mahoney, John. "Critical Methodology and Writing about Religion and Literature." *Religion and the Arts* 1/4 (1997), 89–97.

Maier, Hans. "Sozialdisziplinierung—ein Begriff und seine Grenzen (Kommentar)." In *Glaube und Eid: Treueformeln, Glaubensbekenntnisse und Sozialdisziplinierung zwischen Mittelalter und Neuzeit,* edited by Paolo Prodi with Elisabeth Müller-Luckner. Munich: R. Oldenbourg, 1993, pp. 237–240.

Mallon, Florencia E. "The Promise and Dilemma of Subaltern Studies: Perspectives from Latin American History." *American Historical Review* 99 (1994), 1491–1515.

Mangoni, Luisa. *In partibus infidelium, Don Giuseppe De Luca: Il mondo cattolico e la cultura italiana del Novecento.* Turin: Giulio Einaudi, 1989.

Manselli, Raoul. "Ludwig von Pastor—Der Historiker der Päpste." *Römische historische Mitteilungen* 21 (1979), 111–126.

Marcus, Leah S. "Renaissance/Early Modern Studies." In *Redrawing the Boundaries: The Transformation of English and American Literary Studies,* edited by Stephen Greenblatt and Giles Gunn. New York: Modern Language Association of America, 1992, pp. 41–63.

Maron, Gottfried. "Des [sic] Schicksal der katholischen Reform im 16. Jahrhundert: Zur Frage nach der Kontinuität in der Kirchengeschichte." *Zeitschrift für Kirchengeschichte* 88 (1977), 218–229.

Marsden, George M. *The Soul of the American University: From Protestant Establishment to Established Nonbelief.* New York: Oxford University Press, 1994.

Martin, John. "Recent Italian Scholarship on the Renaissance: Aspects of Christianity in Late Medieval and Early Modern Italy." *Renaissance Quarterly* 48 (1995), 593–610.

Marx, Jakob. *Lehrbuch der Kirchengeschichte,* 4th ed. Trier: Paulinus, 1908.

Maurenbrecher, Wilhelm. *Geschichte der katholischen Reformation.* Nördlingen: C. H. Beck, 1880.

Mayeur, Jean-Marie, et al., eds., *Histoire du Christianisme des origines à nos jours,* 9 vols. to date. Paris: Desclée de Brouwer, 1990–.

Miethke, Jürgen. "Reform, Reformation." in *Lexikon des Mittelalters,* 9 vols. in 15. Munich and Zurich: Artemis-Verlag, 1977–1998, vol. 7, pp. 543–550.

Moeller, Bernd. *Reichstadt und Reformation.* Gütersloh: Gerd Mohn, 1962. English translation in: *Imperial Cities and the Reformation,* translated by H. C. Erik Midelfort and Mark Edwards. Philadelphia: Fortress Press, 1972, pp. 41–115.

———. Review of *Die Entstehung der Konfessionen: Grundlagen und Formen der Konfessionsbildung* by Ernst Walter Zeeden. *Zeitschrift für Kirchengeschichte* 76 (1965), 405–408.

Moreau, E. de, et al. *La Crise religieuse du XVIe siècle.* Vol. 16 of *Histoire de l'Église depuis les origines jusqu'à nos jours,* edited by Augustin Fliche and Victor Martin. Paris: Bloud and Gay, 1951.

Morrison, Karl F. *The Mimetic Tradition of Reform in the West.* Princeton: Princeton University Press, 1982.

Noiriel, Gérard. "Foucault and History: The Lessons of a Disillusion." *Journal of Modern History* 66 (1994), 352–365.

———. *Sur la "crise" de l'histoire.* Paris: Belin, 1996.

Oberman, Heiko A. Review of *Sin and Fear: The Emergence of a Western Guilt Culture, 13th–18th Centuries,* by Jean Delumeau. *Sixteenth Century Journal* 23 (1992), 149–150.

Oestreich, Gerhard. "Strukturprobleme des europäischen Absolutismus." In *Geist und Gestalt des frühmodernen Staates: Ausgewählte Aufsätze.* Berlin: Duncker and Humblot, 1969, pp. 179–197. English translation: "The Structure of the Absolute State." In Gerhard Oestreich, *Neostoicism and the Early Modern State,* edited by Brigitta Oestreich and H. G. Koenigsberger, translated by David McLintock. Cambridge: Cambridge University Press, 1982, pp. 258–273.

———. *Strukturprobleme der frühen Neuzeit: Ausgewählte Aufsätze,* edited by Brigitta Oestreich. Berlin: Duncker and Humblot, 1980.

O'Farrell, Clare. *Foucault: Historian or Philosopher?* New York: St. Martin's Press, 1989.

Olin, John C. *The Catholic Reformation: Savonarola to Ignatius Loyola, Reform in the Church, 1495–1540.* New York: Harper and Row, 1969.

———. *Catholic Reform: From Cardinal Ximenes to the Council of Trent, 1495–1563. An Essay with Illustrative Documents and a Brief Study of St. Ignatius Loyola.* New York: Fordham University Press, 1990.

O'Malley, John W. "De Guibert and Jesuit Authenticity." *Woodstock Letters* 95 (1966), 103–110.

———. "Historical Thought and the Reform Crisis of the Early Sixteenth Century." *Theological Studies* 28 (1967), 531–548.

———. *Giles of Viterbo on Church and Reform: A Study in Renaissance Thought.* Leiden: E. J. Brill, 1968.

———. "Reform, Historical Consciousness, and Vatican II's Aggiornamento." *Theological Studies* 32 (1971), 573–601.

———. "Catholic Reform." In *Reformation Europe: A Guide to Research,* edited by Steven Ozment. St. Louis: Center for Reformation Research, 1982, pp. 297–319.

———. "Developments, Reforms, and Two Great Reformations: Towards a Historical Assessment of Vatican II." *Theological Studies* 44 (1983), 373–406.

———. "Priesthood, Ministry, and Religious Life: Some Historical and Historiographical Considerations." *Theological Studies* 49 (1988), 223–257.

———. "Was Ignatius Loyola a Church Reformer? How to Look at Early Modern Catholicism." *Catholic Historical Review* 77 (1991), 177–193.

———. *The First Jesuits.* Cambridge, Mass.: Harvard University Press, 1993.

———. "The Historiography of the Society of Jesus: Where Does It Stand Today?" In *The Jesuits: Cultures, Sciences, and the Arts, 1540–1773,* edited by John W. O'Malley et al. Toronto: University of Toronto Press, 1999, pp. 1–37.

———. "The Religious and Theological Culture of Michelangelo's Rome, 1508–1512." In Edgar Wind, *The Religious Symbolism of Michelangelo: Studies on the Sistine Ceiling,* edited by Elizabeth Sears. Oxford: Oxford University Press, forthcoming.

———, ed. *Catholicism in Early Modern History: A Guide to Research.* St. Louis: Center for Reformation Research, 1988.

——— et al., eds. *The Jesuits: Cultures, Sciences, and the Arts, 1540–1773.* Toronto: University of Toronto Press, 1999.

Ozment, Steven, ed. *Reformation Europe: A Guide to Research.* St. Louis: Center for Reformation Research, 1982.

Pallavicini, Pietro Sforza. *Istoria del Concilio di Trento,* 2 vols. Rome: G. Casoni, 1656–1657.

Panofsky, Erwin. "Erasmus and the Visual Arts." *Journal of the Warburg and Courtauld Institutes* 32 (1969), 200–227.

Paschini, Pio. "Due episodi della Controriforma in Italia." *Archivio della Società romana di Storia patria* 49 (1926), 303–329.

Pastor, Ludwig von. *Geschichte der Päpste seit dem Ausgang des Mittelalters,* 16 vols. Freiburg i/Br.: Herder, 1886–1933. English translation: *History of*

the Popes: From the Close of the Middle Ages, translated by Frederick Ignatius Antrobus et al., 40 vols. St. Louis: Herder, 1891–1953.

Pevsner, Nicolas. "Gegenreformation und Manierismus." *Repertorium für
Kunstwissenschaft* 46 (1925), 243–262.

Phillippson, Martin. *Les origines du catholicisme moderne: La Contre-révolution religieuse au XVIe siècle.* Brussels and Paris: Librairie Félix Alcan,
1884.

Picchi, Mario. *Don Giuseppe De Luca: Ricordi e testimonianze.* Brescia: Morcelliana, 1963.

Polanco, Juan Alfonso de. *Vita Ignatii Loiolae et rerum Societatis Jesu historia,* 6
vols. Madrid: Typographorum Societas, 1894–1898.

Pollen, J. H. "Counter-Reformation." In *The Catholic Encyclopedia,* edited by
Charles G. Herbermann et al., 15 vols. plus index. New York: Appleton
Company, 1907–1914, vol. 4, pp. 437–445.

Problemi di vita religiosa in Italia nel Cinquecento. Padua: Editrice Antenore,
1960.

Prodi, Paolo. *Il cardinale Gabriele Paleotti (1522–1597),* 2 vols. Rome: Edizioni
di Storia e Letteratura, 1959–1967.

———. "Richerche sulla teorica delle arti figurative nella Riforma cattolica."
Archivio italiano per la storia della pietà 4 (1965), 121–212.

———. "Il binomio jediniano 'Riforma cattolica e Controriforma' e la storiografia italiana." *Annuali dell'Istituto storico italo-germanico in Trento* 6
(1980), 85–98.

———. *Il sovrano pontefice: Un corpo e due anime: La monarchia papale nella prima
età moderna.* Bologna: Il Mulino, 1982. English translation: *The Papal
Prince: One Body and Two Souls, the Papal Monarchy in Early Modern
Europe,* translated by Susan Haskins. Cambridge: Cambridge University
Press, 1987.

———. "Introduzione." In *Strutture ecclesiastiche in Italia e in Germania prima
della Riforma,* edited by Paolo Prodi and Peter Johanek. Bologna: Il
Mulino, 1984, pp. 7–18.

———. "Riforma interiore e disciplinamento sociale in San Carlo Borromeo." *Intersezioni* 5 (1985), 273–285.

―――. "Controriforma e/o Riforma cattolica: Superamento di vecchi dilemmi nei nuovi panorami storiografici." *Römische historische Mitteilungen* 31 (1989), 227–237.

―――. "Il concilio di Trento di fronte alla politica e al diritto moderno: Introduzione." In *Il concilio di Trento e il moderno,* edited by Paolo Prodi and Wolfgang Reinhard. Bologna: Il Mulino, 1996, pp. 7–26.

Prodi, Paolo, and Peter Johanek, eds. *Strutture ecclesiastiche in Italia e in Germania prima della Riforma.* Bologna: Il Mulino, 1984.

Prodi, Paolo, with Elisabeth Müller-Luckner, eds. *Glaube und Eid: Treueformeln, Glaubensbekenntnisse und Sozialdisziplinierung zwischen Mittelalter und Neuzeit.* Munich: R. Oldenbourg, 1993.

Prodi, Paolo, with Carla Penuti, eds. *Disciplina dell'anima, disciplina del corpo e disciplina della società tra medioevo ed età moderna.* Bologna: Il Mulino, 1994.

Prodi, Paolo, and Wolfgang Reinhard, eds. *Il concilio di Trento e il moderno.* Bologna: Il Mulino, 1996.

Prosdocimi, Luigi. "Gabriel Le Bras storico delle istituzioni della cristianità medievale." *Rivista di Storia e Letteratura Religiosa* 3 (1967), 70–80.

Prosperi, Adriano. *Tra evangelismo e Controriforma: G. M. Giberti (1495–1543).* Rome: Edizioni di Storia e Letteratura, 1969.

―――. "Riforma cattolica, Controriforma, disciplinamento sociale." In *Storia dell'Italia religiosa, II: L'età moderna,* edited by Gabriele De Rosa and Tullio Gregory. Bari: Laterza, 1994, pp. 3–48.

―――. "Catholic Reformation." In *The Oxford Encyclopedia of the Reformation,* edited by Hans J. Hillerbrand, 4 vols. New York: Oxford University Press, 1996, vol. 1, pp. 287–293.

―――. "Storia di pietà, oggi." *Archivio italiano per la storia della pietà* 9 (1996), 3–29.

Pullan, Brian. *Rich and Poor in Renaissance Venice: The Social Institutions of a Catholic State.* Cambridge, Mass.: Harvard University Press, 1971.

Pullapilly, Cyriac K. *Caesar Baronius: Counter-Reformation Historian.* Notre Dame: University of Notre Dame Press, 1975.

Pütter, Johann Stephan. *Die Augsburgische confession.* Göttingen: Wittwe Vandenhoeck, 1776.

————. *Teutsche reichtsgeschichte in ihrem hauptfaden entwickelt.* Göttingen: Wittwe Vandenhoeck, 1778.

————. *Historische entwicklung der heutigen staatsverfassung des Teutschen Reichs,* 3 vols. Göttingen: Wittwe Vandenhoeck, 1786–1787.

Rabil, Albert, Jr., ed. *Renaissance Humanism: Foundations, Forms, and Legacy,* 3 vols. Philadelphia: University of Pennsylvania Press, 1988.

Ranke, Leopold von. *Die römischen Päpste, ihre Kirche und ihr Staat im 16. und 17. Jahrhundert,* 3 vols. Berlin: Duncker and Humblot, 1834–1836.

————. *Deutsche Geschichte im Zeitalter der Reformation,* 2nd ed., 6 vols. Berlin: Duncker and Humblot, 1842–1847.

Rapley, Elizabeth. *The Dévotes: Women and Church in Seventeenth-Century France.* Montreal: McGill–Queen's University Press, 1990.

Reinhard, Wolfgang. "Gegenreformation als Modernisierung? Prolegomena zu einer Theorie des konfessionellen Zeitalters." *Archive for Reformation History* 68 (1977), 226–252.

————. "Zwang zur Konfessionalisierung? Prolegomena zu einer Theorie des konfessionellen Zeitalters." *Zeitschrift für historische Forschung* 10 (1983), 257–277.

————. "Reformation, Counter-Reformation, and the Early Modern State: A Reassessment." *Catholic Historical Review* 75 (1989), 383–404.

————. "Disciplinamento sociale, confessionalizzazione, modernizzazione: Un discorso storiografico." In *Disciplina dell'anima, disciplina del corpo e disciplina della società tra medioevo ed età moderna,* edited by Paolo Prodi with Carla Penuti. Bologna: Il Mulino, 1994, pp 101–123.

————. Review of Marc Venard, ed., *Le temps des confessions (1530–1620). Historisches Jahrbuch* 114 (1994), 107–124.

————. "Was ist katholische Konfessionalisierung?" In *Die katholische Konfessionalisierung: Wissenschaftliches Symposion der Gesellschaft zur Herausgabe des Corpus Catholicorum und des Vereins für Reformationsgeschichte, 1993,* edited by Wolfgang Reinhard and Heinz Schilling. Gütersloh: Gütersloher Verlagshaus and Münster: Aschendorff, 1995, pp. 419–452.

————. *Ausgewählte Abhandlungen.* Berlin: Duncker and Humblot, 1997.

Reinhard, Wolfgang, and Heinz Schilling, eds. *Die katholische Konfessionali-*

sierung: Wissenschaftliches Symposion der Gesellschaft zur Herausgabe des Corpus Catholicorum und des Vereins für Reformationsgeschichte, 1993. Gütersloh: Gütersloher Verlagshaus and Münster: Aschendorff, 1995.

Renaudet, Augustin. *Préréforme et humanisme à Paris pendant les premières guerres d'Italie (1494–1517).* Paris: E. Champion, 1916.

Repgen, Konrad. "Hubert Jedin (1900–1980)." *Annali dell'Istituto storico italo-germanico in Trento* 6 (1980), 163–177.

————. "'Reform' als Leitgedanke kirchlicher Vergangenheit und Gegenwart." *Römische Quartalschrift für christliche Altertumskunde und Kirchengeschichte* 84 (1989), 5–30.

————. "Reform." In *The Oxford Encyclopedia of the Reformation,* edited by Hans J. Hillerbrand, 4 vols. New York: Oxford University Press, 1996, vol. 3, pp. 392–395.

Il rinnovamento del francescanesimo: L'Osservanza. Atti dell'XI convegno internazionale della Società internazionale di studi francescani (Assisi, 20–22 ottobre, 1983). Assisi: Università di Perugia, Centro di Studi Francescani, 1985.

Ritter, Moriz. *Deutsche Geschichte im Zeitalter der Gegenreformation und des dreissigjährigen Krieges (1555–1648),* 3 vols. Stuttgart: Cotta, 1889–1908.

Roberts, David D. *Benedetto Croce and the Uses of Historicism.* Berkeley: University of California Press, 1987.

Rosa, Mario. "Problemi di vita religiosa in Italia nel Cinquecento (note ed appunti)." *Bibliothèque d'Humanisme et Renaissance* 23 (1961), 395–414.

Rosso, Luigi. "Avvertenza." In *Contributi alla storia del Concilio di Trento e della Controriforma,* edited by Luigi Rosso. Florence: Vallecchi Editore, 1948, pp. vii–viii.

Rublack, Hans-Christoph, ed. *Die lutherische Konfessionalisierung in Deutschland: Wissenschaftliches Symposion des Vereins für Reformationsgeschichte, 1988.* Gütersloh: Gerd Mohn, 1992.

Russo, Carla. "Studi recenti di storia sociale e religiosa in Francia: Problemi e metodi." *Rivista Storica Italiana* 84 (1972), 625–682.

Salimbeni, Fulvio. "Vescovi, popolo e magia nel Sud: A proposito di un libro recente." *Nuova Rivista Storica* 56 (1972), 453–466.

Sarpi, Paolo (under the pseudonym Pietro Soave Polano). *Historia del Concilio Tridentino*. London: G. Billio, 1619.

Schilling, Heinz. *Konfessionskonflikt und Staatsbildung: Eine Fallstudie über das Verhältnis von religiosem und sozialem Wandel in der Frühneuzeit am Beispiel der Grafschaft Lippe*. Gütersloh: Gerd Mohn, 1981.

————. "Konfessionalisierung als gesellschaftlicher Umbruch: Inhaltliche Perspektiven und massenmediale Darstellung." In *Luther, die Reformation und die Deutschen: Wie erzählen wir unsere Geschichte?*, edited by Siegfried Quant. Paderborn: Schoningh, 1982, pp. 35–51.

————. "'Konfessionsbildung' und 'Konfessionalisierung.'" *Geschichte in Wissenschaft und Unterricht* 42 (1991), 447–463, 779–794.

————. *Religion, Political Culture and the Emergence of Early Modern Society: Essays in German and Dutch History*. Leiden: E. J. Brill, 1992.

————. "Confessionalization in the Empire: Religious and Societal Change in Germany between 1555 and 1620." In his *Religion, Political Culture*, pp. 205–245.

————. "The Second Reformation—Problems and Issues." In his *Religion, Political Culture*, pp. 247–301.

————. "Luther, Loyola, Calvin und die europäische Neuzeit." *Archive for Reformation History* 85 (1994), 5–31.

————. "Confessional Europe." In *Handbook of European History, 1400–1600: Late Middle Ages, Renaissance and Reformation*, edited by Thomas A. Brady et al., 2 vols. Leiden: E. J. Brill, 1994–1995, vol. 2, pp. 641–681.

————. "Disziplinierung oder 'Selbstregulierung der Untertanen'? Ein Plädoyer für die Doppelperspektive von Makro- und Mikro-historie bei der Erforschung der frühmodernen Kirchenzucht." *Historische Zeitschrift* 264 (1997), 675–691.

Schilling, Heinz, ed. *Die reformierte Konfessionalisierung in Deutschland: Das Problem der "Zweiten Reformation": Wissenschaftliches Symposion des Vereins für Reformationsgeschichte 1985*. Gütersloh: Gerd Mohn, 1986.

————. *Kirchenzucht und Sozialdisziplinierung im frühneuzeitlichen Europa*. Berlin: Duncker and Humblot, 1994.

172 *Bibliography*

Schloesser, Stephen. "Mystic Realists: Anti-Modernism in the French Catholic Revival, 1918–1928." Ph.D. diss., Stanford University, 1998.

Schmidt, Heinrich Richard. "Ein Plädoyer für das Ende des Etatismus in der Konfessionalisierungforschung." *Historische Zeitschrift* 265 (1997), 639–682.

Schmidt, Kurt Dietrich. *Die katholische Reform und Gegenreformation,* edited by Manfred Jacobs. Göttingen: Vandenhoeck and Ruprecht, 1975.

Schulze, Winfried. "Gerhard Oestreichs Begriff 'Sozialdisziplinierung in der frühen Neuzeit.'" *Zeitschrift für historische Forschung* 14 (1987), 265–302.

Schutte, Anne Jacobson. "Periodization of Sixteenth-Century Italian Religious History: The Post-Cantimori Paradigm Shift." *Journal of Modern History* 61 (1989), 269–284.

Scribner, Robert W. *The German Reformation.* London: Macmillan Education Ltd., 1988.

Seckendorff, Viet Ludwig von. *Commentarius historicus et apologeticus de Lutheranismo sive de reformatione religionis ductu D. Martini Lutheri in magna Germaniae parte aliisque regionibus.* Frankfurt and Leipzig: J. F. Gleditsch, 1692.

Seidel Menchi, Silvana. "Inquisizione come repressione o inquisizione come mediazione? Una proposta di periodizzazione." *Annuario dell'Istituto storico italiano per l'età moderna e contemporanea* 35–36 (1983–1984), 51–77.

Simoncelli, Paolo. *Il caso Reginald Pole: Eresia e santità nelle polemiche religiose del Cinquecento.* Rome: Edizioni di Storia e Letteratura, 1977.

———. "Pietro Bembo e l'evangelismo italiano." *Critica Storica* 15 (1978), 1–63.

———. *Evangelismo italiano del Cinquecento: Questione religiosa e nicodemismo politico.* Rome: Istituto storico italiano per l'età moderna e contemporanea, 1979.

———. "Inquisizione romana e riforma in Italia." *Rivista Storica Italiana* 100 (1988), 5–125.

———. *Storia di una censura: "Vita di Galileo" e Concilio Vaticano II.* Milan: Franco Angeli, 1992.

―――. *Cantimori, Gentile e la Normale di Pisa: Profili e documenti.* Milan: Franco Angeli, 1994.

―――. *Gentile e il Vaticano, 1943 e dintorni.* Florence: Le Lettere, 1997.

Steinert, Heinz. "The Development of 'Discipline' According to Michel Foucault: Discourse Analysis vs. Social History." *Crime and Social Justice* no. 20 (1984), 83–98.

Stoianovich, Traian. *French Historical Method: The Annales Paradigm.* Ithaca: Cornell University Press, 1976.

Strauss, Gerald. "Ideas of *Reformatio* and *Renovatio* from the Middle Ages to the Reformation." In *Handbook of European History, 1400–1600: Late Middle Ages, Renaissance and Reformation,* edited by Thomas A. Brady et. al., 2 vols. Leiden: E. J. Brill, 1994–1995, vol. 2, pp. 1–30.

Tallon, Alain. *La France et le concile de Trente (1518–1563).* Rome: École Française de Rome, 1997.

Tanner, Norman P., ed. *Decrees of the Ecumenical Councils,* 2 vols. Washington: Georgetown University Press, 1990.

Venard, Marc. "Réforme, Réformation, Préréforme, Contre-réforme: Étude de vocabulaire chez les historiens recents de langue française." In *Historiographie de la Réforme,* edited by Philippe Joutard. Paris: Delachaux and Niestle, 1977, pp. 352–365.

―――. *Réforme protestante, Réforme catholique dans la province d'Avignon, xvie siècle.* Paris: Éditions du Cerf, 1993.

Venard, Marc, ed. *Le temps des confessions (1530–1620).* Paris: Desclée de Brouwer, 1992.

Veyne, Paul. "Foucault Revolutionizes History." In *Foucault and His Interlocutors,* edited by Arnold I. Davidson. Chicago: University of Chicago Press, 1997, pp. 146–182.

Villoslada, Ricardo G. "La Contrarreforma: Su nombre y su concepto histórico." In *Saggi storici intorno al papato.* Rome: Università Pontificia Gregoriana, 1959, pp. 189–242.

Walker, Williston. *The Reformation.* New York: Charles Scribner's Sons, 1900.

Weisbach, Werner. *Der Barock als Kunst der Gegenreformation.* Berlin: P. Cassirer, 1921.

Weiss, Otto. "Chiesa cattolica, religione e società nella più recente storiografia tedesca." *Ricerche di storia sociale e religiosa* 52 (July–Dec. 1997), 169–197.

Westervelt, Benjamin Wood. "Roman Catholicism." In *The Oxford Encyclopedia of the Reformation,* edited by Hans J. Hillerbrand, 4 vols. New York: Oxford University Press, 1996, vol. 3, pp. 439–447.

Whitehead, Alfred North. *The Axioms of Projective Geometry.* Cambridge: Cambridge University Press, 1906.

Willaert, L. *La Restauration catholique (1563–1648).* Vol. 18 of *Histoire de l'Église depuis les origins jusqu'à nos jours,* edited by Augustin Fliche and Victor Martin. Namur: Facultés universitaires, 1960.

Wölfflin, Heinrich. *Renaissance und Barock: Eine Untersuchung über Wesen und Entstehung des Barockstils in Italien.* Munich: T. Ackermann, 1888.

Wolgast, Eike. "Reform, Reformation." In *Geschichtliche Grundbegriffe: Historisches Lexikon zur politisch-sozialen Sprache in Deutschland,* edited by Otto Brunner et al., 9 vols. Stuttgart: Klett-Cotta, 1972–1984, vol 5, pp. 313–360.

Zeeden, Ernst Walter. "Grundlagen und Wege der Konfessionsbildung in Deutschland im Zeitalter der Glaubenskämpfe." *Historische Zeitschrift* 185 (1958), 249–299.

———. *Die Entstehung der Konfessionen: Grundlagen und Formen der Konfessionsbildung im Zeitalter der Glaubenskämpfe.* Munich: R. Oldenbourg, 1965.

———. *Konfessionsbildung: Studien zur Reformation, Gegenreformation und katholischen Reform.* Stuttgart: Klett-Cotta, 1985.

———, ed. *Gegenreformation.* Darmstadt: Wissenschaftliche Buchgesellschaft, 1973.

Zen, Stefano. *Baronio storico: Controriforma e crisi del metodo umanistico.* Naples: Vivarium, 1994.

Zoli, Sergio. *La Controriforma.* Florence: La Nuova Italia Editrice, 1979.

NOTES

✝

Introduction

1. On the origins and development of the term, see Eike Wolgast, "Reform, Reformation," in *Geschichtliche Grundbegriffe: Historisches Lexikon zur politisch-sozialen Sprache in Deutschland,* ed. Otto Brunner et al., 9 vols. (Stuttgart: Klett-Cotta, 1972–1984), 5:313–360, especially 321–335.

2. John W. O'Malley, ed., *Catholicism in Early Modern History: A Guide to Research* (St. Louis: Center for Reformation Research, 1988); and Steven Ozment, ed., *Reformation Europe: A Guide to Research* (St. Louis: Center for Reformation Research, 1982).

3. See my "Was Ignatius Loyola a Church Reformer? How to Look at Early Modern Catholicism," *Catholic Historical Review,* 77 (1991), 177–193.

4. Alfred North Whitehead, *The Axioms of Projective Geometry* (Cambridge: Cambridge University Press, 1906), p. 2, as quoted in Gerhart Ladner, *The Idea of Reform: Its Impact on Christian Thought and Action in the Age of the Fathers* (Cambridge, Mass.: Harvard University Press, 1959), pp. 427–428. Ladner discusses Whitehead's principle as applied to history on pp. 427–432.

5. R. W. Scribner, *The German Reformation* (London: Macmillan Education Ltd., 1988), p. 4.

6. Norman F. Cantor, *Inventing the Middle Ages: The Lives, Works, and*

Ideas of the Great Medievalists of the Twentieth Century (New York: Quill, William Morrow, 1991).

7. Wallace K. Ferguson, *The Renaissance in Historical Thought: Five Centuries of Interpretation* (Cambridge, Mass.: Houghton Mifflin Company, 1948).

8. A. G. Dickens and John M. Tonkin, with Kenneth Powell, *The Reformation in Historical Thought* (Cambridge, Mass: Harvard University Press, 1985).

9. Even before the advent of "social disciplining," Giuseppe Alberigo warned of the danger of "one-dimensional schemes" and called for a "polycentric" approach, "Dinamiche religiose del Cinquecento italiano tra Riforma, Riforma cattolica, Controriforma," *Cristianesimo nella storia,* 6 (1985), 543–560, especially 548–549.

10. O'Malley, "Loyola a Church Reformer?"

11. See, for example, Marc R. Forster, "With and Without Confessionalization: Varieties of Early Modern German Catholicism," *Journal of Early Modern History,* 1 (1998), 315–343; and R. Po-chia Hsia, *The World of Catholic Renewal, 1540–1770* (Cambridge: Cambridge University Press, 1998), pp. 1–7.

12. Florencia E. Mallon, "The Promise and Dilemma of Subaltern Studies: Perspectives from Latin American History," *American Historical Review,* 99 (1994), 1515.

13. See, for example, Philip Benedict, "Between Whig Traditions and New Histories: American Historical Writing about Reformation and Early Modern Europe," in *Imagined Histories: American Historians Interpret the Past,* eds. Anthony Molho and Gordon S. Wood (Princeton: Princeton University Press, 1998), pp. 295–323.

14. Hubert Jedin, *Katholische Reformation oder Gegenreformation? Ein Versuch zur Klärung der Begriffe nebst einer Jubiläumsbetrachtung über das Trienter Konzil* (Lucerne: Josef Stocker, 1946).

15. Hubert Jedin, *Girolamo Seripando: Sein Leben und Denken im Geisteskampf des 16. Jahrhunderts,* 2 vols. (Würzburg: Rita-Verlag, 1937), translated into English as *Papal Legate at the Council of Trent: Cardinal Seripando,* trans. Frederic C. Eckhoff (St. Louis and London: Herder, 1947).

16. Hubert Jedin, *Geschichte des Konzils von Trient,* 4 vols. in 5 (Freiburg i/Br.: Herder, 1949–1975). Only the first two volumes have been translated into English: *A History of the Council of Trent,* trans. Ernest Graf (London: Thomas Nelson and Sons, 1957–1961).

17. Pier Giorgio Camaiani, "Interpretazioni della Riforma cattolica e della Controriforma," in *Grande Antologia Filosofica,* ed. Umberto Antonio Padovani et al., 21 vols. (Milan: Marzorati, 1954–1971), 6:329–386, with illustrative texts, 387–490.

18. See, for example, Geoffrey Barraclough, *Main Trends in History,* rev. by Michael Burns (New York: Holmes and Meier, 1991), especially pp. 1–16, 28–45.

1. How It All Began

1. See Gerhart B. Ladner, *The Idea of Reform: Its Impact on Christian Thought and Action in the Age of the Fathers* (Cambridge, Mass.: Harvard University Press, 1959). For a more wide-ranging study that covers some of the same ground from a different perspective, see Karl F. Morrison, *The Mimetic Tradition of Reform in the West* (Princeton: Princeton University Press, 1982). For the whole subject, the work of Yves Congar was especially important, *Vraie et fausse réforme dans l'Église,* rev. ed. (Paris: Éditions du Cerf, 1968), originally published in 1950.

2. See, for example, *Crises et réformes dans l'Église, de la Réforme grégorienne à la Préréforme* (Paris: Editions du CTHS, 1991).

3. The bibliography on the Investiture Controversy is immense. Especially pertinent to the issue at hand are Gerhart B. Ladner, "Die mittelalterliche Reform-Idee und ihr Verhältnis zur Idee der Renaissance," *Mitteilungen des Instituts für österreichische Geschichtsforschung,* 60 (1952), 31–59; his "Two Gregorian Letters: On the Sources and Nature of Gregory VII's Reform Ideology," *Studi Gregoriani,* 5 (1956), 221–242; and my "Developments, Reforms, and Two Great Reformations: Towards a Historical Assessment of Vatican II," *Theological Studies,* 44 (1983), 373–406.

4. See *Decrees of the Ecumenical Councils,* ed. Norman P. Tanner, 2 vols.

(Washington: Georgetown University Press, 1990), 1:407 (Session III, March 26, 1415).

5. See Jürgen Miethke, "Reform, Reformation," in *Lexikon des Mittelalters,* 9 vols. in 15 (Munich: Artemis-Verlag, 1977–1998), 7:543–550; Konrad Repgen, "Reform als Leitgedanke kirchlicher Vergangenheit und Gegenwart," *Römische Quartalschrift,* 84 (1989), 5–30, and his "Reform" in *The Oxford Encyclopedia of the Reformation,* ed. Hans Hillerbrand, 4 vols. (New York: Oxford University Press, 1996), 3:392–395; John W. O'Malley, "Historical Thought and the Reform Crisis of the Early Sixteenth Century," *Theological Studies,* 28 (1967), 531–548, and his "Reform, Historical Consciousness, and Vatican II's Aggiornamento,*" *ibid., 32 (1971), 573–601; Gerald Strauss, "Ideas of *Reformatio* and *Renovatio* from the Middle Ages to the Reformation," in *Handbook of European History, 1400–1600: Late Middle Ages, Renaissance and Reformation,* eds. Thomas A. Brady et al., 2 vols. (Leiden: E. J. Brill, 1994–1995), 2:1–30; Richard Kieckhefer, "Reform, Idea of," in *Dictionary of the Middle Ages,* ed. Joseph R. Strayer, 12 vols. plus index (New York: Charles Scribner's Sons, 1982–1989), 10:281–288.

6. See Repken, "Reform," and Eike Wolgast, "Reform, Reformation," in *Geschichtliche Grundbegriffe: Historisches Lexikon zur politisch-sozialen Sprache in Deutschland,* ed. Otto Brunner et al., 9 vols. (Stuttgart: Klet-Cotta, 1972–1997), 5:313–360, especially 321–335.

7. Veit Ludwig von Seckendorff, *Commentarius historicus et apologeticus de Lutheranismo sive de reformatione religionis ductu D. Martini Lutheri in magna Germaniae parte aliisque regionibus* (Frankfurt and Leipzig: J. F. Gleditsch, 1692). See especially the *Praeloquium.* For the origins of distinctively Catholic and Protestant historiographies, see Eduard Fueter, *Geschichte der neueren Historiographie,* Handbuch der mittelalterlichen und neueren Geschichte, Abt. I, eds. G. von Below et al. (Munich: R. Oldenbourg, 1936), pp. 246–291.

8. See Wallace K. Ferguson, *The Renaissance in Historical Thought: Five Centuries of Interpretation* (Boston: Houghton Mifflin Company, 1948), especially pp. 74–77.

9. See Karl Heussi, *Altertum, Mittelalter und Neuzeit in der Kirchengeschichte:*

Ein Beitrag zum Problem der historischen Periodisierung (1921; reprint ed. Darmstadt: Wissenschaftliche Buchgesellschaft, 1969).

10. Johann Stephan Pütter, *Die Augsburgische confession* (Göttingen: Wittwe Vandenhoeck, 1776), p. 10; see also his *Teutsche reichtsgeschichte in ihrem hauptfaden entwickelt* (Göttingen: Wittwe Vandenhoeck, 1778), p. 429, and *Historische entwicklung der heutigen staatsverfassung des Teutschen Reichs,* 3 vols. (Göttingen: Wittwe Vandenhoeck, 1786–1787), 2:18, 33, 36, as cited in Albert Elkan, the first scholar to identify Pütter's importance in this regard, "Entstehung und Entwicklung des Begriffs 'Gegenreformation,'" *Historische Zeitschrift,* 112 (1914), 473–493, especially p. 475. Contrary to what Elkan knew, the term was used as early as 1654; see Wolgast, "Reform, Reformation," p. 330. For what follows in this chapter, see especially Hubert Jedin, *Katholische Reformation oder Gegenreformation? Ein Versuch zur Klärung der Begriffe nebst einer Jubiläumsbetrachtung über das Trienter Konzil* (Lucerne: Josef Stocker, 1946), and Pier Giorgio Camaiani, "Interpretazioni della Riforma cattolica e della Controriforma," in *Grande Antologia Filosofica,* ed. Umberto Antonio Padovani et al., 21 vols. (Milan: Marzorati, 1954–1971), 6:329–499.

11. Leopold von Ranke, *Deutsche Geschichte im Zeitalter der Reformation,* 6 vols. (Berlin: Duncker and Humblot, 1842–1847), 5:501: "Auf das Zeitalter der Reformation folgte das der Gegenreformationen."

12. Johannes Janssen, *Geschichte des deutschen Volkes seit dem Ausgang des Mittelalters* (Freiburg i/Br.: Herder, 1876–1894); English translation by M. A. Mitchell and A. M. Christie, 17 vols. (London: K. Paul, Trench, Trübner, 1896–1910). On Janssen, see Fueter, *Geschichte,* pp. 571–575; A. G. Dickens and John Tonkin with Kenneth Powell, *The Reformation in Historical Thought* (Cambridge, Mass.: Harvard University Press, 1985), pp. 183–184; and Hubert Jedin, *Die Erforschung der kirchlichen Reformationsgeschichte seit 1876: Leistungen und Aufgaben der deutschen Katholiken* (Münster: Aschendorff, 1931), pp. 5–10.

13. Joseph Hergenröther, *Handbuch der allgemeinen Kirchengeschichte,* ed. Johann Peter Kirsch, 5th ed., 4 vols. (Freiburg i/Br.: Herder, 1911–1917), 4:1.

14. For the achievement of Catholic historians in nineteenth-century Ger-

many, see Hubert Jedin, *Erforschung Reformationsgeschichte*, and his "General Introduction to Church History," in *Handbook of Church History*, eds. Hubert Jedin et al., 10 vols. (New York: Herder and Herder; Crossroad, 1965–1981), 1:1–56, especially 35–37.

15. Jedin, "Introduction to Church History," p. 36.

16. See Dickens and Tonkin, *Reformation*, pp. 154–161.

17. Leopold von Ranke, *Die römischen Päpste, ihre Kirche und ihr Staat im 16. und 17. Jahrhundert*, 3 vols. (Berlin: Duncker and Humblot, 1834–1836).

18. Eberhard Gothein, *Ignatius von Loyola und die Gegenreformation* (Halle: Max Niemeyer, 1895).

19. Moriz Ritter, *Deutsche Geschichte im Zeitalter der Gegenreformation und des dreissigjährigen Krieges (1555–1648)*, 3 vols. (Stuttgart: Cotta, 1889–1908).

20. See Wolfgang Reinhard, "Gegenreformation als Modernisierung? Prolegomena zu einer Theorie des konfessionellen Zeitalters," *Archive for Reformation History*, 68 (1977), 226–252, especially 227.

21. Wilhelm Maurenbrecher, *Geschichte der katholischen Reformation* (Nördlingen: C. H. Beck, 1880). On the use of the term in the eighteenth century, see Elkan, "Entstehung," p. 475.

22. See Ricardo G. Villoslada, "La Contrarreforma: Su nombre y su concepto histórico," in *Saggi storici intorno al papato*, Miscellanea Historiae Pontificiae 21 (Rome: Pontificia Università Gregoriana, 1959), pp. 189–242, especially p. 207.

23. Constantin R. von Höfler, *Die romanische Welt und ihr Verhältnis zu den Reformideen des Mittelalters*, found in *Sitzungsberichte der kaiserlichen Akademie der Wissenschaften* (Vienna) phil.-hist. Classe, 91 (1878), 257–538, especially 460ff. On Höfler, see A. Dürrwächter, "Konstantin von Höfler und die fränkische Geschichtsforschung: Zu seinem 100. Geburtstage," *Historisches Jahrbuch*, 33 (1912), 1–53.

24. Joseph Kerker, "Die kirchliche Reform in Italien unmittelbar vor dem Tridentinum," *Tübinger theologische Quartalschrift*, 41 (1859), 3–56.

25. Alfons Bellesheim, "Professor Maurenbrecher über die katholischer Reformation," *Historisch-politische Blätter für das katholische Deutschland*, 88

(1881), 608–622; review by Franz Dittrich, *Historische Jahrbuch,* 2 (1881), 602–617.

26. Gothein, *Ignatius von Loyola,* p. 40.

27. Ibid., p. 92.

28. Review by H. Baumgarten, *Historische Zeitschrift,* 46 (1881), 154–164.

29. See, for example, the popular text by Jakob Marx, *Lehrbuch der Kirchengeschichte,* 4th ed. (Trier: Paulinus, 1908), p. 685.

30. Jacob Burckhardt, *The Civilization of the Renaissance in Italy,* trans. S. G. C. Middlemore (New York: Harper and Brothers, 1958), p. 143. For recent interpretations, see Anthony Molho, "The Italian Renaissance: Made in the USA," in *Imagined Histories: American Historians Interpret the Past,* ed. Anthony Molho and Gordon S. Wood (Princeton: Princeton University Press, 1998), pp. 263–294.

31. Eberhard Gothein, "Staat und Gesellschaft des Zeitalters der Gegenreformation," in *Staat und Gesellschaft der neueren Zeit (bis zur französischen Revolution),* in the series *Die Kultur der Gegenwart,* Teil II, Abt. V,1 (1908), 137–230.

32. Burckhardt, *Civilization of the Renaissance,* p. 540. For Burckhardt's appreciation of Spain's religious importance, see Werner Kaegi, "La Spagna e la Controriforma nel pensiero di J. Burckhardt," *Annali della Scuola Normale Superiore di Pisa,* series II, 21 (1952), 158–173.

33. Gustav Droysen, *Geschichte der Gegenreformation* (Berlin: G. Grote, 1893). He is not to be confused with his more distinguished father, Johann Gustav Droysen (1808–1884).

34. See the first volume of Janssen, *Geschichte.*

35. See Jedin, *Erforschung Reformationsgeschichte,* especially pp. 10–18, and Owen Chadwick, *Catholicism and History: The Opening of the Vatican Archives* (Cambridge: Cambridge University Press, 1978).

36. The first volume appeared in the series by Juan Alfonso de Polanco, *Vita Ignatii Loiolae et rerum Societatis Jesu historia,* 6 vols. (Madrid: Typographorum Societas, 1894–1898).

37. Peter Canisius, *Beati Petri Canisii Societatis Iesu Epistulae et Acta,* ed. Otto Braunsberger, 8 vols. (Freiburg i/Br.: Herder, 1896–1923).

38. *Concilium Tridentinum: Diariorum, actorum, epistolarum, tractatuum nova collectio,* 13 vols. in 18 to date (Freiburg i/Br.: Herder, 1901–); the last volume to appear bore a 1985 imprint. See Jedin, *Erforschung Reformationsgeschichte.*

39. Paolo Sarpi (under the pseudonym Pietro Soave Polano), *Historia del Concilio Tridentino* (London: G. Billio, 1619).

40. Bernhard Duhr, *Geschichte der Jesuiten in den Ländern deutscher Zunge,* 4 vols. (Freiburg i/Br.: Herder, 1907–1913; Munich-Regensburg: G. J. Manz, 1921–1928).

41. On Pastor, see Chadwick, *Catholicism and History,* especially pp. 116–127, and Raoul Manselli, "Ludwig von Pastor—Der Historiker der Päpste," *Römische historische Mitteilungen,* 21 (1979), 11–26.

42. Ludwig von Pastor, *Geschichte der Päpste seit dem Ausgang des Mittelalters,* 16 vols. (Freiburg i/Br.: Herder, 1886–1933); English translation, *History of the Popes: From the Close of the Middle Ages,* trans. Frederick Ignatius Antrobus et al., 40 vols. (St. Louis: Herder, 1891–1953). Pastor died in 1928; the last volume was published posthumously.

43. Ferguson, *Renaissance,* p. 343.

44. See Jedin, *Reformation oder Gegenreformation?,* p. 20.

45. See Camaiani, "Interpretazioni," pp. 350–54.

46. See, for example, Pio Paschini, "Due episodi della Controriforma in Italia," *Archivio della Società romana di Storia patria,* 49 (1926), 303–329. On Paschini, see Michele Maccarrone, "Mons. Pio Paschini (1878–1962)," *Rivista di Storia della Chiesa in Italia,* 17 (1963), 181–221, and Giuseppe Alberigo, "Il Cinquecento religioso italiano nell'opera storica di Pio Paschini," ibid., 234–247.

47. Arturo Carlo Jemolo, "Controriforma," *Enciclopedia Italiana,* 11:260–263.

48. Hubert Jedin, "Riforma cattolica," in *Enciclopedia Cattolica,* 10:904–907. The entry "Controriforma" simply refers the reader to "Riforma cattolica."

49. See Francesco De Sanctis, *Storia della letteratura italiana,* ed. Niccolò Gallo, 2 vols., Opere di Francesco De Sanctis 8 and 9 (Turin: G. Einaudi, 1958), 2:792–804, first published in 1871.

50. See, for example, Benedetto Croce, "La crisi italiana del Cinquecento e il legame del Rinascimento col Risorgimento," *La Critica,* 37 (1939), 401–411.

51. Benedetto Croce, "Controriforma," *La Critica,* 22 (1924), 325–333. He repeats the idea in *Storia dell'età barocca in Italia: Pensiero, poesia e letteratura, vita morale* (Bari: G. Laterza, 1929), pp. 10–11, 15–17.

52. Ibid.

53. See Otto Kurz, "Barocco: Storia di una parola," *Lettere italiane,* 12 (1960), 414–444. For art history the turning point in assessment was Heinrich Wölfflin, *Renaissance und Barock: Eine Untersuchung über Wesen und Entstehung des Barockstils in Italien* (Munich: T. Ackermann, 1888). For applications of the term to historiography, see Eric W. Cochrane, "The Transition from Renaissance to Baroque: The Case of Italian Historiography," *History and Theory,* 19 (1980), 21–38.

54. See Croce, *Età barocca,* especially pp. 3–51. See also Delio Cantimori, "Il dibattito sul Barocco," *Rivista Storica Italiana,* 72 (1960), 489–500. More broadly, see David D. Roberts, *Benedetto Croce and the Uses of Historicism* (Berkeley: University of California Press, 1987).

55. Werner Weisbach, *Der Barock als Kunst der Gegenreformation* (Berlin: P. Cassirer, 1921). For a challenge to Weisbach that proposes Mannerism as the more characteristic style of the Counter Reformation, see Nicolaus Pevsner, "Gegenreformation und Manierismus," *Repertorium für Kunstwissenschaft,* 46 (1925), 243–262; and for a direct confrontation between the two scholars, ibid., 49 (1928), 16–28, 225–246. See also Paolo Prodi, "Richerche sulla teorica delle arti figurative nella Riforma cattolica," *Archivio italiano per la storia della pietà,* 4 (1965), 121–212, especially 123–140; see also the exhaustive historiographical survey by Gauvin Alexander Bailey, "'Le style jésuite n'existe pas:' Jesuit Corporate Culture and the Visual Arts," in *The Jesuits: Cultures, Sciences, and the Arts, 1540–1773,* ed. John W. O'Malley et al. (Toronto: University of Toronto Press, 1999), pp. 38–89.

56. See Villoslada, "La Contrarreforma," especially pp. 189–191.

57. See, for example, Alain Tallon, *La France et le concile de Trente (1518–1563)* (Rome: École Française de Rome, 1997), pp. 10–12.

58. Augustin Renaudet, *Préréforme et humanisme à Paris pendant les premières guerres d'Italie (1494–1517)* (Paris: E. Champion, 1916).

59. Pierre Imbart de La Tour, *L'Évangelisme (1521–1538)* (Paris: Librairie Hachette, 1914), which was the third volume of the four in his series, *Les origines de la Réforme* (1905–1935).

60. Camaiani, "Interpretazioni," p. 355.

61. Henri Bremond, *Histoire littéraire du sentiment religieux en France depuis la fin des guerres de religion jusqu'à nos jours,* 11 vols. (Paris: Bloud et Gay, 1916–1933). On Bremond, see Michel de Certeau, "Henri Bremond et 'la Métaphysique des Saints': Une interprétation de l'expérience religieuse moderne," *Recherches de science religieuse,* 54 (1966), 23–60, and Émile Goichot, *Henri Bremond, historien du sentiment religieux: Genèse et stratégie d'une entreprise littéraire* (Paris: Éditions Ophrys, 1982). Bremond himself developed an earlier tradition represented by Charles Dejob, *De l'influence du Concile de Trente sur la littérature et les beaux arts chez les peuples catholiques: Essai d'introduction à l'histoire littéraire du siècle de Louis XIV* (1884; reprint ed. Geneva: Slatkine Reprints, 1969).

62. Bremond, *Histoire,* 1:vi.

63. Roger Aubenas and Robert Ricard, *L'Église et la Renaissance (1449–1517)* (Paris: Bloud and Gay, 1951); E. de Moreau et al., *La Crise religieuse du XVIe siècle* (1950); Léon Cristiani, *L'Église à l'époque du Concile de Trente* (1948); and Léon E. Halkin and L. Willaert, *La Restauration catholique, 1563–1648* (Namur: Facultés universitaires, 1960).

64. See Tallon, *Le concile de Trente,* p. v, and Marc Venard, "Réforme, Réformation, Préréforme, Contre-Réforme: Étude de vocabulaire chez les historiens recents de langue française," in *Historiographie de la Réforme,* ed. Philippe Joutard (Paris: Delachaux and Niestle, 1977), pp. 352–365. For a polemic against Counter Reformation, 1936, see Léon Cristiani, "Réforme catholique ou Contre-Réforme," *Dictionnaire de théologie catholique,* 13:2097–2098.

65. Martin Phillippson, *Les origines du catholicisme moderne: La Contre-révolution religieuse au XVIe siècle* (Brussels and Paris: Librairie Félix Alcan, 1884).

66. See, for example, Williston Walker, *The Reformation* (New York: Charles Scribner's Sons, 1900).

67. For an analysis of Laurence, see Camaiani, "Interpretazioni," pp. 349–350.

68. B. J. Kidd, *The Counter-Reformation, 1550–1600* (London: Society for Promoting Christian Knowledge, 1933).

69. H. Outram Evennett, *The Cardinal of Lorraine and the Council of Trent: A Study in the Counter-Reformation* (Cambridge: Cambridge University Press, 1930), pp. 465–466.

70. Hubert Jedin, *Riforma cattolica o Controriforma?: Tentativo di chiarimento dei concetti con riflessioni sul Concilio di Trento,* trans. Marola Guarducci (Brescia: Morcelliana, 1957).

71. *Revue d'Histoire Ecclésiastique,* 41 (1946), 667–668. The only other notice in a Francophone publication was in *Nouvelle Revue Théologique,* 69 (1947), 990.

72. Kurt Dietrich Schmidt, a Lutheran historian, accepted it but with notable qualifications; see *Die katholische Reform und Gegenreformation,* ed. Manfred Jacobs (Göttingen: Vandenhoeck and Ruprecht, 1975), especially pp. 4–6. By contrast, Gottfried Maron, also a Protestant, was far more critical; see "Des [sic] Schicksal der katholischen Reform im 16. Jahrhundert: Zur Frage nach der Kontinuität in der Kirchengeschichte," *Zeitschrift für Kirchengeschichte,* 88 (1977), 218–229. Earlier reviews appeared in *Historisches Jahrbuch,* 52–69 (1949), 870–871; *Zeitschrift für schweizer Kirchengeschichte,* 40 (1946), 148–149; *Mitteilungen des Instituts für österreichische Geschichtsforschung,* 56 (1948), 461–462; *Theologische Quartalschrift,* 128 (1948), 369–372; *Theologie und Glaube,* 40 (1950), 558; and *Verkündigung und Forschung* (1951–1952), 156ff.

73. Delio Cantimori, "Riforma cattolica," *Società* 2 (1946), 820–834. Other reviews published in Italy were *Archivum Historicum Societatis Iesu,* 14 (1945), 151–153; *Antonianum,* 22 (1947), 302–303; *Humanitas,* 1 (1946), 711. There is a judicious summary of reactions in Camaiani, "Interpretazioni," pp. 377–378.

74. "Counter-Reformation," *The Oxford Dictionary of the Christian Church,* ed. E. A. Livingstone (Oxford: Oxford University Press, 1997), 423–424.

75. Adriano Prosperi, "Catholic Reformation," in *Oxford Encyclopedia,* 1:287–293; Benjamin Wood Westervelt, "Roman Catholicism," ibid., 3:439–447.

76. See Eric W. Cochrane, "Counter Reformation or Tridentine Reformation? Italy in the Age of Carlo Borromeo," in *San Carlo Borromeo: Catholic Reform and Ecclesiastical Politics in the Second Half of the Sixteenth Century,* ed. John M. Headley and John B. Tomaro (Washington: Folger Books, The Folger Shakespeare Library, 1988), pp. 31–46, and William V. Hudon, "Religion and Society in Early Modern Italy: Old Questions, New Insights," *American Historical Review,* 101 (1996), 783–804.

77. R. Po-chia Hsia, *The World of Catholic Renewal, 1540–1770* (Cambridge: Cambridge University Press, 1998).

78. Pierre Janelle, *The Catholic Reformation* (Milwaukee: The Bruce Publishing Company, 1949).

79. John C. Olin, *The Catholic Reformation: Savonarola to Ignatius Loyola, Reform in the Church, 1495–1540* (New York: Harper and Row, 1969).

80. John C. Olin, *Catholic Reform: From Cardinal Ximenes to the Council of Trent, 1495–1563. An Essay with Illustrative Documents and a Brief Study of St. Ignatius Loyola* (New York: Fordham University Press, 1990).

2. Hubert Jedin and the Classic Position

1. The best source for Jedin's life is his own account, finished just before his death and published posthumously, *Lebensbericht,* ed. Konrad Repgen (Mainz: Matthias-Grünewald Verlag, 1984). See also Repgen's brief but astute account, "Hubert Jedin (1900–1980)," *Annali dell'Istituto storico italo-germanico in Trento,* 6 (1980), 163–177. Virtually all the contributions in this volume of the *Annali* (or *Jahrbuch,* its alternative German title) deal with Jedin, and they are frequently cited below.

2. For the general ecclesio-political background during these formative

years of Jedin's life, see Martin Conway, *Catholic Politics in Europe, 1918–1945* (New York: Routledge, 1997).

3. Jedin wrote the history of the Nazi regime, 1933–1939, for the *Seconda appendice* to the *Enciclopedia Italiana*, 2 vols. (1948): 1035–1042.

4. Paolo Sarpi (under the pseudonym Pietro Soave Polano), *Historia del Concilio Tridentino* (London: G. Billio, 1619; Pietro Sforza Pallavicini, *Istoria del Concilio di Trento*, 2 vols. (Rome: G. Casoni, 1656–1657).

5. See Hubert Jedin, "Kardinal Giovanni Mercati 80 Jahre alt," in the collection of Jedin's studies, *Kirche des Glaubens, Kirche der Geschichte: Ausgewählte Aufsätze und Vorträge*, 2 vols. (Freiburg i/Br.: Herder, 1966), 1:95–98.

6. Hubert Jedin, ed., *Handbuch der Kirchengeschichte*, 7 vols. in 10 (Freiburg im/Br.: Herder, 1962–1979); English-language edition, *Handbook of Church History*, 10 vols. (New York: Herder and Herder; Crossroad, 1965–1981).

7. The acts of the conference were published as *Il concilio di Trento e la riforma tridentina*, 2 vols. (Rome and Freiburg i/Br.: Herder, 1965).

8. Jedin, *Lebensbericht*, pp. 194–195.

9. He has left in print two lectures he delivered on the subject. The first is a lecture that he gave in different forms in a number of different places between 1959 and 1962, before Vatican II began: "Das II. Vatikanische Konzil in historischer Sicht," in *Kirche des Glaubens*, 2:589–603. The second was delivered in Düsseldorf in 1968 and is particularly interesting because the printed text includes comments from some distinguished scholars who were present, such as Karl Rahner, Heinrich Lausberg, and Joseph Ratzinger: "Vaticanum II und Tridentinum: Tradition und Fortschritt in der Kirchengeschichte," *Arbeitsgemeinschaft für Forschung des Landes Nordrhein-Westfalen*, no. 146 (Cologne: Westdeutscher Verlag, 1968).

10. See Georg G. Iggers, *New Directions in European Historiography*, rev. ed. (London: Methuen, 1985), pp. 80–92.

11. See Jedin, *History of the Church*, continuation of the *Handbook* under a new title, 5:623–645.

12. See Giuseppe Alberigo, "La 'riforma' come criterio della Storia della Chiesa," *Annali dell'Istituto storico italo-germanico in Trento*, 6 (1980), 25–33.

13. See Jedin, *History of the Church,* continuation of his *Handbook* under new title, 5:431.

14. Delio Cantimori, "Riforma cattolica," *Società,* 2 (1946), 831.

15. Hubert Jedin, *Katholische Reformation oder Gegenreformation? Ein Versuch zur Klärung der Begriffe nebst einer Jubiläumsbetrachtung über das Trienter Konzil* (Lucerne: Josef Stocker, 1946), p. 38: "Die katholische Reform ist die Selbstbesinnung der Kirche auf das katholische Lebensideal durch innere Erneuerung, die Gegenreformation ist die Selbstbehauptung der Kirche im Kampf gegen den Protestantismus."

16. See Alberigo, "La 'riforma,'" p. 27, with note 6.

17. Jedin, *Katholische Reformation,* p. 32: "Um den Gegner abzuwehren, schafft sich die Kirche neue Methoden und neue Waffen, mit denen sie schliesslich zum Gegenangriff übergeht, um das Verlorene widerzugewinnen. Der Inbegriff der durch diese Reaktion an der Kirche ausgebildeten Merkmale und ihre Betätigung heisst *Gegenreformation.*"

18. Jedin, *Katholische Reformation,* p. 36.

19. Ibid., p. 37; see also ibid., p. 35.

20. See Jedin, "Zur Aufgabe des Kirchengeschichtesschreibers," in *Kirche des Glaubens,* pp. 23–35, especially pp. 27–28. For the immediate background constructive of this ecclesiological viewpoint, see Francis Schüssler Fiorenza, *Foundational Theology: Jesus and the Church* (New York: Crossroad, 1992), especially pp. 64–81.

21. See, for example, *Römische Quartalschrift für christliche Altertumskunde und Kirchengeschichte,* 80 (1985); the entire volume is dedicated to the issue. For a wider context for the debate, see Otto Weiss, "Chiesa cattolica, religione e società nella più recente storiografia tedesca," *Ricerche di storia sociale e religiosa,* 52 (July-Dec. 1997), 169–197.

22. See Hubert Jedin, "Gewissenerforschung eines Historikers," in *Kirche des Glaubens,* 1:13–22. In 1952 he expressed himself on the subject again, in reaction to some criticisms by Josef Lortz of the first volume of his history of Trent, "Zur Aufgabe," ibid., 1:23–35, for example, p. 24: " . . . die Kirchengeschichte zunächst und vor allem Theologie, und zwar historische

Theologie ist, durch den Gegenstand, den sie behandelt, die Kirche Christi, deren Begriff sie von der Dogmatik empfängt." See also his "General Introduction to Church History," in *Handbook of Church History,* 1:1–56, especially 1–3, and the article written the year before his death, "Kirchengeschichte als Theologie und Geschichte," *Internationale katholische Zeitschrift,* 8 (1979), 496–507.

23. For a summary of his position see Erwin Iserloh, "Kirchengeschichte als Geschichte und Theologie in der Sicht Hubert Jedins," in *Annali dell'Istituto storico italo-germanico in Trento,* 6 (1980), 35–39, with transcription of discussion, 40–64.

24. See Jedin, "Zur Aufgabe," p. 35. See also Iserloh, "Kirchengeschichte," especially p. 35.

25. Jedin, *Katholische Reformation,* p. 50.

26. See, for example, Jedin, "Zur Aufgabe," p. 24.

27. Jedin, "General Introduction to Church History," *Handbook of Church History,* 1:10.

28. Jedin, *Katholische Reformation,* p. 52.

29. Ibid., p. 66: "Die Erneuerung der Kirche im Zeitalter des Konzils von Trient ist ein Vorgang, so überraschend, so wunderbar, dass eine rein natürliche, nur rationale Erklärung mit ihm nicht fertig wird. Sie ist letzten Endes ein übernatürliches Geheimnis, dessen letzte Ursachen wir nicht vollständig zu durchdringen vermögen. Man ist versucht, sie ein Wunder zu nennen." See also Jedin, "Vaticanum II und Tridentinum," p. 23; "Das II. Vatikanische Konzil," p. 596; and "Il significato del Concilio di Trento nella storia della Chiesa," *Gregorianum,* 26 (1945), 117–136, especially 133–134, "miracolo."

30. See Jedin, *History of the Church,* continuation of the *Handbook* under new title, 5:644–645.

31. Josef Lortz, *Die Reformation in Deutschland,* 4th ed., 2 vols. (Freiburg i/Br.: Herder, 1962); *The Reformation in Germany,* trans. Ronald Walls, 2 vols. (New York: Herder and Herder, 1968). I was unable to consult the 1939 imprint. On Lortz (1887–1975), see Michael B. Lukens, "Lortz's View of the Reformation and the Crisis of the True Church," *Archive for Reformation His-*

tory, 81 (1990), 20–31, and Eric W. Gritsch, "Joseph Lortz's Luther: Appreciation and Critique," ibid., 32–49. See also Lortz's review of the first volume of Jedin's history of Trent, *Theologische Revue,* 47 (1951), 157–170, to which Jedin replied with "Zur Aufgabe."

32. See Jedin, "Vaticanum II und Tridentinum," p. 10, and *Lebensbericht,* pp. 266–72.

33. See, for example, Jedin, "Vaticanum II und Tridentinum," pp. 15, 19, 34, 41.

34. See, for example, Jedin, "Zur Aufgabe," p. 33, and "Vaticanum II und Tridentinum," p. 19; Alberigo, "La 'riforma,'" p. 30; Repgen, "Jedin," p. 66.

35. See, for example, Jedin, "Zur Aufgabe," p. 33.

36. See, for example, Jedin, "Vaticanum II und Tridentinum," pp. 15, 52.

37. See ibid., p. 23.

38. See Alain Tallon, *La France et le concile de Trente (1518–1563)* (Rome: École Française de Rome, 1997), pp. 12–15.

39. See Jedin, "Vaticanum II und Tridentinum," p. 34.

40. See ibid., p. 23.

41. See ibid., especially pp. 38–49.

42. See Cyriac K. Pullapilly, *Caesar Baronius: Counter-Reformation Historian* (Notre Dame: University of Notre Dame Press, 1975); Romeo De Maio et al., eds., *Baronio storico e la Controriforma: Atti del convegno internazionale di studi, Sora, 6–10 ottobre 1979* (Sora: Centro di Studi Sorani "Vincenzo Patriarca," 1982); Stefano Zen, *Baronio storico: Controriforma e crisi del methodo umanistico* (Naples: Vivarium, 1994).

43. See, for example, John W. O'Malley, "Developments, Reforms, and Two Great Reformations: Towards a Historical Assessment of Vatican II," *Theological Studies,* 44 (1983), 373–406.

44. See Jedin, *Katholische Reformation,* p. 37. For a helpful distinction between "renewal" *(renovatio)* and "reform" *(reformatio),* see Adriano Prosperi, "Riforma cattolica, Controriforma, disciplinamento sociale," in *Storia dell'Italia religiosa, II: L'età moderna,* ed. Gabriele De Rosa and Tullio Gregory (Bari: Laterza, 1994), pp. 3–48, especially pp. 16–19.

45. Jedin, *Katholische Reformation,* p. 59: "Salus animarum suprema lex esto.

In Trient entscheidet sich, dass die Kirche der Neuzeit Seelsorgs- und Missionskirche wird. Es ist ein Wendepunkt, der in der Geschichte der Kirche nicht viel weniger bedeutet als die Entdeckungen des Kopernikus und Galilei für das naturwissenschaftliche Weltbild." See also ibid., p. 30, and "Il significato," p. 128.

46. See, for example, the works of John Bossy cited below in Chapter 3. See also Tallon, *Le concile de Trente,* pp. 813–814; Lawrence G. Duggan, "The Unresponsiveness of the Late Medieval Church: A Reconsideration," *Sixteenth Century Journal,* 9 (1978), 3–26; John Van Engen, "The Christian Middle Ages as an Historiographical Problem," *American Historical Review,* 91 (1986), 519–552; and the case study that is Eamon Duffy's *The Stripping of the Altars: Traditional Religion in England, c.1400–c.1580* (New Haven: Yale University Press, 1992). For a bibliographical survey of another reevaluation, see John W. O'Malley, "The Religious and Theological Culture of Michelangelo's Rome, 1508–1512," in Edgar Wind, *The Religious Symbolism of Michelangelo: Studies on the Sistine Ceiling,* ed. Elizabeth Sears (Oxford: Oxford University Press, forthcoming). See also John Martin, "Recent Italian Scholarship on the Renaissance: Aspects of Christianity in Late Medieval and Early Modern Italy," *Renaissance Quarterly,* 48 (1995): 593–610.

47. See Hubert Jedin and Giuseppe Alberigo, *Il tipo ideale di vescovo secondo la Riforma cattolica* (Brescia: Morcelliana, 1985), pp. 91–97.

48. See, for example, Jedin and Alberigo, *Il tipo ideale,* especially pp. 61–66, 83–98.

49. The bibliography of confraternities is now huge. For current trends and information, see the series *Confraternitas,* published by the Society for Confraternities Studies. See also John W. O'Malley, "Priesthood, Ministry, and Religious Life: Some Historical and Historiographical Considerations," *Theological Studies,* 49 (1988), 223–257.

50. See, for example, Joseph Bergin, *The Making of the French Episcopate, 1589–1661* (New Haven: Yale University Press, 1996), and Oliver Logan, *The Venetian Upper Clergy in the 16th and Early 17th Centuries: A Study of Religious Culture* (Lewiston, N.Y.: Edwin Mellen Press, 1996).

51. See, for example, Elizabeth Rapley, *The Dévotes: Women and Church in*

Seventeenth-Century France (Montreal: McGill–Queen's University Press, 1990).

52. See Jedin, *Katholische Reformation,* p. 62.

53. Ibid., p. 26.

3. England and Italy in Jedin's Wake

1. H. Outram Evennett, *The Cardinal of Lorraine and the Council of Trent: A Study in the Counter-Reformation* (Cambridge: Cambridge University Press, 1930).

2. A concise summary of Evennett's life can be found in David Knowles's "Foreword" to H. Outram Evennett, *The Spirit of the Counter-Reformation,* ed. John Bossy (Cambridge: Cambridge University Press, 1968), pp. vii–xi.

3. John Bossy, "Postscript," in Evennett, *Spirit of the Counter-Reformation,* p. 133.

4. Evennett, *Spirit of the Counter-Reformation,* p. 1.

5. Bossy, "Postscript" in *Spirit of the Counter-Reformation,* p. 126.

6. Evennett, *Spirit of the Counter-Reformation,* p. 3.

7. See Ibid., pp. 18, 20, 39. Henri Bremond, *A Literary History of Religious Thought in France from the Wars of Religion down to Our Own Times,* trans. K. L. Montgomery, 3 vols. (London: Society for Promoting Christian Knowledge, 1928–1936). No further volumes were translated into English.

8. *Dictionnaire de spiritualité ascétique et mystique: Doctrine et histoire,* 16 vols. in 22 (Paris: Beauchesne, 1937–94).

9. Joseph de Guibert, *La spiritualité de la Compagnie de Jésus: Esquisse historique* (Rome: Institutum Historicum Societatis Iesu, 1953); English: *The Jesuits, Their Spiritual Doctrine and Practice: A Historical Study,* trans. William J. Young (Chicago: The Institute of Jesuit Sources/Loyola University Press, 1964). See John W. O'Malley, "De Guibert and Jesuit Authenticity," *Woodstock Letters,* 95 (1966), 103–110.

10. Evennett, *Spirit of the Counter-Reformation,* p. 9.

11. Ibid., p. 93.

12. Delio Cantimori, "Riforma cattolica," *Società,* 2 (1946), 820–834, reprinted in his *Studi di storia* (Turin: Giulio Einaudi, 1959), pp. 537–553.

13. See Hubert Jedin, *Lebensbericht,* ed. Konrad Repgen (Mainz: Matthias-Grünewald Verlag, 1984), pp. 121, 129, 133, 141, 158.

14. On Cantimori, see the article by Piero Craveri in the *Dizionario biografico degli Italiani* (Rome: Istituto della Enciclopedia Italiana, 1960–), 18:283–290, with bibliography, and now Paolo Simoncelli, *Cantimori, Gentile e la Normale di Pisa: Profili e documenti* (Milan: Franco Angeli, 1994).

15. See, for example, Adriano Prosperi, "Riforma cattolica, Controriforma, disciplinamento sociale," in *Storia dell'Italia religiosa: II. L'età moderna,* ed. Gabriele De Rosa and Tullio Gregory (Bari: Laterza, 1994), pp. 3–48, especially 3–16.

16. See the tracing of this tradition by Pier Giorgio Camaiani, "Cinquecento religioso italiano e concilio di Trento," *Critica Storica,* 3 (1964), 432–465.

17. See, for example, Luisa Mangoni, *In partibus infidelium, Don Giuseppe De Luca: Il mondo cattolico e la cultura italiana del Novecento* (Turin: Giulio Einaudi, 1989), and Paolo Simoncelli, *Gentile e il Vaticano, 1943 e dintorni* (Florence: Le Lettere, 1997).

18. Luigi Rosso, "Avvertenza" to *Contributi alla Storia del Concilio di Trento e della Controriforma,* ed. Luigi Rosso (Florence: Vallecchi Editore, 1948), p. vii.

19. See Pedro de Leturia, "Il Concilio di Trento nel Quaderno Primo di 'Belfagor,'" *Civiltà Cattolica,* 100/2 (1949), 82–98, especially 97–98.

20. Cantimori, "Riforma cattolica," p. 550.

21. The papers of the conference were published as *Problemi di vita religiosa in Italia nel Cinquecento* (Padua: Editrice Antenore, 1960). On the conference, see Paolo Prodi, "Il binomio jediniano 'riforma cattolica e controriforma' e la storiografia italiana," *Annali dell'Istituto storico italo-germanico in Trento,* 6 (1980), 85–98, especially 88–89, and Mario Rosa, "Problemi di vita religiosa in Italia nel Cinquecento (note ed appunti)," *Bibliothèque d'Humanisme et Renaissance,* 23 (1961), 395–414.

22. See Prodi, "Il binomio jediniano," p. 89; Paolo Prodi, *Il cardinale Gabriele Paleotti (1522–1597)*, 2 vols. (Rome: Edizioni di Storia e Letteratura, 1959–1967).

23. Giuseppe Alberigo, *I vescovi italiani al Concilio di Trento (1545–1547)* (Florence: G. C. Sansoni, 1959).

24. Adriano Prosperi, *Tra evangelismo e Controriforma: G. M. Giberti (1495–1543)* (Rome: Edizioni di Storia e Letteratura, 1969).

25. The proceedings were published as *Il Concilio di Trento e la riforma tridentina*, 2 vols. (Rome and Freiburg i/Br: Herder, 1965).

26. See Prodi, "Il binomio jediniano," p. 90. For broad perspectives on Italian historiography from the mid-1960s forward, see Sergio Bertelli, "Il Cinquecento," in *La storiografia italiana degli ultimi vent'anni*, ed. Luigi De Rosa, 3 vols. (Bari: Laterza, 1989), 2:3–62; Romeo De Maio, "La storia religiosa: Il Rinascimento," ibid., 2:85–95; and, with observations more pertinent to our subject, Giuseppe Giarrizzo, "Il Seicento," ibid., 2:63–84.

27. See Prodi, "Il binomio jediniano," p. 90, and Paolo Simoncelli, "Inquisizione romana e riforma in Italia," *Rivista Storica Italiana*, 100 (1988), 5–125, especially 98–99, n.285.

28. Paolo Prodi, "Riforma interiore e disciplinamento sociale in San Carlo Borromeo," *Intersezioni*, 5 (1985), 273–285, specifically 273.

29. Ibid., p. 274.

30. For a discussion of the issue, with bibliography, see Anne Jacobson Schutte, "Periodization of Sixteenth-Century Italian Religious History: The Post-Cantimori Paradigm Shift," *Journal of Modern History*, 61 (1989), 269–284.

31. See Delio Cantimori, "'Nicodemismo' e speranze conciliari nel Cinquecento italiano," in his *Studi di storia*, pp. 518–536. See now Silvana Seidel Menchi, "Inquisizione come repressione o inquisizione come mediazione? Una proposta di periodizzazione," *Annuario dell'Istituto storico italiano per l'età moderna e contemporanea*, 35–36 (1983–1984), 53–77, as well as Schutte, "Periodization."

32. Massimo Firpo and Dario Marcatto, eds., *Il processo inquisitoriale del Cardinal Giovanni Morone,* 6 vols. (Rome: Istituto storico italiano per l'età moderna e contemporanea, 1981–1995).

33. See, for example, Elisabeth G. Gleason, *Gasparo Contarini: Venice, Rome and Reform* (Berkeley: University of California Press, 1993), and William V. Hudon, *Marcello Cervini and Ecclesiastical Government in Tridentine Italy* (DeKalb: Northern Illinois University Press, 1992).

34. See Massimo Firpo, *Inquisizione romana e Controriforma: Studi sul cardinal Giovanni Morone e il suo processo d'eresia* (Bologna: Il Mulino, 1992).

35. See Paolo Simoncelli, for example, *Il caso Reginald Pole: Eresia e santità nelle polemiche religiose del Cinquecento* (Rome: Edizioni di Storia e Letteratura, 1977); "Pietro Bembo e l'evangelismo italiano," *Critica Storica,* 15 (1978), 1–63; and *Evangelismo italiano del Cinquecento: Questione religiosa e nicodemismo politico* (Rome: Istituto storico italiano per l'età moderna e contemporanea, 1979).

36. See Simoncelli, "Inquisizione romana."

37. Ibid., p. 91.

38. Sergio Zoli, *La Controriforma* (Florence: La Nuova Italia Editrice, 1979), especially pp. 10–27, 136–139.

39. See Prodi, "Il binomio jediniano," pp. 85–98.

40. Paolo Prodi, *Il sovrano pontefice: Un corpo e due anime: La monarchia papale nella prima età moderna* (Bologna: Il Mulino, 1982); English translation by Susan Haskins, *The Papal Prince: One Body and Two Souls, the Papal Monarchy in Early Modern Europe* (Cambridge: Cambridge University Press, 1987).

41. Barbara McClung Hallman, *Italian Cardinals, Reform, and the Church as Property, 1492–1563* (Berkeley: University of California Press, 1985).

42. Prodi, *Papal Prince,* p. viii.

43. See ibid., especially pp. 123–156.

44. See ibid., especially pp. 90–101.

45. See ibid., especially pp. 166–171.

46. Ibid., p. viii.

47. Paolo Prodi, "Controriforma e/o Riforma cattolica: Superamento di vecchi dilemmi nei nuovi panorami storiografici," *Römische historische Mitteilungen,* 31 (1989), 227–237.

48. See Prodi, "Riforma interiore"; "Controriforma e/o Riforma cattolica;" Prodi, "Introduzione," in *Strutture ecclesiastiche in Italia e in Germania prima della Riforma,* ed. Paolo Prodi and Peter Johanek (Bologna: Il Mulino, 1984), pp. 7–18; Prodi with Elisabeth Müller-Luckner, eds., *Glaube und Eid: Treueformeln, Glaubensbekenntnisse und Sozialdisziplinierung zwischen Mittelalter und Neuzeit* (Munich: R. Oldenbourg, 1993); Prodi with Carla Penuti, eds., *Disciplina dell'anima, disciplina del corpo e disciplina della società tra medioevo ed età moderna* (Bologna: Il Mulino, 1994); Prodi, "Il concilio di Trento di fronte alla politica e al diritto moderno: Introduzione," in *Il concilio di Trento e il moderno,* ed. Paolo Prodi and Wolfgang Reinhard (Bologna: Il Mulino, 1996), pp. 7–26.

49. Prodi, "Controriforma e/o Riforma cattolica," p. 229.

50. On De Luca, see Mangoni, *In partibus infidelium;* the biographies by Romana Guarnieri, *Don Giuseppe De Luca: Tra cronica e storia* (Milan: Edizioni Paoline, 1991), and Giovanni Antonazzi, *Don Giuseppe De Luca, uomo cristiano e prete (1898–1962)* (Brescia: Morcelliana, 1992); the collection of reminiscences by friends and colleagues edited by Mario Picchi, *Don Giuseppe De Luca: Ricordi e testimonianze* (Brescia: Morcelliana, 1963); and the entry on him by Gabriele De Rosa in *Dizionario biografico degli italiani,* 38:353–359, with further bibliography. For a discussion on De Luca's publications, recent editions of his correspondence, and related matters, see Guarnieri, *De Luca,* pp. 7–42. See also the several articles on De Luca in *Archivio italiano per la storia della pietà,* 9 (1996), especially Adriano Prosperi, "Storia di pietà, oggi," pp. 3–29; and Carlo Delcorno, "Don Giuseppe De Luca e gli studi recenti sulla letteratura religiosa medievale," pp. 323–337.

51. See Paolo Simoncelli, *Storia di una censura: "Vita di Galileo" e Concilio Vaticano II* (Milan: Franco Angeli, 1992).

52. See Mangoni, *In partibus infidelium,* pp. 307–308.

53. For the pertinent documentation, see Picchi, *De Luca,* pp. 331–335.

54. See Giuseppe De Luca and Giovanni Battista Montini, *Carteggio, 1930–1962* (Rome: Edizioni di Storia e Letteratura, 1993).

55. See Guarnieri, *De Luca,* pp. 34–42, 136–145.

56. See Michele Cassese, "Giuseppe De Luca e John H. Newman," *Ricerche di storia sociale e religiosa,* n.s. 28 (1985), 131–146.

57. See Giuseppe De Luca, "Introduzione," *Archivio italiano per la storia della pietà,* 1 (1951), pp. lxx–lxxv.

58. See Romana Guarnieri, "Tra storia della pietà e sensibilità religiosa: Don Giuseppe De Luca e Lucien Febvre," in *Società e religione in Basilicata nell'età moderna: Atti del Convegno di Potenza-Matera (25–28 settembre 1975),* 2 vols. (n.p.: D'Elia, 1977), 1:81–129.

59. Much has been written on the relationship between De Luca and Bremond. See especially *Ricerche di storia sociale e religiosa,* n.s. 28 (1985), which contains the papers from a conference held at Vicenza, 1984, and entitled "Giuseppe De Luca e la storia della spiritualità"; and, most recently, Émile Goichot, "Don Giuseppe De Luca et l'histoire de la pieté," ibid., n.s. 48 (1995), 91–111.

60. See De Luca, "Introduzione," pp. xxxviiff.

61. The last, up to now, was volume 9 (1996).

62. His introduction to the first volume of the *Archivio* has, for instance, recently been translated into French, with a preface by André Vauchez and an introduction by Émile Goichot, *La piété: Approche historique,* trans. Elisabeth Arnoulx and Émile Goichot (Paris: Letouzey & Ané, 1995).

63. See De Luca, "Introduzione," pp. xiv, xvii, xxx, xxxiv.

64. Ibid., p. lxii.

65. Gabriele De Rosa, *Vescovi, popolo e magia nel Sud: Ricerche di storia socio-religiosa dal XVII al XIX secolo* (Naples: Guida, 1971). See Fulvio Salimbeni, "Vescovi, popolo e magia nel Sud: A proposito di un libro recente," *Nuova Rivista Storica,* 56 (1972), 453–466.

66. See De Rosa's "Premessa" to the first volume (1972), pp. 5–8.

67. See David Gentilcore, "Methods and Approaches in the Social History of the Counter-Reformation in Italy," *Social History,* 17 (1992), 73–98. For

some astute observations about the study of Italian religious history, see John Martin, "Recent Italian Scholarship on the Renaissance: Aspects of Christianity in Late Medieval and Early Modern Italy, *Renaissance Quarterly,* 48 (1995), 593–610. More broadly, see Craig Harline, "Official Religion—Popular Religion in Recent Historiography of the Catholic Reformation," *Archive for Reformation History,* 81 (1990), 239–262.

4. *France, Germany, and Beyond*

1. For general background, see Guy Bourdé and Hervé Martin, *Les écoles historiques* (Paris: Éditions du Seuil, 1983), pp. 181–214.

2. See, for example, Marc Fumaroli, *L'âge de l'éloquence: Rhétorique et "res literaria" de la Renaissance au seuil de l'époque classique* (Geneva: Droz, 1980), and Luce Giard, ed., *Les jésuites à la Renaissance: Système éducatif et production de savoir* (Paris: Presses Universitaires de France, 1995). For the origins of this tradition in the Enlightenment, see Wallace K. Ferguson, *The Renaissance in Historical Thought: Five Centuries of Interpretation* (Boston: Houghton Mifflin Company, 1948), pp. 67–72.

3. Marc Venard, "Réforme, Réformation, Préréforme, Contre-Réforme: Étude de vocabulaire chez les historiens récents de lange française," in *Historiographie de la Réforme,* ed. Philippe Joutard (Paris: Delachaux and Niestle, 1977), pp. 352–365, especially 361, and Alain Tallon, *La France et le concile de Trente (1518–1563)* (Rome: École Française de Rome, 1997), p. v.

4. See, for example, Frédéric Gugelot, *La conversion des intellectuels au catholicisme en France, 1885–1935* (Paris: CNRS, 1998); Stephen Schloesser, "Mystic Realists: Anti-Modernism in French Catholic Revival, 1918–1928," Ph.D. diss., Stanford University, 1998; and the volume entitled "Les intellectuels catholiques: Histoire et débats" of the serial *Mil neuf cent: Revue d'histoire intellectuelle (Cahiers Georges Sorel)* 13 (1995).

5. Peter Burke, *The French Historical Revolution: The Annales School, 1929–89* (Stanford: Stanford University Press, 1990), p. 1. For a lucid and concise description of the development of historical studies in France, see Gérard

Noiriel, "Foucault and History: The Lessons of a Disillusion," *Journal of Modern History,* 66 (1994), 547–568.

6. A great deal has been written about the origins and character of the *Annales* school. See especially Burke's *French Historical Revolution,* with its excellent bibliography, as well as Traian Stoianovich, *French Historical Method: The Annales Paradigm* (Ithaca: Cornell University Press, 1976), and François Dosse, *New History in France: The Triumph of the "Annales,"* trans. Peter V. Conroy, Jr. (Urbana: University of Illinois Press, 1994). For treatments in broader historical contexts, see Bourdé and Martin, *Écoles historiques,* pp. 215–270; Georg G. Iggers, *New Directions in European Historiography,* rev. ed. (London: Methuen, 1985), pp. 43–79; Norman F. Cantor, *Inventing the Middle Ages* (New York: Quill, William Morrow, 1991), pp. 118–160. Especially valuable are reflections coming from within the "school" such as Emmanuel Le Roy Ladurie, *The Territory of the Historian,* trans. Ben and Siân Reynolds (Chicago: The University of Chicago Press, 1979), as well as those appearing in the journal itself; see, for example, the several on the fiftieth anniversary, *Annales ESC,* 34 (1979), and also ibid., 44 (1989).

7. See Bourdé and Martin, *Écoles historiques,* pp. 182–188.

8. Lucien Febvre, "Une question mal posée: Les origines de la Réforme française et le problème des causes de la Réforme," *La Revue Historique,* 159 (1929), 1–73, reprinted in his *Au coeur religieux du XVIe siècle* (Paris: Sevpen, 1957), pp. 1–70.

9. The title is shortened and inverted as "The Origins of the French Reformation: A Badly-Put Question?" in Febvre, *A New Kind of History: From the Writings of Febvre,* ed. Peter Burke, trans. K. Folca (New York: Harper and Row, 1973), pp. 44–107.

10. Febvre, "Origins," p. 59.

11. Ibid., p. 65.

12. Dermot Fenlon, *"Encore une Question:* Lucien Febvre, the Reformation and the School of *Annales,"* in *Historical Studies: Papers Read before the Irish Conference of Historians,* IX, May 29–31, 1971 (Belfast: Blackstaff Press, 1974), pp. 65–81, especially p. 67.

13. Febvre, "Origins," p. 80.

14. Fenlon, *Encore Une Question,* p. 65.

15. See Febvre, "Origins," pp. 54–57.

16. Lucien Febvre, *Le problème de l'incroyance au XVIe siècle: La religion de Rabelais* (Paris: A. Michel, 1942); English translation, *The Problem of Unbelief in the Sixteenth Century: The Religion of Rabelais,* trans. Beatrice Gottlieb (Cambridge, Mass.: Harvard University Press, 1982).

17. Marc Bloch, *La société féodale,* 2 vols. (Paris: A. Michel, 1939–1940); English translation, *Feudal Society,* trans. L. A. Manyon, 2 vols. (Chicago: The University of Chicago Press, 1961).

18. See, for example, Luce Giard, "S'il faut conclure, ou comment l'histoire intellectuelle de la Renaissance est encore à écrire," in *Sciences et religions, de Copernic à Galilée (1540–1610)* (Rome: École Française de Rome, 1999), pp. 493–524; and Hartmut Lehmann, "Zur Bedeutung von Religion und Religiosität im Barockzeitalter," in *Religion und Religiosität im Zeitalter des Barock,* ed. Dieter Breuer, 2 vols. (Wiesbaden: Harrassowitz, 1995), 1:3–22, especially 3–8.

19. For broader perspectives, see Bourdé and Martin, *Écoles historiques;* Giard, "S'il faut conclure"; Pierre Blet, "France," in *Catholicism in Early Modern History: A Guide to Research,* ed. John W. O'Malley (St. Louis: Center for Reformation Research, 1988), pp. 49–67; and Gérard Noiriel, *Sur la "crise" de l'histoire* (Paris: Belin, 1996).

20. On Delaruelle, see the introductory essays by Philippe Wolff, Raoul Manselli, and André Vauchez in the collection of his studies, *La piété populaire au Moyen Âge* (Turin: Bottega d'Erasmo, 1975).

21. Vauchez in Delaruelle, *La piété,* p. xix.

22. See J. F. Lemarignier, "Gabriel Le Bras (1891–1970)," *Aevum,* 46 (1972), 1–8; Luigi Prosdocimi, "Gabriel Le Bras storico delle istituzioni della cristianità medievale," *Rivista di Storia e Letteratura Religiosa,* 3 (1967), 72–80; Gabriel Le Bras, "'Discours synthétique' d'un récipiendaire," *Archives de sociologie des religions,* no. 29 (1970), 7–14.

23. Gabriel Le Bras, "Statistique et histoire religieuses: Pour un examen

détaillé et pour une explication historique de l'état du catholicisme dans les diverses régions de la France," *Revue d'Histoire de l'Église de France,* 17 (1931), 425–449. He outlined the program in his *Introduction à l'histoire de la pratique religieuse en France,* 2 vols. (Paris: Presses Universitaires de France, 1942–1945). See also his *Études de sociologie religieuse,* 2 vols. (Paris: Presses Universitaires de France, 1955–1956).

24. See Le Bras, "'Discours synthétique,'" p. 9; and "Religion légale et religion vécue: Entretien avec Gabriel Le Bras," *Archives de sociologie des religions,* no. 29 (1970), 15–20.

25. Gabriel Le Bras, "Sociologie religieuse et science des religions," *Archives de sociologie des religions,* 1 (1956), 3–17, p. 6.

26. See, for example, Agostino Borromeo, "The Inquisition and Inquisitorial Censorship," in O'Malley, *Catholicism,* pp. 253–272.

27. See Lucien Febvre's enthusiastic review of the first volume of Le Bras's *Introduction à l'histoire de la pratique religieuse en France,* "La pratique religieuse et l'histoire de la France," *Mélanges d'histoire sociale,* 4 (1943), 31–35.

28. Le Bras, "'Discours synthétique,'" p. 10: " . . . montrant l'origine sociale des règles et l'effet des règles sur la société."

29. See Le Groupe de Sociologie des Religions, "Quinze ans de vie et de travail (1954–1969)," *Archives de sociologie des religions,* no. 28 (1969), 3–92.

30. See, for example, Gabriel Le Bras, "L'historiographie contemporaine du catholicisme en France," in *Mélanges Pierre Renouvin: Études d'histoire des relations internationales* (Paris: Presses Universitaires de France, 1966), pp. 23–32; Jean Delumeau, *Catholicism between Luther and Voltaire: A New View of the Counter-Reformation,* with an introduction by John Bossy, trans. Jeremy Moiser (Philadelphia: Westminster Press, 1977), pp. 129–153; Carla Russo, "Studi recenti di storia sociale e religiosa in Francia: Problemi e metodi," *Rivista Storica Italiana,* 84 (1972), 625–682.

31. Delumeau, *Catholicism,* p. 129. Originally published in French in 1971; see note 32.

32. Jean Delumeau, *Le Catholicisme entre Luther et Voltaire* (Paris: Presses Universitaires de France, 1971).

33. John Bossy, "The Counter-Reformation and the People of Catholic Europe," *Past and Present,* no. 47 (May 1970), 51–70.

34. Brian Pullan, *Rich and Poor in Renaissance Venice: The Social Institutions of a Catholic State* (Cambridge, Mass.: Harvard University Press, 1971).

35. Jean Delumeau, *Vie économique et sociale de Rome dans la second moitié du XVIe siècle,* 2 vols. (Paris: De Boccard, 1957–1959). See also his *L'alun de Rome, XVe-XIXe siècle* (Paris: S.E.V.P.E.N., 1962).

36. Jean Delumeau, *Naissance et affirmation de la Réforme* (Paris: Presses Universitaires de France, 1965).

37. The list of his publications is long. Among the more important, in addition to those listed in other notes, are: *La Civilisation de la Renaissance* (Paris: Arthaud, 1967); *Rome au XVIe siècle* (Paris: Hachette, 1975); *Le christianisme va-t-il mourir?* (Paris: Hachette, 1977); *Le cas Luther* (Paris: Desclée de Brouwer, 1983). There are, besides, his personal statement of faith, *Ce que je crois* (Paris: B. Grasset, 1985), and, among the volumes he has edited, *L'historien et la foi* (Paris: Fayard, 1996).

38. Jean Delumeau, *La peur en Occident (XIVe-XVIIIe siècles): Une cité assiégée* (Paris: Fayard, 1978); *Le péché et la peur: La culpabilisation en Occident (XIIIe-XVIIIe siècles)* (Paris: Fayard, 1983), English translation, *Sin and Fear: The Emergence of a Western Guilt Culture, 13th-18th Centuries,* trans. Eric Nicholson (New York: St. Martin's Press, 1990); *Rassurer et protéger: Le sentiment de sécurité dans l'Occident d'autrefois* (Paris: Fayard, 1989). To these must now be added his projected trilogy, *Une histoire du paradis,* 2 vols. to date (Paris: Fayard, 1992–), English translation of vol. 1, *History of Paradise: The Garden of Eden in Myth and Tradition,* trans. Matthew O'Connell (New York: Continuum, 1995).

39. See especially Jean Delumeau, *Un chemin d'histoire: Chrétienté et christianisation* (Paris: Fayard, 1981).

40. See, for example, Michel Despland, "How Close Are We to Having a Full History of Christianity? The Work of Jean Delumeau," *Religious Studies Review,* 9 (1983), 24–33; Robert Bireley, "Two Works by Jean Delumeau,"

Catholic Historical Review, 77 (1991), 78–88; Heiko A. Oberman, review of *Sin and Fear, Sixteenth Century Journal,* 23 (1992), 149–150.

41. On the large issue, see the brilliant article by John Van Engen, "The Christian Middle Ages as an Historiographical Problem," *American Historical Review,* 91 (1986), 519–552.

42. See Louis Châtellier, *The Religion of the Poor: Rural Missions in Europe and the Formation of Modern Catholicism, c.1500–c.1800,* trans. Brian Pearce (Cambridge: Cambridge University Press, 1997), p. 235.

43. Bossy, "Counter-Reformation and People of Europe," pp. 52–53.

44. See, for example, John Bossy, "The Counter-Reformation and the People of Catholic Ireland, 1596–1641," *Historical Studies: Papers Read before the Irish Conference of Historians,* ed. T. D. Williams, VIII, May 17–30, 1969 (Dublin: Gill and MacMillan, 1971), pp. 155–169; "The Social History of Confession in the Age of the Reformation," *Transactions of the Royal Historical Society,* 5th series, 25 (1975), 21–38; "The Mass as a Social Institution, 1200–1700," *Past and Present,* no. 100 (1983), 29–61; "Christian Life in the Later Middle Ages: Prayers," *Transactions of the Royal Historical Society,* 6th series, 1 (1991), 137–148, with Virginia Reinburg's commentary, pp. 148–150.

45. John Bossy, *The English Catholic Community, 1570–1850* (New York: Oxford University Press, 1976).

46. Bossy, "Counter-Reformation and People of Europe," p. 68.

47. John Bossy, *Christianity in the West, 1400–1700* (Oxford: Oxford University Press, 1985).

48. Ibid., p. 91.

49. See ibid., pp. 168–171.

50. Ernst Walter Zeeden, ed., *Gegenreformation* (Darmstadt: Wissenschaftliche Buchgesellschaft, 1973), pp. 46–81.

51. Bernd Moeller, *Reichstadt und Reformation* (Gütersloh: Gerd Mohn, 1962); English translation in *Imperial Cities and the Reformation: Three Essays,* trans. H. C. Erik Midelfort and Mark U. Edwards (Philadelphia: Fortress Press, 1972), pp. 41–115.

52. See Otto Weiss, "Chiesa cattolica, religione e società nella più recente storiografia tedesca," *Ricerche di storia sociale e religiosa,* 52 (July–Dec. 1997), 169–197.

53. Kurt Dietrich Schmidt, *Die katholische Reform und die Gegenreformation,* ed. Manfred Jacobs (Göttingen: Vandenhoeck and Ruprecht, 1975), a separately printed fascicle of Bernd Moeller, ed., *Die Kirche in ihrer Geschichte: Ein Handbuch,* Band 3, Leiferung L. (1. Teil).

54. It was published the next year: Gottfried Maron, "Des [sic] Schicksal der katholischen Reform im 16. Jahrhundert: Zur Frage nach der Kontinuität in der Kirchengeschichte," *Zeitschrift für Kirchengeschichte,* 88 (1977), 218–229.

55. Ernst Walter Zeeden, "Grundlagen und Wege der Konfessionsbildung in Deutschland im Zeitalter der Glaubenskämpfe," *Historische Zeitschrift,* 185 (1958), 249–299.

56. See, for example, Ernst Walter Zeeden, *Die Entstehung der Konfessionen: Grundlagen und Formen der Konfessionsbildung im Zeitalter der Glaubenskämpfe* (Munich: R. Oldenbourg, 1965), and *Konfessionsbildung: Studien zur Reformation, Gegenreformation und katholischen Reform* (Stuttgart: Klett-Cotta, 1985). For misgivings and reservations about Zeeden's approach, see the review by Bernd Moeller of the former book, *Zeitschrift für Kirchengeschichte,* 76 (1965), 405–408.

57. See, for example, Peter Thaddäus Lang, "Konfessionsbildung als Forschungsgegenstand," *Historisches Jahrbuch,* 100 (1980), 480–493, and Heinz Schilling, "'Konfessionsbildung' und 'Konfessionalisierung?" *Geschichte in Wissenschaft und Unterricht,* 42 (1991), 447–463, 779–794.

58. See Wolfgang Reinhard, for example, "Gegenreformation als Modernisierung? Prolegomena zu einer Theorie des konfessionellen Zeitalters," *Archive for Reformation History,* 68 (1977), 226–252; "Zwang zur Konfessionalisierung? Prolegomena zu einer Theorie des konfessionellen Zeitalters," *Zeitschrift für historische Forschung,* 10 (1983), 257–277; "Reformation, Counter-Reformation, and the Early Modern State: A Reassessment," *Catholic Historical Review,* 75 (1989), 383–404: "Disciplinamento sociale, confession-

alizzazione, modernizzazione: Un discorso storiografico," in *Disciplina dell'anima, disciplina del corpo e disciplina della società tra medioevo ed età moderna*, ed. Paolo Prodi with Carl Penuti (Bologna: Il Mulino, 1994), pp. 101–123; "Was ist katholische Konfessionalisierung?" in *Die katholische Konfessionalisierung: Wissenschaftliches Symposion der Gesellschaft zur Herausgabe des Corpus Catholicorum und des Vereins für Reformationsgeschichte, 1993*, ed. Wolfgang Reinhard and Heinz Schilling (Gütersloh: Gütersloher Verlagshaus and Münster: Aschendorff, 1995), pp. 419–452. For a complete bibliography of Reinhard's publications as of December 31, 1996, see his *Ausgewählte Abhandlungen* (Berlin: Duncker and Humblot, 1997), pp. 437–463.

59. See Heinz Schilling, for example, *Konfessionskonflikt und Staatsbildung: Eine Fallstudie über das Verhältnis von religiosem und sozialem Wandel in der Frühneuzeit am Beispiel der Grafschaft Lippe* (Gütersloh: Gerd Mohn, 1981); "Konfessionalisierung als gesellschaftlicher Umbruch: Inhaltliche Perspektiven und massenmediale Darstellung," in *Luther, die Reformation und die Deutschen: Wie erzählen wir unsere Geschichte?*, ed. S. Quandt (Paderborn: Schoningh, 1982), pp. 35–51; "Confessionalization in the Empire: Religious and Societal Change in Germany between 1555 and 1620," in his *Religion, Political Culture and the Emergence of Early Modern Society: Essays in German and Dutch History* (Leiden: E. J. Brill, 1992), pp. 205–245; "The Second Reformation—Problems and Issues," ibid., pp. 247–301; "Luther, Loyola, Calvin und die europäische Neuzeit," *Archive for Reformation History*, 85 (1994), 5–31; "Confessional Europe," in *Handbook of European History, 1400–1600: Late Middle Ages, Renaissance and Reformation*, ed. Thomas A. Brady et al., 2 vols. (Leiden: E. J. Brill, 1994–1995), 2:641–670; "Disziplinierung oder 'Selbsregulierung der Untertanen'? Ein Plädoyer für die Doppelperspektive von Makro- und Mikro-historie bei der Erforschung der frühmodernen Kirchenzucht," *Historische Zeitschrift*, 264 (1997), 675–691. See also the volumes Schilling has edited, *Die reformierte Konfessionalisierung in Deutschland: Das Problem der "Zweiten Reformation": Wissenschaftliches Symposion des Vereins für Reformationsgeschichte, 1985* (Gütersloh: Gerd Mohn, 1986), and *Kirchenzucht und So-*

zialdisziplinierung im frühneuzeitlichen Europa (Berlin: Duncker and Humblot, 1994).

60. Schilling, "Confessional Europe," p. 642. See also Reinhard, "Was ist?," p. 420: " . . . Ernst Walter Zeedens 'Konfessionsbildung' sozialwissenschaftlich angereichert als 'Konfessionalisierung' von einem Vorgang der Kirchengeschichte zu einem sozialgeschichtlichen Fundamentalprozess der Frühneuzeit zu erheben."

61. Febvre, "Origins," p. 47.

62. See Reinhard, for example, "Zwang," pp. 268–277.

63. Schilling, "Confessional Europe," p. 645.

64. Reinhard, "Gegenreformation," p. 231.

65. See Reinhard, "Reformation," pp. 388–389.

66. See Reinhard, "Zwang," pp. 263–268, and "Was ist?," pp. 428–431. See also Robert Bireley, "Early Modern Germany," in *Catholicism,* ed. O'Malley, pp. 11–30, especially pp. 11–13.

67. Reinhard, "Gegenreformation," p. 226.

68. Reinhard, "Reformation," p. 384. See also "Zwang," pp. 258–262.

69. Schilling, *Die reformierte Konfessionalisierung.*

70. Reinhard and Schilling, eds., *Die katholische Konfessionalisierung.* See also Hans-Christoph Rublack, ed., *Die lutherische Konfessionalisierung in Deutschland: Wissenschaftliches Symposion des Vereins für Reformationsgeschichte, 1988* (Gütersloh: Gerd Mohn, 1992).

71. See Schilling, "Luther, Loyola," pp. 28–29.

72. Schilling, "Confessionalization," pp. 209–210.

73. Ibid., pp. 241–242.

74. See Reinhard, "Was ist?," p. 422.

75. Ibid., pp. 433–434.

76. As early as 1982, vol. 8 (1982) of the *Annali dell'Istituto storico italo-germanico in Trento* contained several articles on the subject.

77. See Lehmann, "Zur Bedeutung," especially pp. 8–13; Marc R. Forster, "With and Without Confessionalization: Varieties of Early Modern German Catholicism," *Journal of Early Modern History,* 1 (1998), 315–343, and

"Kirchenreform, katholische Konfessionalisierung und dörfliche Religion um Kloster Salem 1650–1750," *Rottenburger Jahrbuch für Kirchengeschichte,* 16 (1997), 93–110.

78. Reinhard, "Was ist?," p. 427.

79. See, for example, Reinhard, "Was ist?," p. 421.

80. See Gerhard Oestreich, "Strukturprobleme des europäischen Absolutismus," in *Geist und Gestalt des frühmodernen Staates: Ausgewählte Aufsätze* (Berlin: Duncker and Humblot, 1969), pp. 179–197, translated into English as "The Structure of the Absolute State," in Gerhard Oestreich, *Neostoicism and the Early Modern State,* ed. Brigitta Oestreich and H. G. Koenigsberger, trans. David McLintock (Cambridge: Cambridge University Press, 1982), pp. 258–273; see as well Oestreich's *Strukturprobleme der frühen Neuzeit: Ausgewählte Aufsätze,* ed. Brigitta Oestreich (Berlin: Dunker and Humblot, 1980). See also the basic study by Winfried Schulze, "Gerhard Oestreichs Begriff 'Sozialdisziplinierung in der frühen Neuzeit,'" *Zeitschrift für historische Forschung,* 14 (1987), 265–302, and the excellent analysis by Stefan Breuer, "Sozialdisziplinierung: Probleme und Problemverlangerungen eines Konzeps bei Max Weber, Gerhard Oestreich und Michel Foucault," in *Soziale Sicherheit und soziale Disziplinierung: Beiträge zu einer historischen Theorie der Sozialpolitik,* ed. Christoph Sachsse and Florian Tennstedt (Frankfurt a/M: Suhrkamp Verlag, 1986), pp. 45–69.

81. Quoted in Schulze, "Oestreichs Begriff," p. 301: "Disziplinierung des Einzelnen für die gesellschaftliche Ordnung."

82. See Schultze, "Oestreichs Begriff," p. 266.

83. See, for example, Breuer, "Sozialdisziplinierung"; Hans Maier, "Sozialdisziplinierung—ein Begriff und seine Grenzen (Kommentar)," in *Glaube und Eid: Treueformeln, Glaubensbekenntnisse und Sozialdisziplinierung zwischen Mittelalter und Neuzeit,* ed. Paolo Prodi with Elisabeth Müller-Luckner (Munich: R. Oldenbourg, 1993), pp. 237–240; Heinrich Richard Schmidt, "Sozialdisziplinierung? Ein Plädoyer für das Ende des Etatismus in der Konfessionalisierungforschung," *Historische Zeitschrift,* 265 (1997), 639–682.

84. Michel Foucault, *Surveiller et punir: Naissance de la prison* (Paris: Galli-

mard, 1975); English translation, *Discipline and Punish: The Birth of the Prison*, trans. Alan Sheridan (New York: Pantheon Books, 1977). See Breuer, "Sozialdisziplinierung," and his "Die Formierung der Disziplinargesellschaft: Michel Foucault und die Probleme einer Theorie der Sozialdisziplinierung," *Sozialwissenschaftliche Informationen für Unterricht und Studium,* 4 (1983), 257–264; Heinz Steinert, "The Development of 'Discipline' According to Michel Foucault: Discourse Analysis vs. Social History," *Crime and Social Justice,* no. 20 (1984), 83–98; Clare O'Farrell, *Foucault: Historian or Philosopher?* (New York: St. Martin's Press, 1989), especially pp. 101–112. For an important defense of Foucault as a historian, see Paul Veyne, "Foucault Revolutionizes History," in *Foucault and His Interlocutors,* ed. Arnold I. Davidson (Chicago: University of Chicago Press, 1997), pp. 146–182, but see as well Noiriel, "Foucault and History." See also Bourdé and Martin, *Écoles historiques,* pp. 324–332, and Thomas Flynn, "Foucault's Mapping of History," in *The Cambridge Companion to Foucault,* ed. Gary Gutting (Cambridge: Cambridge University Press, 1994), pp. 28–46. As an introduction to writing by and about Foucault, see Michael Clark, *Michel Foucault: An Annotated Bibliography—Tool Kit for a New Age* (New York: Garland Publishing, Inc., 1983).

85. See, for example, James W. Bernauer, "Michel Foucault's Ecstatic Thinking," *Philosophy and Social Criticism,* 12 (1987), 156–193.

86. Foucault, *Discipline,* p. 215.

87. Ibid., p. 216.

88. See, for example, Hans Baron, *Calvin's Staatsanschauung und das konfessionelle Zeitalter* (Berlin: R. Oldenbourg, 1924).

89. Jean-Marie Mayeur et al., eds., *Histoire du Christianisme des origines à nos jours,* 9 vols. to date (Paris: Desclée de Brouwer, 1990–). See the review by Wolfgang Reinhard of the German translation of vol. 8, *Historisches Jahrbuch,* 114 (1994), 107–124, especially the comparison with the corresponding volume of Jedin's *Handbuch,* pp. 110–111.

90. Venard, "Introduction," *Temps des confessions,* p. 11.

91. See Venard, *Temps des confessions,* p. 223. See also, however, Venard's *Réforme protestante, Réforme catholique dans la province d'Avignon, XVIe siècle*

(Paris: Éditions du Cerf, 1993), the unrevised text of a *doctorat d'État* submitted in 1977, in which *Réforme catholique* as well as, in a more limited way, *Contre-réforme* play more obvious functions.

Conclusion

1. R. Po-chia Hsia, *The World of Catholic Renewal, 1540–1770* (Cambridge: Cambridge University Press, 1998).

2. See, for example, Pamela M. Jones, *Federico Borromeo and the Ambrosiana: Art Patronage and Reform in Seventeenth-Century Milan* (Cambridge: Cambridge University Press, 1993).

3. The title of Louis Châtellier's book conveys the point, *The Religion of the Poor: Rural Missions in Europe and the Formation of Modern Catholicism, c. 1500–c. 1800,* trans. Brian Pearce (Cambridge: Cambridge University Press, 1997).

4. See John W. O'Malley, "Reform, Historical Consciousness, and Vatican II's Aggiornamento," *Theological Studies,* 32 (1971), 573–601, especially 581–583.

5. *Invasion mystique* was the title of the second volume of Henri Bremond, *Histoire littéraire du sentiment religieux en France depuis la fin des guerres de religion jusqu'à nos jours,* 11 vols. (Paris: Bloud et Gay, 1916–1933).

6. See, for example, Marc Fumaroli, "Baroque et classicisme: L'*Imago Primi Saeculi Societatis Jesu* (1640) et ses adversaires," in his *L'école du silence: Le sentiment des images au XVIIe siècle* (Paris: Flammarion, 1994), pp. 343–365, and "The Fertility and Shortcomings of Renaissance Rhetoric: The Jesuit Case," in *The Jesuits: Cultures, Sciences, and the Arts, 1540–1773,* ed. John W. O'Malley et al. (Toronto: Toronto University Press, 1999), pp. 90–106.

7. See, for example, O'Malley et al., eds., *The Jesuits,* and Gauvin Alexander Bailey, *Art on the Jesuit Missions in Asia and Latin America, 1542–1773* (Toronto: University of Toronto Press, 1999).

8. See John W. O'Malley, "The Historiography of the Society of Jesus: Where Does It Stand Today?" in *The Jesuits,* ed. O'Malley et al., pp. 1–37.

9. See, for example, Erwin Panofsky, "Erasmus and the Visual Arts," *Journal of the Warburg and Courtauld Institutes,* 32 (1969), 200–227.

10. See John W. O'Malley, "Developments, Reforms, and Two Great Reformations: Towards a Historical Assessment of Vatican II," *Theological Studies,* 44 (1983), 373–406, in which I try to describe some features that made the Reformation a reformation. See also O'Malley, "Reform, Historical Consciousness," in which I analyze the conservative nature of the language of the councils of the church, including Trent.

11. The scholarship of Paul Oskar Kristeller is of course central to this development. See, for example, his *Renaissance Thought: The Classic, Scholastic, and Humanistic Strains* (New York: Harper, 1961), as well as Albert Rabil, Jr., ed., *Renaissance Humanism: Foundations, Forms, and Legacy,* 3 vols. (Philadelphia: University of Pennsylvania Press, 1988). For evidence of continuing debate within defined parameters, see Kenneth Gouwens, "Perceiving the Past: Renaissance Humanism after the 'Cognitive Turn,'" *American Historical Review,* 103 (1998), 55–82. For an even broader perspective on the Renaissance, see Claire Farago, ed., *Reframing the Renaissance: Visual Culture in Europe and Latin America, 1450–1650* (New Haven: Yale University Press, 1995).

12. See, for example, John W. O'Malley, *Giles of Viterbo on Church and Reform: A Study in Renaissance Thought* (Leiden: E. J. Brill, 1968); *Il rinnovamento del francescanesimo: l'Osservanza, Atti dell'XI convegno internazionale della Società internazionale di studi francescani (Assisi, 20–22 ottobre, 1983)* (Assisi: Università di Perugia, Centro di Studi Francescani, 1985); and Kaspar Elm, ed., *Reformbemühungen und Observanzbestrebungen im spätmittelalterlichen Ordenswesen* (Berlin: Duncker and Humblot, 1989).

13. See, for example, John W. O'Malley, "Was Ignatius Loyola a Church Reformer? How to Look at Early Modern Catholicism," *Catholic Historical Review,* 77 (1991), 177–193.

14. See, for example, Joseph Bergin, *The Making of the French Episcopate, 1589–1661* (New Haven: Yale University Press, 1996); Oliver Logan, *The Venetian Upper Clergy in the Sixteenth and Seventeenth Centuries: A Study of Religious Culture* (Lewiston, N.Y.: Edwin Mellen Press, 1996); Agostino Bor-

romeo, "I vescovi italiani e l'applicazione del concilio di Trento," in *I Tempi del concilio: Religione, cultura e società nell'Europa tridentina,* ed. Cesare Mozzarelli and Danilo Zardin (Rome: Bulzoni Editore, 1997), pp. 27–105; and the comparative essay, Joseph Bergin, "L'Europe des évêques au temps de la Réforme catholique," *Bibliothèque de l'École des Chartes* 154 (1996), 509–531.

15. See, for example, Marc R. Forster, "With and Without Confessionalization: Varieties of Early Modern German Catholicism," *Journal of Early Modern History,* 1 (1998), 315–343.

16. See, for example, Caroline Walker Bynum, "Wonder," *American Historical Review,* 102 (1997), 1–26; Eugene Goodheart, "Reflections on the Culture Wars," *Daedalus,* 126 (Fall 1997), 153–175, especially 168; John L. Mahoney, "Critical Methodology and Writing about Religion and Literature," *Religion and the Arts,* 1/4 (1997), 89–95; and, from a different viewpoint, George M. Marsden, *The Soul of the American University: From Protestant Establishment to Established Nonbelief* (New York: Oxford University Press, 1994).

17. See O'Malley, "Loyola a Church Reformer?"

18. See, for example, Marc R. Forster, "With and Without Confessionalization"; his "Clericalism and Communalism in German Catholicism," in *Infinite Boundaries: Order, Disorder, and Reorder in Early Modern German Culture,* ed. Max Reinhart (Kirksville, Mo.: Sixteenth Century Journal Publishers, 1998), pp. 55–75; and Benjamin Wood Westervelt, "Roman Catholicism," in *The Oxford Encyclopedia of the Reformation,* ed. Hans J. Hillerbrand, 4 vols. (New York: Oxford University Press, 1996), 3:439–447.

19. See "Early Modernities," subject of a full number of *Daedalus,* 127 (Summer 1998).

20. See, for example, Leah S. Marcus, "Renaissance/Early Modern Studies," in *Redrawing the Boundaries: The Transformation of English and American Literary Studies,* ed. Stephen Greenblatt and Giles Gunn (New York: The Modern Language Association of America, 1992), pp. 41–63; Paula Findlen and Kenneth Gouwens, "Introduction: The Persistence of the Renaissance," *American Historical Review,* 103 (1998), 51–54; and William J. Bouwsma, "Eclipse of the Renaissance," ibid., pp. 115–117.

ACKNOWLEDGMENTS

✠

As mentioned, this book originated as the D'Arcy Lectures that I gave in 1993 at Campion Hall, Oxford. I am grateful to the then Master of the Hall, Joseph Munitz, and to the Senior Tutor, Norman Tanner, for inviting me to deliver them. I am also grateful to the Association of Theological Schools for awarding me a Lilly Faculty Fellowship, 1997, which provided me with leisure and other resources to turn the lectures into a book. I have profited from the criticism of a number of colleagues and students who in formal and informal situations have listened patiently as I expounded my views. Luce Giard of the Centre National de Recherche Scientifique, Paris, read two chapters of an earlier draft, and Robert Bireley of Loyola University, Chicago, read the whole manuscript. They offered valuable comments and saved me from embarrassing mistakes. The two anonymous readers for Harvard University Press did the same. Patricia Gross helped me at the final stage of checking references. Everyone mentioned above contributed to whatever merits the book has; I alone am responsible for its defects.

In admiration and gratitude I dedicate this book to Helen and Mary North, whom I met at the American Academy in Rome thirty-five years ago. They have been great friends, tried and true.

INDEX

✣